Achieving
Impossible Things
With Free Culture and
Commons-Based Enterprise

Achieving Impossible Things

With Free Culture and Commons-Based Enterprise

by

Terry Hancock

FSM
FREE SOFTWARE MAGAZINE
PRESS

First Edition (Print-on-Demand), Prepared 2009

The chapters of this book were originally serialized in a slightly modified form in Free Software Magazine.

This book is enriched by a large number of photos and drawings which were released under free licenses. Special thanks to all of those who contributed their work to the intellectual commons, making this usage possible. Separate credit lines are provided alongside the figures containing them. These notations must be retained (or new ones provided).

Trademarks and tradenames are used at many points in this book to refer to or represent the companies and/or organizations to whom they belong. Ownership of the marks is hereby acknowledged. It is the opinion of the author and publisher that using these marks in this way (to illustrate and refer to their various antecedants) is constitutionally protected speech and requires no additional permission. This usage does not represent any endorsement of this book or author by those companies or organizations.

This book was written, designed, pre-pressed, and submitted for press entirely using free software tools, including: LyX, Gvim, PyChart, Inkscape, Gimp, Blender, ImageMagick, Scribus, and Mozilla Seamonkey. All running on Debian GNU/Linux. Thank you to all the people who have made these tools possible.

ISBN: 978-0-578-03272-6 (paperback only)

Lulu ID: 7298616 (paperback)
           7337310 (casewrap hardcover)

Published by Free Software Magazine Press
(http://www.freesoftwaremagazine.com/books).
Editor-in-Chief: Tony Mobily

Print-on-demand services provided by Lulu
(http://lulu.com).

Pre-press services by Anansi Spaceworks
(http://www.anansispaceworks.com)

Cover Image Credits (clockwise from top): GNU/Linux image from Free Software Foundation, Wikipedia logo from Wikipedia, Screen capture of Dogmazic music sharing site and Creative Commons logo, Big Buck Bunny from Blender Foundation, Car design sketches from OScar project, and children using an XO computer from the OLPC Project.

Table of Contents

"At first people refuse to believe that a strange new thing can be done. Then they begin to hope it can be done. Then they see it can be done. Then it is done, and all the world wonders why it was not done centuries ago."
—— *Frances Hodgson Burnett,* **The Secret Garden**

Magic or Method?

L argely triggered by improvements in computer technology, the internet, and especially the world wide web, there has emerged a growing movement of collaborative efforts in many areas of human endeavor, including such diverse areas as software, art, technology, and science. At its core, the movement emphasizes the free exchange of information, without the imposition of artificial legal or technical barriers to impede innovation and inspiration. This broad, though similarly patterned, collection of activities has come to be known as **"free culture."**

In the mainstream, this free culture is regarded with varying degrees of skepticism, disdain, and dewy-eyed optimism. It violates the rules by which we imagine our world works, and many people react badly to that which they don't understand.

If the system of rules that we have based our entire industrial civilization on is wrong, will we have to face the prospect of re-ordering that society from the ground up? Will that civilization now collapse (like Wile E. Coyote falling once he notices there's no ground underneath him)?

On the opposite extreme, for those who've given up on the rationalizations, preferring a "faith-based" approach, there is a great tendency to leap to magical thinking. Perhaps there are gods of freedom reordering the world to make it a happier place? If we shake our rattles hard enough, will *all* our dreams come true?

But where is genuine reason in all of this? In this book, I'll present six "impossible" achievements of free culture, each representing a particular challenge to the old paradigm. Then I'll present a set of five basic rules to help understand "how the magic works," and give a more realistic framework for what can and can't be expected from free culture and the commons-based enterprises which spring from it.

This knowledge can make the "impossible" possible, enabling the realization and improvement of this new paradigm of **commons-based enterprise**. In the end, thriving in the new, deeply-networked world of information freedom, this new kind of productivity shows the potential to surpass all prior forms of productive enterprise, including those of governments and corporations.

Conventions

Textboxes, like this one, with a wrench icon in the upper right corner contain practical applications advice (in case the other observations and rules seem a little too abstract).

Jargon words and some proper names are marked in **bold text** when introduced and can be found in the Glossary.

A superscript number,[0] indicates a note at the end of the chapter.

Illustration or photo credits are provided in an abbreviated form: "PD" for "public domain," "PR" for "press release," "CC" for "Creative Commons," "By" for "Attribution," and "SA" for "ShareAlike," along with a version number if applicable.

[0]Like This.

Part I:
Six Impossible Things Before
Breakfast

Six Impossible Things

> "Why, sometimes I've believed as many as six impossible things before breakfast."
>
> —— *The White Queen, from **Through the Looking Glass** by Lewis Carroll*

Most of the assumptions on which our present economic system is based are based on nothing much better than "conventional wisdom": which is a fancy way of saying "it just sounds plausible." Sometimes conventional wisdom is wrong, and that's what the first part of this book is meant to show: six things that ought to be impossible if conventional wisdom were correct. But if the foundational assumptions of our economy are false, then where does that leave the economy? And if it's no longer standing on a firm foundation, then what are the new rules?

Here are six "impossible things" that challenge six myths raised in defense of the old paradigm. First, it is claimed that free culture is limited in scope to small projects—and yet somehow free software is completely reshaping the computing landscape. Failing that, there is the idea that at least it cannot possibly compete with the existing corporate enterprise paradigm—and yet free knowledge resources already dwarf similar products in the corporate world.

Then are the myths that try to limit the *breadth* of free culture's impact: That it is only useful for utilitarian projects, and yet there is an enormous swell of free-licensed aesthetic content on the internet. That it cannot apply to commercial projects and will fail the minute money is introduced, and yet there is successful community financing for free-licensed projects. That it can't have any effect on the material marketplace, and yet there is open hardware. That it will somehow run into a wall, being the product of some fringe community or that it benefits only a small privileged class, and yet it is being used to tear down the old class divisions and build a vastly larger system on the international stage.

The old paradigm of a world dominated by corporate enterprise and the division of financial wealth is cracking apart at the seams. Beyond it is a new paradigm of **commons-based enterprise**, driven not so much by the accumulation and dispersal of *monetary* wealth, but by the accumulation and dispersal of *knowledge* and individual *effort*; coordinated by worldwide information networks; formalized and protected by a legal framework of free licenses and the ideal of the commons; and sharable among all of its participants, simply because that is the intrinsic nature of information.

The new paradigm obsoletes the old ideas of "work" and "play," combining them into a new form which is both more satisfying to the human spirit and more productive. We no longer have to choose between having fun and getting things done, because in this new world, people are often more productive in "leisure" than in "labor."

Of course, it's not a perfect utopia. The new paradigm has its own limitations and rules. There will be a few losers in this new economy, and there has already been some outcry from a few of them, as they struggle to hold on to their old cash cows. But commerce will not evaporate and society will not implode, as some doomsayers have suggested. Rather, new commerce will arise to fill the needs of the new system, just as it did for the old. The trick, for those who want to make it in this new economy, is to look closely at the successes in order to understand where new opportunities will arise, and to discover how to build new businesses and organizations that will thrive in a commons-based free market.

Impossible Thing #1:

Free Software
Debian GNU/Linux

L et's look at some solid evidence for the success of what is probably the most obvious "impossible" achievement of **commons-based peer production**: **free software**, as exemplified by the **Debian GNU/Linux distribution**.

First, of course, we need to start with the myth that commons-based development is limited to small projects—an idea promulgated by a couple of decades of **proprietary software** dominance with an economic model founded on the manufacturing analogy.

How Big is "Big"?

It's difficult for people to compare the scale of free and proprietary products with each other. First of all, it's tempting to say that software is "worth what you charge"—that is to say, that you could evaluate it by its sale price. In that case, proprietary software is a multi-billion dollar industry, so how can you even compare it to the **free-licensed** software industry which doesn't charge per-copy costs?

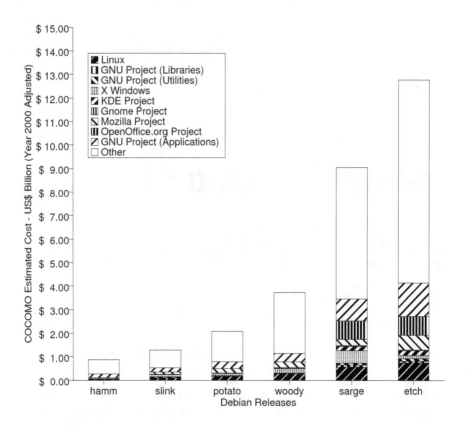

Figure 1.1:
Equivalent cost of producing Debian GNU/Linux if it were to be developed in a conventional centrally-managed development setting. This can be regarded as an approximate lower bound for its "use value" (because the community had to want it that much to spend that much effort on it)

However, we don't value software for software's sake. We value using it to do stuff. Thus, **use value** is the relevant metric, not **sale value**. Unfortunately, that too is hard to count, though you can look at the figures for how many people are using free software.

But there is another way to ask the question: if you had to start from scratch and re-build the existing body of software, using a proprietary development company, how much would it cost you? At the very least, free software must be worth the effort that people are putting into it (or they'd stop working on it). So, how much is that?

Myth #1:

"Free development is only adequate for small scale projects"

This may seem almost comic in a Free Software Magazine book, but I *still* hear this myth from otherwise intelligent people in other communities. It's such a strongly held belief because it is all that conventional wisdom allows for works created by "amateurs" in their "spare time." The professionalist belief is that only paid professionals can produce quality, well-engineered designs and that professionals cannot possibly be paid to work on something you can get "for free."

Measuring the size of "free software" is not easy. First of all, it's hard enough to find it all. Then there's deciding what is worth counting and what is just cruft. Fortunately, this has largely already been done for us—in the form of Debian GNU/Linux, the world's most complete free software GNU/Linux distribution.

There is a project being conducted by the LibreSoft Research Group[1] to collect and analyze metrics data for free software projects based on "**source lines of code**" (**SLOC**), a relatively easy-to-measure statistic for any kind of software. These data are generated by David Wheeler's SLOCCount[2] program, which uses COCOMO[3], a long-standing and fairly simple model, to estimate the costs of software projects under the assumptions of centralized, managed software development. Now this is probably not an accurate measure of the actual

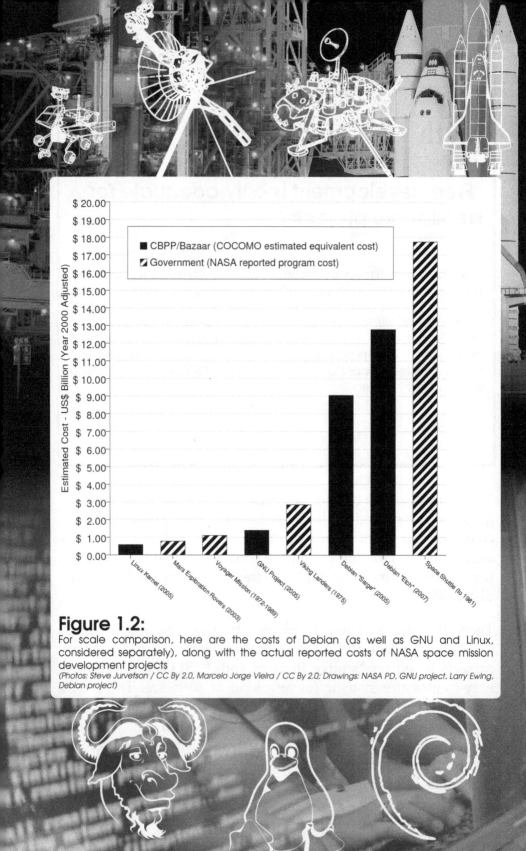

Figure 1.2:
For scale comparison, here are the costs of Debian (as well as GNU and Linux, considered separately), along with the actual reported costs of NASA space mission development projects
(Photos: Steve Jurvetson / CC By 2.0, Marcelo Jorge Vieira / CC By 2.0; Drawings: NASA PD, GNU project, Larry Ewing, Debian project)

effort cost of developing free software (although I leave it as an exercise for the reader to guess whether it's too high or too low), but it does provide an order-of-magnitude estimation and a consistent metric which allows for comparisons. Figure 1.1 shows the results of this estimation, showing the growth of the distribution with each release.

Now these are very large numbers. It's easy to lose perspective. So let's throw in some comparable project costs to give an idea of the scale of project we are talking about (Figure 1.2).

The estimated equivalent cost of developing the 4.0 "Etch" release of Debian was not quite three-quarters of the actual development cost of the Space Shuttle.[4] And that's in adjusted dollars[5] (inflation has been applied to these numbers to make for a fair comparison, otherwise Etch would seem much more expensive than the Shuttle). The GNU project alone represents more equivalent value than the cost of the Voyager space probe missions to the outer planets. If that doesn't convince you that free software projects can be large and complex, I don't know what would.

But is it *Better?*

> *"Measuring programming progress by lines of code is like measuring aircraft building progress by weight."*
> —— *Bill Gates*

The large size of free software projects could simply be due to inefficiency. After all, both Microsoft Windows and Mac OS X have been criticized on these grounds as being "bloated." However, comparing the size of Microsoft Windows to the entire Debian GNU/Linux distribution is like comparing an apple to an entire orchard: Debian is not an "operating system," it's a complete collection of software. The equivalent in the proprietary world would be something like "the entire inventory of a retail software store."

So, to make things comparable, let's strip down the Debian numbers so that we only include the things that provide equivalent function to what comes out of the box with, say, Microsoft Windows "Vista" (estimated at 50 million SLOC). So, we'll need what computer scientists (as opposed to marketing executives) call the **operating system**—which includes the Linux **kernel**, the GNU **libraries**, and the GNU **utilities** (not the entire GNU project, which today is dominated by **application** software **packages** like Gimp). Then we'll also need the graphical windowing environment, which means the X

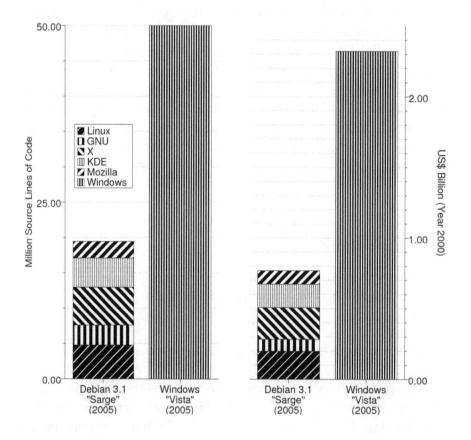

Figure 1.3:

The free software stack providing the same functionality as Microsoft Windows does "out of the box." The left side compares by source lines of code, while the right compares COCOMO-estimated cost (based on the assumption that the free software projects are developed as independent projects and Windows is developed as one unit)

server packages, and—since Microsoft continues to bundle it—the web browser, which is from the Mozilla project. Microsoft Office is not bundled with Windows, so we'll leave out OpenOffice.org. This allows us to compare "equivalent stacks" of software (see Figure 1.3).

Not only is the free software stack (at 19 million SLOC) less than half the size of Windows, but, because it is factored into distinct packages, it is even easier to maintain. It could be that the need to divide the work among independent projects forces engineering discipline to be followed, and it is apparent that this pays off in the long run in more compact code (it's also interesting to note that this Debian source code supports eleven **binary** builds for different **CPU architectures**, while Windows only supports one).

So, not only does free software represent a vast amount of effort, but it is apparently very well-engineered and efficient effort leading to an even higher use value than equivalent proprietary products! Not only can free software manage large, complex projects, but it appears to do it better than proprietary methods.

Notes

1 LibreSoft Research Group: Debian Counting. The published numbers include the overall totals and the results for each Debian source package. I have grouped packages using dependency rules and string-searches (taking advantage of Debian's package naming conventions) in order to produce the aggregates used in the Windows comparison as well as the divisions in the bar charts.
`http://libresoft.es/debian-counting`

2 SLOCCount (Software Package). Program used by the Debian Counting project to generate their results.
`http://www.dwheeler.com/sloccount/`

3 The COnstructive COst MOdel or COCOMO is used by the SLOCCount program to estimate costs.
`http://en.wikipedia.org/wiki/COCOMO`

4 Space Shuttle Program Cost based on testimony of Mr. Robert F. Thompson, taken from the Columbia Accident Investigation Board public hearing on Wednesday, April 23, 2003. Places the cost of the Shuttle at an estimated $5.15 billion in 1971 dollars or an actual $8.5 billion in 1981 dollars.
`http://caib.nasa.gov`

5 Measuring Worth. Online source and calculator, demonstrating six different deflation formulae used to compare different kinds of cost over time. The one most appropriate for large government projects is the "GDP Deflator", which is what I used here to adjust space project costs. All of the cost numbers have been converted to year 2000 dollars for comparison purposes.

`http://www.measuringworth.com/uscompare`

Impossible Thing #2:

Free Knowledge
Wikipedia & Project Gutenberg

W ikipedia is the largest and most comprehensive encyclopedic work ever created in the history of mankind. It's common to draw comparisons to Encyclopedia Britannica, but they are hardly comparable works—Wikipedia is dozens of times larger and covers many more subjects. Accuracy is a more debatable topic, but studies have suggested that Wikipedia is not as much less accurate than Britannica as one might naively suppose. Project Gutenberg is a less well known, but much older part of the free culture movement, having been started in 1971. Today it contains over 25,000 e-texts.

Measuring Wikipedia

It's actually a bit hard to say what the exact size of Wikipedia is today, because the log engine that the site used to measure its size started to fail in 2006, due to the enormous size of the database! Since then, there is no direct data available on the total size of Wikipedia, nor even on the English language

Figure 2.1:

Growth of Wikipedia by word count. Late in 2006, the size of the database exceeded the capacity of the logging engine and less systematic estimates have to be used. The diamonds show estimates based on article counts, with an assumption that mean article size remained the same (in the previous data, there is a gradual trend upwards in mean article size).

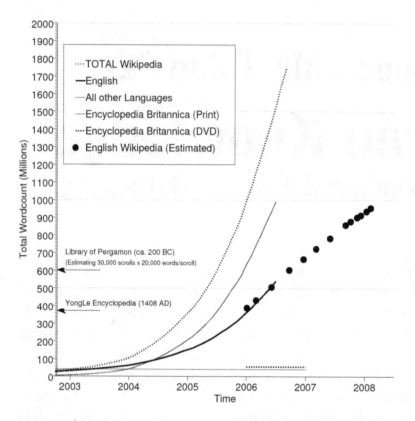

version (the largest language version, unsurprisingly). There is data on some of the less highly populated language versions, simply because they haven't grown so large yet.

However, we can make some estimates based on the evidence before 2006 and the somewhat less complete statistics which continue to be available. 2006 was a pivotal year for Wikipedia. It was the year its size surpassed the *Yong-Le Encyclopedia*.

The *Yong-Le Encyclopedia* was the former largest encyclopedic work ever created, commissioned by the Emperor of China in 1403.[1] It was so large it was only ever possible to make two

Myth #2:

"Commons-based projects can't possibly compete with what corporations can do"

Unlike the previous myth, this one is largely unchallenged. Even inside the free culture community there is a strong perception of the community as a rebel faction embattled against a much more powerful foe. Yet, some projects challenge this world view!

copies of it (including the original). It was bound into approximately 23,000 volumes, and unfortunately, though there are still some scattered volumes in collections around the world, it has not survived intact into the present day.

The year 2006 was also the year when Wikipedia apparently finally transitioned from "exponential" to approximately "linear" growth, which can be regarded as an important maturation step. Instead of growing explosively, as it did in its first few years of existence, Wikipedia is now moving into a more sustainable growth pattern, with an increasing effort being put into improving the quality of existing articles rather than adding new ones. This is not to say that new articles aren't being written: the growth may be linear, but it's linear at an amazing rate—Wikipedia adds something close to an entire new *Yong-Le Encyclopedia* every year! Figure 2.1 illustrates the growth and size of Wikipedia, compared to some other significant works.

In many situations, growth follows a "sigmoid" curve (so named, because it is "S-shaped"), with an initial period of exponential growth when there is no retarding force whatsoever, followed by linear growth, and finally an asymptotic taper as the phenomenon runs into environmental limits. Thus far, Wikipedia appears to have exhausted the potential for rapidly increasing labor and has already picked all of the "low-hanging fruit" of encyclopedic entries.

Now, it is moving into a phase of growth represented primarily by the effort of the existing interested "Wikipedians" (now a fairly stable population, with growth balanced by attrition). Thus the growth rate now represents a fairly constant effort put into improving the encyclopedia. Also, evidence suggests that maintenance and quality-control now represent a much larger fraction of the work as more edits are now dedicated to revisions (and reversions) of existing pages rather than adding new ones.[2] There is also, of course, continuing exponential growth among the less-well-represented languages in Wikipedia, which contributes to the total growth.

Quantity and Quality

Of course, if Wikipedia were, as some have suggested, just an "enormous pile of rumors", then its size would not necessarily be a good thing. In fact though, Wikipedia is surprisingly accurate. A study in 2005 by the editorial staff of *Nature* (one of the world's most respected scientific journals) demonstrated that in the area of science, Wikipedia was only slightly less accurate than Encyclopedia Britannica, although it found a number of mistakes in both publications.[3] It is interesting to note that, after publication of this study, all of the Wikipedia articles objected to in the study were quickly edited to fix the problems, while the same cannot be said for Britannica, since it is harder to change.

There are many areas of knowledge which Wikipedia covers, such as popular culture, which other encyclopedias cannot possibly hope to keep up with (try looking up episode summaries for *Buffy the Vampire Slayer* in Britannica!). It is understandably unmatched in computer-related subject areas.

Probably the weakest thing about Wikipedia is its susceptibility to intentional bias: many individuals, organizations, and governments have been known to edit Wikipedia articles to put themselves in a more favorable light. On the other hand, critical organizations may edit them to be more harsh, and in the end, these effects appear to balance out for all but the most controversial topics. Even in most such cases, however, Wikipedia fairly depicts controversial topics in all of their controversy (try looking up "Evolution", "Creationism", or "George W. Bush" in Wikipedia for interesting examples of what happens with controversial topics).

More to the point, these weaknesses describe what might be dubbed the "editorial bias" of Wikipedia, which represents the collective bias of the society of people willing to contribute to the project. It has to be remembered, though, that conventional encyclopedic works are also subject to editorial bias, and usually the bias of one organization. As it stands, researchers using Wikipedia need to take the same kind of critical approach that they've always applied to encyclopedias as sources of information, and they must follow up the sources themselves for serious scholarly work.

Although there has always been a concern with the problems caused by intentional vandalism—especially by anonymous contributors, this is not as much of a problem as many would imagine. A study at Dartmouth[4] concluded that anonymous contributors improved articles roughly as much as signed-in users. Thus, it appears likely that the Delphi effect[5] is out-competing vandalism and intentional bias in Wikipedia. In other words, distributed, community-based editorial review works, just as distributed debugging does for free software. Biases and judgement calls are a problem, but in the end they appear to balance out for almost all articles.

Project Gutenberg

Started in 1971, Project Gutenberg is the grand-daddy of free culture projects. It predates much of the thought about the

Figure 2.2:

Growth of Project Gutenberg, measured in number of works, from Wikipedia (Hellisp@Wikipedia / PD).

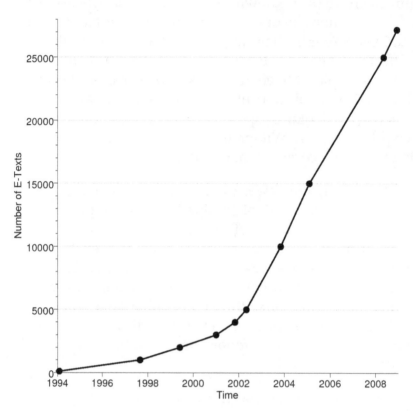

"intellectual commons" and it came thirteen years before the **GNU Manifesto** was written. As such it does not reflect modern ideas about free-licensing, and instead focuses on public domain works. That, along with the insistence on "plain text" representations of the works included reflect attitudes some may regard as dated. This situation has been mollified somewhat in recent years, with the inclusion of some graphics and other e-book formats.

Project Gutenberg measures its size in terms of numbers of e-texts, which can be somewhat confusing since e-texts are of many different lengths. However, a rough estimate of the size of the repository in number of words suggests that it may be similar in size to the fabled Library of Alexandria[6] and it is certainly larger than many modern community libraries.

The collection started fairly small, limited by the relatively small amount of networking and human labor available to the project in its early years.

However, as the internet and the web matured, so did the community supporting Project Gutenberg. Today, there is a significant volunteer scanning and distributed proof-reading[7] effort going on which has accounted for the tremendous growth that the project has seen over the last decade or so (see Figure 2.2). It has also been joined by a number of like-minded organizations around the world, forming the Project Gutenberg Affiliates organization which operates internationally, and today includes some 100,000 e-books.[8]

The size of Project Gutenberg today is probably more limited by the availability of public domain works than by the labor pool willing to digitize them. The public domain has been starved multiple times in the last few decades by copyright term extensions which have effectively frozen the public domain in the mid 1920s. As more works do move into the public domain, Gutenberg will certainly be capable of capturing them.

Understanding the Scale

Like the Debian GNU/Linux project in the previous chapter, Wikipedia and Project Gutenberg force us to readjust our preconceived notions of what a loosely-organized group of volunteers can achieve. Debian GNU/Linux is on the same scale of US space projects in terms of the labor represented. Wikipedia is more than an *order of magnitude* larger than the largest works of encyclopedic information created by corporate enterprise, more than twice the size of the largest encyclopedia ever created by a government, and growing by that much every year, even as it moves into a linear growth phase.

Figure 2.3:

Logarithmic chart of various works, compared by estimated word count. Works grouped on the left side are individual works (although the Bible can be regarded as a collection); works in the middle are original encyclopedic works; and works on the right are entire libraries of works.

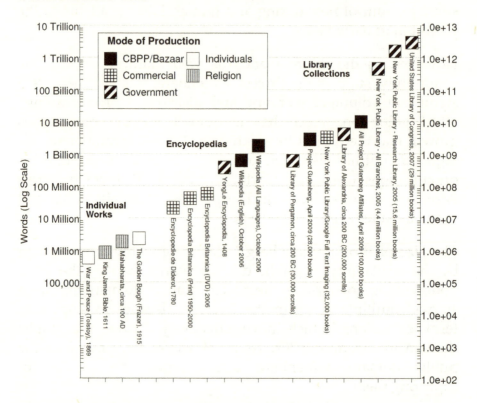

Figure 2.3 attempts to display all of these information projects on a single chart, spanning many orders of magnitude, through the use of a logarithmic scale. Though not useful for making fine comparisons, such a chart is fairly forgiving of estimation errors (because errors of less than a factor of two don't amount to much change on the chart). For this chart, "scrolls" have been estimated at 20,000 words and "books" at 100,000, allowing library collections to be placed on the same scale with individual works and encyclopedias (which, as collective works, are somewhat intermediate between the two).

This chart should make it clearer just where these commons-based enterprise projects fall on the scale of human endeavors, from individually authored works up to the entire U.S. Library of Congress. Project Gutenberg, along with the Distributed Proofreading Project, is a long way from challenging the world's major print libraries like the US Library of Congress or the New York Public Library, but compares very favorably with public domain digitization projects such as the recent collaboration between Google and the New York Public Library, to make NYPL books in the public domain available electronically.[9]

Much more dramatically, Wikipedia is far larger than the largest comparable works of government or corporate production, and is indeed approaching the scale of entire library collections. The greatest encyclopedic work of corporate production is probably the Encyclopedia Britannica, yet it falls far behind in this comparison. The greatest encyclopedic work of government production was the *Yong-Le Encyclopedia*. Yet even that was several times smaller than the whole of Wikipedia (note also that the Wikipedia numbers are the last reliable numbers from 2006, not the later estimates—Wikipedia is considerably larger today).

The conventional wisdom sees corporations and governments as the most powerfully productive organizations in existence—institutions we still regard with awe, reverence, and even fear. However, in just a few short years, a new player—the commons-based enterprise—has far out-produced them in important fields, as illustrated here by the Wikipedia and Project Gutenberg examples (and by Debian GNU/Linux in the previous chapter).

Clearly, the conventional wisdom needs adjusting.

Notes

1 The *Yong-Le Encyclopedia*
http://www.chinaculture.org/gb/
   en_aboutchina/2003-09/24/content_26624.htm

2 These trends can be seen in the Wikipedia statistics pages.
http://stats.wikimedia.org

3 "Internet encyclopaedias go head to head"Jim Giles. Nature 438, 900 – 901 (2005).
`http://www.nature.com/doifinder/10.1038/438900a`

4 A Dartmouth study found that contributions from anonymous visitors to Wikipedia show a similar quality to those from logged-in, named contributors.
`http://www.sciam.com/article.cfm`
    `?id=good-samaritans-are-on-the-money`

5 The Delphi effect or Delphi method is an observed tendency for a group of experts (or even people in general) to produce better answers when queried collectively than any one could do by themselves. This contrasts with the idea of relying on specialization. Further information can be found in several sources, including Wikipedia.
`http://en.wikipedia.org/wiki/Delphi_method`

6 This statement is difficult to test because no one really knows exactly how big the Library of Alexandria was, and there are estimates that are probably huge exaggerations. The number used here is 200,000 scrolls, one of the largest believable figures quoted. Scrolls are generally somewhat smaller than books (or Project Gutenberg e-texts which are mostly based on books). For this article, I've used 20,000 words per scroll and 100,000 per book in order to make comparisons. Fortunately, changing these figures by as much as a factor of two either way does not really affect the big picture. Converting all of the sizes to word counts makes it possible to compare them direclty, which is instructive, even with these inaccuracies.

7 Distributed Proof-reading is a collaborative system for sharing the load of proof-reading optical character recognition scans of original works.
`http://www.pgdp.net/c`

8 Project Gutenberg and Project Gutenberg Affiliates sizes are availabled from the project website.
`http://www.gutenberg.org/wiki/Main_Page`

`http://www.gutenberg.org/wiki/`
    `Gutenberg:Partners%2C_Affiliates_and_Resources`

9 The New York Public Library, with sponsorship from Google, has begun a digitization project, making many of the public domain works in their collection available online
`http://catnyp.nypl.org/screens/help_googlebooks_about.html`

`http://catnyp.nypl.org/search/XGoogle+Books+Library+Project`

Impossible Thing #3:
Free Art &
Music
Creative Commons Culture

A new conventional wisdom began to spring up around free software, led in part by theorists like Eric Raymond, who were interested in the economics of free software production. Much of this thought centered around service-based and other ancillary sales for supporting free software. Based on this kind of thinking, it's fairly easy to imagine extending free licensing ideas to **utilitarian works**. But what about **aesthetic works**? The Creative Commons was established in 2002, largely to solve the kinds of licensing problems that aesthetic works might encounter, and it has been remarkably successful, pushing the envelope of even this newer wave of thought. Today, Creative Commons licensed works number in at least the tens of millions. And more than a quarter of those are using the "**Attribution**" or "**Attribution-ShareAlike**" free licenses (see also Appendix F).

The Problems with
Free-licensing Aesthetic Works

The economics of free software is not so difficult to understand. After all, we don't value software for what it is, but for what it does. No one really just sits and admires Microsoft Word, or LyX, or AbiWord. They use one of these programs to create written works. An interoffice memo written in AbiWord may be indistinguishable from one written in MS Word. If AbiWord is also, from the user's point of view, cheaper and more flexible, then it may be a complete replacement of Microsoft Word.

If, on the other hand, you were putting together a museum collection of "word processing programs" (figure 3.1), AbiWord would not be interchangeable with Microsoft Word: only Microsoft Word can stand in such an aesthetic role for Microsoft Word. Works, when valued aesthetically, are never interchangeable.

That was a contrived example, because software usually isn't valued aesthetically. But this is the norm for artistic works. If you are a Beatles fan, you will never be satisfied with a free-licensed song that just "sounds a lot like a Beatles song" or "can be used the same way as a Beatles song."

It is also fundamentally impossible to prove the relative objective worth of aesthetic works. For utilitarian works, we can always list a set of objective criteria, test different products, and evaluate which is "best" according to those criteria. However, for aesthetic works, such judgements must always be subjective. At best, we ask a larger or more representative group of people to give their opinion (in other words, we can report objective facts about collected subjective opinions), but that's the best we can do (see figure 3.2).

At the same time, aesthetic works lack many of the ancillary funding opportunities of utilitarian works like free software. It's pretty hard to sell a service contract on a painting or a music track (figure 3.3). So, while there is still great public benefit in creating free-licensed aesthetic works, the economic

Figure 3.1:
In a notional Museum of Software, software is displayed for aesthetic value, rather than utilitarian. The presence of one piece of software in such a collection doesn't invalidate another, because no piece can "replace" the aesthetic value of another (only its utilitarian value)

support structure, which ensures that the artists will get paid for their efforts, is missing.

Aesthetic works have one other important property, which is that they are used to communicate opinions and make political statements. With aesthetic works, we directly influence people's opinions and sometimes their actions. Such statements also

Figure 3.2:

Is the Mona Lisa a great work of Renaissance art or just a lady with no eyebrows? Are SF pulp illustrations cheap genre sketches or classic works of imagination? Does this art electronic head make you think of modern society's inundation with technology, or just that some people have way too much time on their hands? Is Edvard Munch's "The Scream" a classic expressionist work, or just a really bad painting of a very disturbed person? Is the image below just a photo of some pipes and a fire escape or is it a lyrical architectural impression? Beauty is in the eye of the beholder

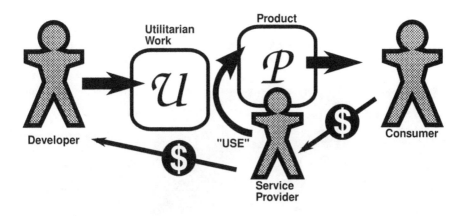

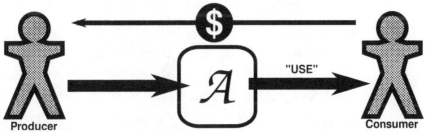

Figure 3.3:

For aesthetic works, "use" means only "to appreciate or sense directly" by the consumer, while for utilitarian works it means that the work is involved in processing to create another work or product (sometimes immaterial) which is actually directly of value to the consumer. This indirection provides a more complex environment and more possible business models. However, for aesthetic works, it is hard to escape the direct sale model as the principle means to make income from professional production

reflect on the author's reputation (for both intent and talent), which can lead to strong positive or negative consequences (figure 3.4).

Thus, aesthetic works present special challenges for free licensing and economics. Which leads to the myth that it can't be done.

The Creative Commons

In 2002, Larry Lessig founded the **Creative Commons** (**CC**) to solve artistic licensing problems with a modular system of

Figure 3.4:

Given the extreme subjectivity of artistic value, some artists may not appreciate seeing their work "improved" by others. What if this derivative work of Leonardo da Vinci's famous painting had contained offensive language or pornographic content? Would such a derivative reflect poorly on Da Vinci? What about on a less-well-known artist?

licenses designed to accommodate the needs of creators of "creative"—or more accurately, "aesthetic"—works. Since then, the mission of the Creative Commons has been to simplify the existing network of use cases by defining a finite set of license modules, and then combining those into generally useful licenses for all kinds of media. Figure 3.5 illustrates some of the possible uses for these licenses.

The organization provides three types of information products for each of its licenses: the actual license, which CC calls the "legal code" (meant to be understood by lawyers and

---

Myth #3:

"The service model limits free production to utilitarian, not aesthetic, works (so it can't work for art or music)"

This is one of the most sophisticated objections to free culture, and the hardest to refute. But we will see that there are ways that free culture continues to produce aesthetic works.

---

meticulously detailed in meaning); a brief set of descriptions intended to help licensors and licensees to understand what they are choosing, which CC calls the "deed"; and a machine-readable **RDF** representation which helps search engines and other AI tools to recognize and sort CC licensed material (Figure 3.6).

In addition to creating new licenses principly targeted at aesthetic works, the Creative Commons has also subsumed the pre-existing GPL and LGPL licenses for software, by providing the "deed" and RDF code to complement the existing licenses' "legal code."

Measuring the Success of Creative Commons Licenses

It is extremely difficult to find any accurate figures on the total adoption of Creative Commons licenses. The existing studies worked by doing search queries through major commercial search engines (Yahoo and Google), using features which allow tracing "**backlinks**" to the Creative Commons license pages. However, the Creative Commons has published these statistics, which are intriguing, despite the intrinsic inaccuracy of the methods.[1]

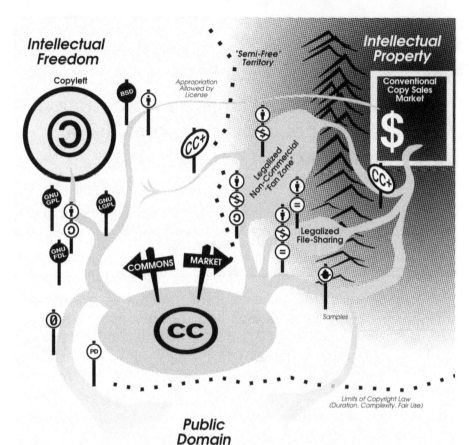

Intellectual Freedom

Copyleft

Appropriation Allowed by License

"Semi-Free" Territory

Intellectual Property

Conventional Copy Sales Market

Legalized Non-Commercial "Fan Zone"

Legalized File-Sharing

COMMONS   MARKET

Samples

Limits of Copyright Law
(Duration, Complexity, Fair Use)

Public Domain

Figure 3.5:

Creative Commons licenses span a plethora of use-cases and user communities. The free licenses (left) are of the most interest to advocates of the "Commons" (or the "Bazaar"). For many artistic producers who are professional or semi-professional, however, the "Non-Commercial" "semi-free" licenses are of more interest. These mostly legalize practices that have already existed for some time, such as "fan fics" and "fan art" (served by the NC and NC-SA licenses) and file-sharing distribution of verbatim works (served by ND and NC-ND licenses). The new "CC+" initiative aims to improve the ease with which these works can be monetized by transferring them to individual non-free licenses in the copy-sales marketplace. Another use of CC+ might be to transfer them to the free commons

Attribution (By)

Requires that works be attributed to the author in a requested way (within reasonable limits).

ShareAlike (SA)

Requires that derivatives bear a similar license. In other words, a minimal copyleft (no source code requirement is made).

NonCommercial (NC)

The work can't be used for commercial gain (for example, it can't be sold or used in advertising or in advertising-sponsored media).

NoDerivatives (ND)

No derivatives can be made from the work; it must be preserved as-is (excepting derivatives allowed by fair-use).

Sampling

The Sampling license allows samples or excerpts of the work to be used in new works, but does not allow the whole work to be copied without permission.

Public Domain (PD)

Public domain works are not licensed or owned at all. CC uses this symbol simply to mark such works clearly.

deed

RDF

```
<rdf:RDF    xmlns="http://web.resource.org/cc/"
            xmlns:rdf="http://www.w3.org/1999/02/22-rdf-syntax-ns#">
    <License rdf:about="http://creativecommons.org/licenses/by-sa/2.5/">
        <permits rdf:resource="http://web.resource.org/cc/Reproduction"/>
        <permits rdf:resource="http://web.resource.org/cc/Distribution"/>
        <requires rdf:resource="http://web.resource.org/cc/Notice"/>
        <requires rdf:resource="http://web.resource.org/cc/Attribution"/>
        <permits rdf:resource="http://web.resource.org/cc/DerivativeWorks"/>
        <requires rdf:resource="http://web.resource.org/cc/ShareAlike"/>
    </License>
</rdf:RDF>
```

legal code

Figure 3.6:

The Creative Commons products include the license icons (at left), used to identify their licenses in a modular way. For each of the licenses, three main items are maintained: a "deed," meant to make the license terms apparent to users of the work; an RDF code meant to make the work indexable by search engines which check for licensing; and the full text of the license, which CC calls the "legal code." The Attribution-ShareAlike-2.5 license (CC-By-SA-2.5) is shown here as an example (Above)

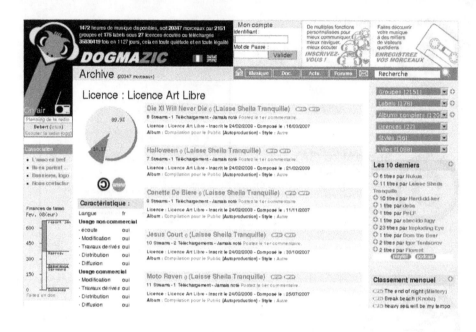

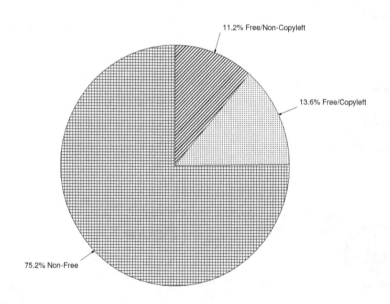

11.2% Free/Non-Copyleft

13.6% Free/Copyleft

75.2% Non-Free

Figure 3.7:

This music download site contains about 21,000 tracks under a wide variety of licenses, including free and non-free (about 75% are from Creative Commons) (Web capture and site statistics data from http://www.dogmazic.net, taken in Spring 2008)

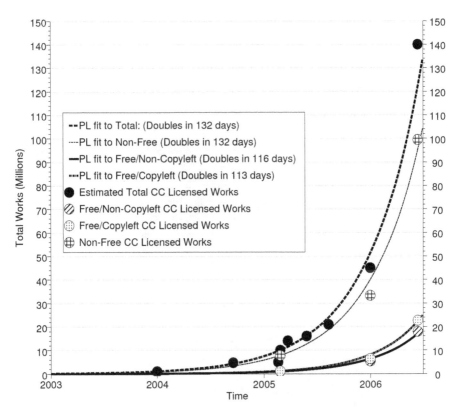

Figure 3.8:
Estimated CC licenses by license category, plotted over time, with exponential growth curves overlaid, showing what appears to be good fits to the available data. The "free" licenses are gaining slightly against the "non-free" licenses. It must be emphasized that the data is poor, however, since there are many poorly-controlled variables in the collection process

There are several things that are suspect about this approach, including the incompleteness of search engine databases, the uncertainty in determining that backlinks necessarily equate to license assertions, and the assumption that there is a one-to-one relationship between **license assertions** and licensed works. However, in the absence of better data, it's worth looking at the statistics that Creative Commons has been able to publish.

Creative Commons' own analysis of the data is somewhat misleading, because it treats the separate license modules as if

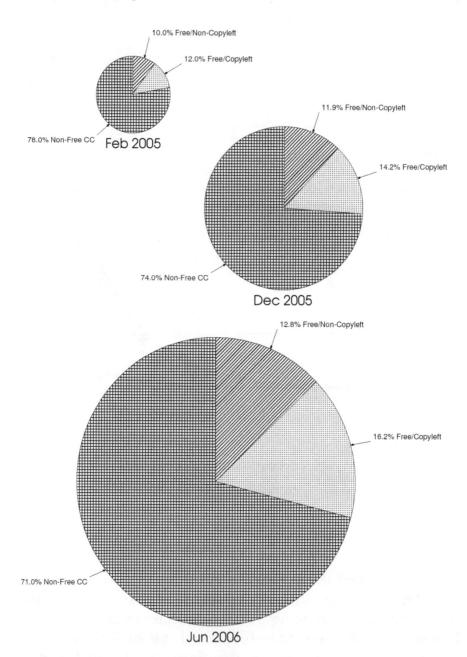

Figure 3.9:

Information about the preferences of one type of license over another are more solid than the total values. These pie charts show the percentages of free, copyleft, and non-free licenses. Note that the free licenses start out at a bit under one quarter of the total in early 2005, and finish at well over one quarter in 2006. The charts are scaled to represent correct areas for the total license figures that were published at the same time (but this total scale figure is less reliable than the license ratios)

they were orthogonal (i.e. as if use of the "ShareAlike" module meant the same thing, regardless of whether the "Non-Commercial" module is used or not). So, I have re-classified the data for my own analysis, dividing the licenses into "Free/Non-Copyleft" ("Public Domain" and "Attribution"), "Free/Copyleft" ("Attribution-ShareAlike"), and "Non-Free CC" (all licenses with "Non-Commercial" or "Non-Derivative" modules). Figure 3.8 shows the results of such search-engine based measurements.

In general, the "Non-Free CC" licenses have been very successful, probably reflecting a general dissatisfaction with decreasing fair use, increasingly closed "**intellectual property**" legislation, and attacks on file sharing over the internet. However, these licenses are not "free" in the same sense as "free software," and represent a distinct phenomenon from the growth of the "Free" licenses.

From early on in the Creative Commons' history there has been a political debate over whether the "Non-Free" licenses are helping or harming the adoption of "Free" licenses. The data doesn't necessarily support either position, but it's clear that the free licenses are succeeding, whether because of or in spite of the other Creative Commons licenses.

A 2007 study on the Creative Commons licenses was conducted by an outside research group at Singapore Management University. It estimated a lower bound of about 60 million CC license backlinks, based on data from Yahoo and Flickr (this is somewhat smaller than the estimates CC created, but the numbers are not directly comparable because of the difference in technique). In this study, the "Free/Non-Copyleft" group represents 12%; the "Free/Copyleft" is 18%; and the "Non-Free" group is 70%.[2] Figure 3.9 shows the change in license-preference over time. The free licenses are gradually gaining in relative popularity to the non-free licenses, while both are growing together at a substantial rate.

Freedom for the Mainstream

Despite the shakiness of the theoretical foundation for producing aesthetic works professionally and releasing them under free licenses, a lot of material is nevertheless being produced. Is this material created just by amateurs? Or is it the result of business models we have not considered? Do the non-free licenses from Creative Commons signal a broader, more mainstream cultural phenomenon of people who are disenchanted with the "more is better" attitude towards copyright that the proprietary industry has shown?

There are still many questions, but the Creative Commons and the free culture surrounding it is going strong.

Notes

1 Creative Commons License Statistics, from the CC wiki.
   `http://wiki.creativecommons.org/License_statistics`

2 Giorgos Cheliotis Singapore Management University Study
   `http://hoikoinoi.wordpress.com/2007/07/02/cc-stats/`

Impossible Thing #4:

Community
Financing
Blender Foundation &
Open Movies

T he **bazaar** development model turns out to be amazingly versatile: it seems that most software, even things you wouldn't think would be feasible, can be developed using such an approach. But there has to be some working core software before the community will have enough interest to contribute to a project, and there are some projects where that is really too much work for one person to do.

One such area is sophisticated 3D graphics applications, like Blender (and also **Computer Aided Design** applications, like BRL-CAD). Such projects typically need some sort of seed project in a "**cathedral**" mode in order to get started. Other projects, such as creative endeavors, are simply not going to be as successful in the committee atmosphere of a community-driven project.

In such cases, there's a need to accumulate capital and simply pay people for their work. You might think that this is surely

Figure 4.1:

The Blender program is a sophisticated 3D animation program. Such programs can be difficult to start in a bazaar mode
(*Example file is from Orange Project*)

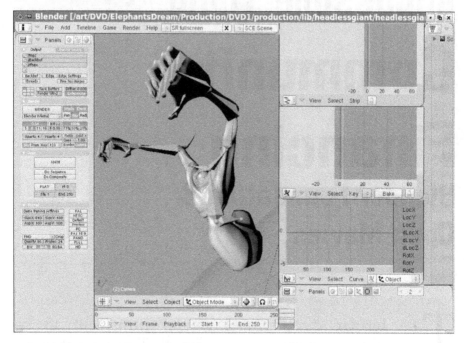

impractical for a loosely-bound group like the free culture community, but let's look at some important examples of how it can be done.

Starting Commercial with Blender

A number of large-scale projects in the free software world—such as Mozilla, Zope, OpenOffice.org, and Blender—started out as fairly standard commercial/proprietary development projects. During their incubation phase, the simplicity and structure of a commercial environment with capital investment and salaried programmers made their development fairly straightforward. It was only after these programs had released operational software that their supporting companies made the decision to go to free software licensing.

Figure 4.2:
The Blender Foundation is now the community-based steward for the Blender free software package

> # Myth #4:
>
> ## "Sometimes projects have to have money, and commons-based projects can't raise it"
>
> The truth is that it *is* hard for the free culture community to raise actual cash for projects, but it has been done. And there are parallels with mainstream culture that suggest it can be taken even further.

Most of them did this as part of a successful business plan, and their mother companies continued on in a "support and services" business model that continues into the present. Sadly, Blender was a little different. In 2002, its authoring company, "Not a Number" (which provided services based on the Blender application) folded. In the proceedings, the stockholders (who owned the copyright) agreed that they would let Blender be released under a free license, if they were given a fixed payoff of €100,000 to cover the company's remaining debts.[1]

This was feasible because at that time, Blender was already **"freeware"**—that is, an application you could freely download, though no source code was provided. So there were already many people using it. As a result, the **Blender Foundation** was created and started taking donations (electronically "passing the hat," in a process that has come to be called the **street performer protocol** or **SPP**). In just *seven weeks*, enough money was raised to pay off the Not a Number investors, and Blender was released under the GPL as promised, with all of its **source code**.

Afterwards, the Blender Foundation continued to work and receive donations, and those donations are spent on improving the now-free Blender. This has proved to be a very successful operation, and Blender has continued to improve both in capability and usability.

Starting Free with the Blender Foundation Movies

So, is it necessary to start such capital-intensive projects in a commercial environment with proprietary licensing to protect the bottom line? Or are there ways in which the community can collectively patronize such activities from the outset?

This is trickier than a traditional company startup, but again, the Blender Foundation provides interesting examples.

Since the best way to improve software like Blender is to use it in actual production projects, driving the development process by the demonstrated needs of users, the Blender Foundation reasoned that the best way to promote and improve Blender was to make movies with it.

Orange

Thus started the Orange Movie Project. With a projected budget of €120,000, no script and no definite story idea, but with a talented group of animators, the Blender Foundation proposed to pre-sell DVDs of the finished movie—which they would finish in about eight months. Everything the project produced would be released under a free license (the Creative Commons Attribution license).

Then, when 1000 DVDs had been sold (raising about €35,000 of seed money), the project would start work. The animators were not paid top dollar, but they did have stipends, computers, and plenty of creative space. They brainstormed, designed characters, wrote a script, developed Blender models, new tools for animating them, and ultimately created an 11 minute film, called *Elephants Dream*.[2]

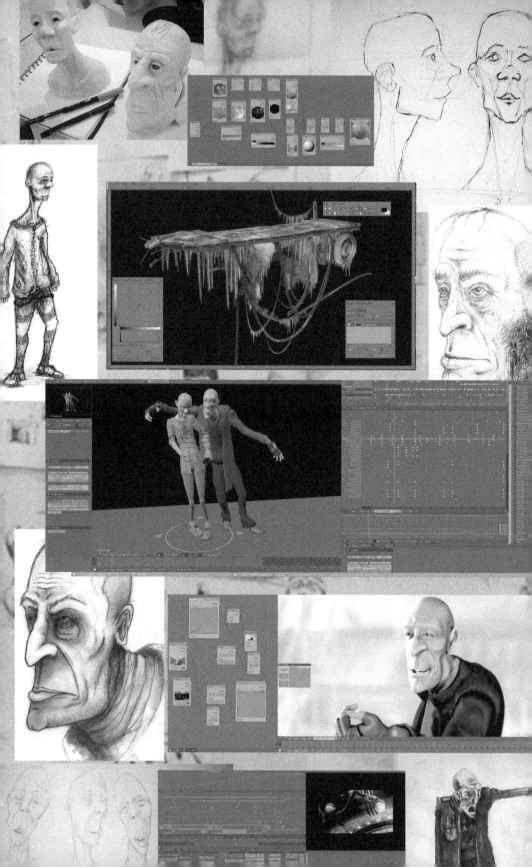

The movie *Elephants Dream* itself is in some ways a mixed bag. It's clearly not the greatest work of fiction ever animated, but it does have creative merit. The characters are engaging and the environment is fascinating. The story is artistic almost to the point of incomprehensibility, but there is a point lying underneath about the nature of sharing, artistic works, and the imagination.

It is clear, though, that the real star of the show is Blender and the models that the Orange Project was able to create. More importantly, when you bought a DVD of *Elephants Dream*, you weren't just buying an 11 minute movie. You were buying approximately seven gigabytes of production files: models, textures, python scripts for Blender, screenplays, translations, animatics, and (with the exception of the cast and crew!) everything you could possibly need to produce a derivative work from *Elephants Dream* (and I mean real derivatives, not "mix-ups").

The movie *Elephants Dream* can be thought of as just a "demo," a reference implementation of what can be done with the tools and artistic resources contained on the DVD. Legally, of course, all of that is enabled by the Creative Commons Attribution license: as long as you credit the people on the Orange Movie Project for their work, you can use it all to make your own derivative works.

Peach

Since the Orange Project was so successful, both in terms of the popularity of the movie produced and in the improvements to Blender that it facilitated, the Blender Foundation moved on to make a second film.

Figure 4.3:

(Facing Page) The Blender Orange Movie project is best known for producing the short film *Elephants Dream*, but the most remarkable product of the project is the production materials which can be used to freely create derivative works using the characters, digital models, matte paintings, and other material used in the movie
(Blender Foundation | www.blender.org / CC-By 2.5)

The Peach Open Movie project had specific orders to strike a more populist chord: it had to be cute, furry, and funny. No doubt this was partly to compensate for the shortcomings of *Elephants Dream*, but it was also simply to stay diverse, so as to cover more technical territory for Blender.

It was also self-consciously decided that the mark should not be set too high, lest the film never get made. After all, "best is the enemy of good enough," and all the people pre-ordering the DVDs would be more disappointed by a film that was never finished than by one that lacked a certain artistic edge.

The Peach Project's *Big Buck Bunny* did aim for a lower artistic mark—it was, with neither prentence nor shame, a cartoon. However, unlike *Elephants Dream*, it squarely hit the mark it set: the film is funny, cute, and genuinely entertaining to watch.

Clearly, lessons were learned from *Elephants Dream* and applied to later projects.

Apricot

Shortly after completing *Big Buck Bunny*, another project, called "Apricot" produced a game based on the resources from Peach, titled *Yo, Frankie!* ("Frankie" is the name of the flying squirrel in *Big Buck Bunny*). The game development process promoted development on the Blender game engine, the CrystalSpace game engine, and the support for CrystalSpace in Blender.

Relative scales

Each of these projects (and the community purchase of Blender) were capitalized within a community foundation setting, using some pioneering fund-raising techniques. There's plenty of room for improvement in these techniques, and yet they are already producing results. So it seems that indeed, it is possible to raise funds within the community for more traditional, capitalized, "cathedral" endeavors. We can do it when we need to.

Figure 4.4:

As of this writing, the Blender Foundation has successfully funded and released two movies, *Elephants Dream* and *Big Buck Bunny*, as well as a game based on the resources from *Big Buck Bunny*, called *Yo, Frankie!* An instructional video on *Character Animation* has also been produced as a spin-off of these projects.

Figure 4.5:

Comparison of costs on a logarithmic scale, emphasizing Blender both as a software project and a license buy-out, as well as some other foundation-funded projects

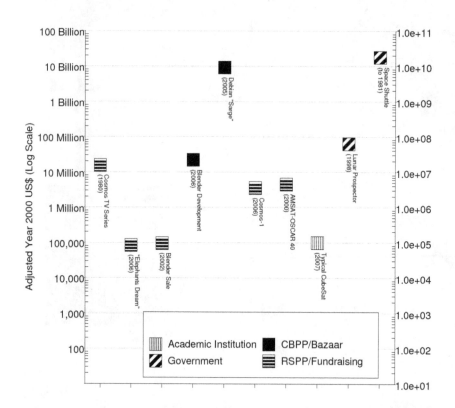

It is true, however, that the scale is still much smaller than the support the community can raise in "in kind" donations of time and effort. To illustrate this, and also to give some perspective to the project, I've created a logarithmic plot of the relative monetary and monetary-equivalent investments represented by several projects, in Figure 4.5.

This chart includes a number of different kinds of valuations. The free software projects are evaluated in terms of estimated cost using the same "Constructive Cost Model" (COCOMO) that was used earlier to evaluate the effort on Debian GNU/Linux and other software projects. Also on this chart are some comparable reported final budgets for space development projects (on the right) and other kinds of media projects (left).

Blender appears twice on this chart: once as a software project, with a COCOMO-estimated equivalent effort cost, and once as the actual Blender Foundation buy-out sale price. Also appearing is the budget for the Orange Project (the Peach budget was not available at the time of writing).

These can be seen as estimates of what the community can raise in terms of actual cash capital, as opposed to the "sweat capital" represented by free software project effort estimates. As you can see, there is a difference of nearly two orders of magnitude between the in-kind contributions to a software project like Blender and the actual cash that could be raised to buy out its license.

On the other hand, foundation funding has been used before. Also appearing on this chart are two much larger foundation-funded projects: *Cosmos*, the television series featuring Carl Sagan, with a reported budget of approximately US$6 million for production and US$2 million for promotion, which was funded by voluntary contributions to the American Public Broadcasting System (PBS), and the *Cosmos-1* solar sail project, with a reported project cost of US$4 million, funded by voluntary contributions to the Planetary Society.

We might be inclined to discount these as comparables, but PBS's fund-raising scheme is really just another kind of street performer protocol: every so often, they "pass the hat" through their periodic "pledge drives," in order to get viewers to contribute to their projects. They do also receive funding from other foundations and a certain amount from US federal government grants (but these are possible sources of funding for free software or open hardware projects as well).

Communities certainly can raise funds if the community is large enough and there is a high level of trust that the contributions will produce results. The free culture community has about an order of magnitude to go to catch up to such mainstream funding levels, but there's every reason to believe that the potential for that kind of growth is there.

Notes

1 The Blender Foundation's History webpage explains this in detail.
   `http://www.blender.org/blenderorg/blender-foundation/history/`

2 *Elephants Dream* figures from Wikipedia (which is based on information from the Blender Foundation).
   `http://en.wikipedia.org/wiki/Elephants_Dream`

   `http://www.blender.org`

Impossible Thing #5:

Open Hardware
Chips, Computers, Cards, and Cars

S o far, I've identified examples of free, commons-based production of several pure information products. And that leads to the next question: what about the material marketplace? Can commons-based methods be used to design, prototype, and manufacture physical products? The answer, according to a growing group of open hardware developers is a resounding "Yes!" From computer hardware to automobiles, the **open hardware** revolution is on.

Open Hardware Electronics

Although there have been "**homebrew**" projects for many years, one of the first really successful complex electronic designs to be released under a free-license was the LART.[1] It was an embedded ARM-based computer designed for

Myth #5:

"Free development only works for pure information projects—so it can't work for hardware"

Part of this myth is true, of course: you can't really share physical products the way we do with free-licensed information products. That's a fundamental property of information. However, the designs for physical products are just a special kind of information product, and they can be shared.

multimedia **set-top boxes** (but of course, it could be adapted to many uses). The complete design was released under a GPL license, including all of the plans and **CAD/CAM** files used to construct it.

There was one problem, which was that the StrongARM SA-1100 **CPU** used was not a free-licensed product, and it was eventually discontinued, which essentially orphaned the LART design. Although work continued for some time on new designs, the project's website hasn't been updated since 2003. Closed design and limited availability of important components is a serious problem for higher level designs.

Getting Inside the Chip: FPGA Designs

Much of the recent success of popularizing free hardware design has come from the introduction of the **Field Programmable Gate Array** (**FPGA**). These chips store huge arrays of logic gates whose connectivity and functionality can be altered in software as if they were memory addresses. This allows a **hardware description language** (**HDL**) to be used to

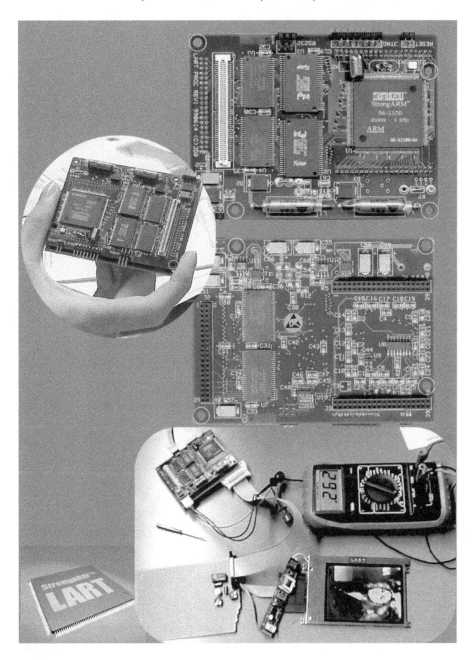

Figure 5.1:
The LART was an embedded open hardware computer designed for multimedia applications
(LART project PR Photos)

Figure 5.2:
(Below) An Altera FPGA
(Credit: Mike1024@Wikipedia/PD)

Figure 5.3:
(Facing Page Top) The Open Cores project hosts a large number of open hardware chip designs, called "cores"

Figure 5.4:
(Facing Page Bottom) A prototype Open Graphics Development board (OGD1), developed by the Open Graphics project
(Credit: Open Graphics project / CC By-SA 3.0)

describe the functionality of a circuit, then compile (or "**synthesize**") the result into an actual **gate** layout which can be loaded onto one of these chips. Xilinx and Altera are the biggest names today in FPGA manufacturing. Once a design has been tested in FPGA, it is possible to create an **Application Specific Integrated Circuit** (**ASIC**) made for much lower unit costs. Thus an FPGA serves a similar role for chip designers as breadboarding does for printed circuit board designers.

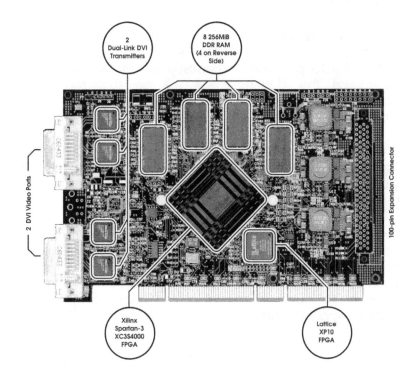

Realizing Open Hardware

Because of the realities of hardware manufacturing and the resulting cost structures, it's often a challenge to actually get open hardware made, once it has been designed. This is usually because manufacturing setup costs are high, while marginal production costs are low: the classical reason for mass production.

Strategies differ, but the Open Graphics project presents a practical example, illustrated in figure 5.5.

First the project will create the OGD1 (this was essentially completed in 2008, although at the time of this writing in 2009, the project is still raising funds to build the first run). Then the project will develop the Open Graphics Architecture on this platform, while selling the OGD1 cards (which are powerful, low-cost general-purpose FPGA boards in addition to their special input/output features).

Once the architecture is complete, the project hopes to use seed capital from the OGD1 sales and venture capital investment to produce a modest-sized run of ASIC chips based on the design. These will be sold mostly to embedded developers, for whom the open source design is a strong selling point.

Even a small number of these chips will provide ample supplies for short runs of an ASIC-based "Open Graphics Card," designed to be competitive enough to attract the market of free software operating system users.

Production runs and collective purchasing are a common problem for open hardware projects. Even runs of circuit boards often need to be in the hundreds or thousands in order to be cost-effective (figure 5.6). Despite the difficulty, however, a number of projects manage to get their products manufactured.

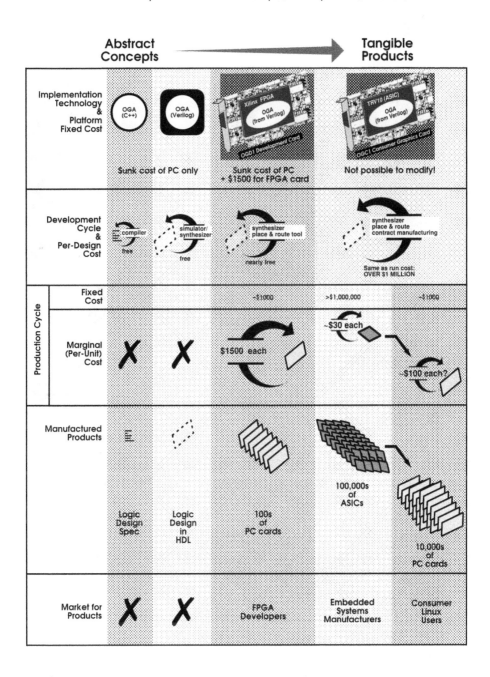

Figure 5.5:
Open Graphics project's production and financing strategy

Figure 5.6:

Remainder from a LART production run
(From LART website)

Joseph Black, a developer on the **Open Graphics** project described the experience of working with FPGA designs and hardware description languages in 2008:

> *"When I did a short course about FPGAs and VHDL (a hardware language) I found to my surprise that I could download a datasheet of any chip I found and make my FPGA do the same job. And this is not very difficult. I tried a certain 8 bit RISC processor, and after two months of work, I realized that I had implemented a sizable portion of it. And it ran fast! So fast, I could envision that it was possible to run their chip faster on my FPGA. Then I searched the net and found others had already begun similar work on other chips and designs and I then had a lightbulb moment. Hardware design was now possible for the average man.*

> *"With the ability to create and test open hardware designs, it's possible to develop a bazaar development community around open hardware chip designs. Such a site is Open Cores."*
>
> —— *Joseph Black*

The **Open Cores**[2] project now hosts approximately 280 open hardware chip "**cores**," varying in complexity from frequently-used interface and register logic up to entire **microcontroller** and **microprocessor** systems (several legacy processor specifications have been implemented as well as some new designs such as the "OpenRISC 1000" CPU, which has already seen some commercial applications).

Taking FPGA a step further, the Open Graphics project, started by Timothy Miller of Tech Source (and now of Traversal Technology), aims to design a high-speed 3D-accelerated graphics subsystem, for tasks such as 3D design, data visualization, and desktop support (as well as some games). As a first step in the project, the Open Graphics community has completed design of a specialized FPGA development board that will be usable as a graphics card (albeit a very expensive one) when its FPGA is loaded with the Open Graphics Architecture (OGA).

Later products of this project should include a cheaper ASIC graphics chip directly useful for embedded designers and a 3D accelerated graphics card suitable for consumer personal computers, where the open design will enable free software graphics drivers, thus eliminating a major nuisance for users of free software operating systems.

Less and Less Ephemeral: Open Hardware Cars

So far, however, we haven't strayed far from the realm of computers and computing. These are still quite ephemeral

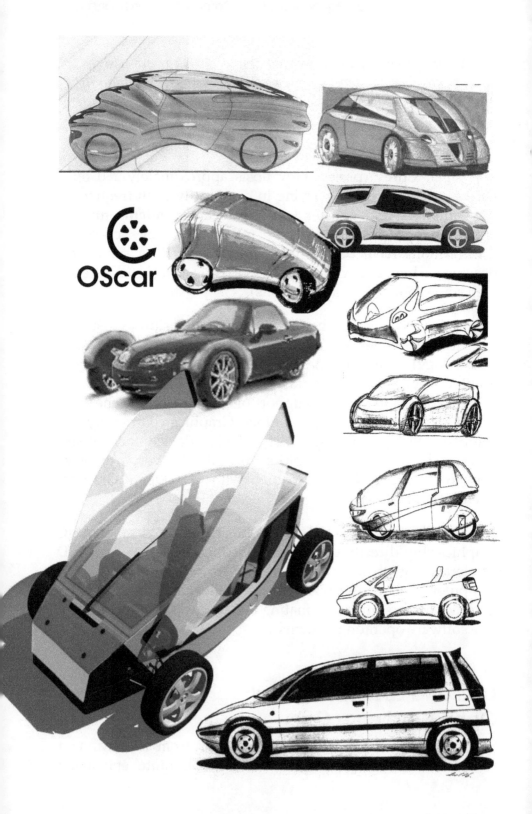

OScar

"high information content" designs. But open hardware can go much further.

So far, few projects self-consciously identify themselves as "open hardware": there are a lot of "homebrew" designs out there for technology ranging from windmills to airplanes which are usable for hobbyists, but limited somewhat in collaboration because no consideration has been made of the licenses.

However, some people are getting the idea. For example, three separate groups have started attempts to develop a next-generation automobile design using open source methods: the "OScar" project, the "Open Source Green Vehicle," and the "C,mm,n" project. Arising from different communities, each has a unique character which is worth exploring.

OScar[3] is a true community-driven project, very much in the amateur spirit (Figure 5.7). The project's originator, Markus Merz, was motivated to do the project largely out of a desire to create something physical using bazaar methodology. The result is less a car development project, and more a forum for sharing ideas on car design and construction. Very likely, the result (or results) of the OScar project will be in the form of "kit cars" which can be manufactured using fairly simple tools, by individuals or small organizations, though it's still unclear exactly what the project will try to produce.

The Society for Sustainable Mobility has proposed creating an "Open Source Green Vehicle" (OSGV[4]) primarily out of a self-conscious desire to counter perceived market pressure for the *status quo*, and the community reflects this outlook. The license is not a true free-license, as it prohibits manufacture of the design (although it's not clear that such restrictions are

Figure 5.7:

(Facing Page) A collection of design concepts from the OScar project site. The rendered 3D concept on the lower left is by Tiago do Vale. The three-wheel concept above it is the dart-footed monster (Detalidon) by Arak Leatham

(Credits: OSCar Project / theoscarproject.org/PR, Arak Leatham / detalidon.com/PR, Tiago do Vale/PD)

enforceable). The rationale for this is based in liability and safety concerns (and a faith in professional training): they claim that only "professionals" should do such tasks and fear that people might "kill themselves" by attempting to manufacture the cars themselves.

This attitude is a big contrast from the do-it-yourselfer attitude of the OScar project, but it is not an unfounded fear, and something that free-licensed hardware designers must consider in licenses for high-powered equipment. As Lourens Veen of the Open Hardware Foundation reflected in a 2008 interview:

> *"One possible problem is a legal one. As the devices we buy have become more complex and more proprietary, their manufacturers have become more powerful. In response to that, consumer protection laws have become more and more strict, especially in the European Union. These laws are not designed with the Open Hardware ecosystem of loosely organized design groups and small, independent manufacturers in mind, and they could well become an obstacle.*
>
> *"There are precedents for more Open Hardware-friendly legislation however, such as the Single Vehicle Approval that is required for kit cars in the UK, and the 'experimental' category air worthiness certificate in the US."*
>
> —— *Lourens Veen*

The OSGV site does suggest that its restrictions might be lifted in the future, and the overall focus on community involvement in the engineering process merits mentioning on the subject of open hardware. The OSGV focuses on a "kernel" of drive train development, with localized projects developing the "look and feel" of the designs with a focus on regional car markets.

Figure 5.8:

(Facing Page) C,mm,n project prototypes from the 2007 and 2009 AutoRAI auto shows in Holland as well as a technology demonstrator with frame and fuel cell / electric motor drive system
(Photos credit: Jacco Lammers / CC-By-SA 2.0)

c,mm,n

your mobility. our c,mm,n future.

(Above) 2009 C,mm,n Technology Demonstrator

(Right) 2009 control panel mock-up

(Above and Right) Body-style mock-up for the 2007 AutoRAI show

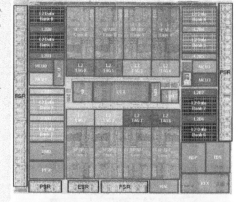

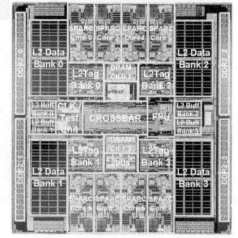

Figure 5.9:
The OpenSPARC project supports the community of hardware developers around Sun's GPL release of their UltraSPARC T1 and T2 CPU cores (the chips are shown at right)
(Photo Credit: Sun Microsystems / PR)

Finally, the C,mm,n[5], with its too-clever-for-its-own-good name, was born in a university engineering environment at TU Delft in Holland, providing it with a strong brick-and-mortar support system (Figure 5.8). Thus, although the project started later than OScar, it was able to produce a non-working prototype of the design for display at the Dutch biannual AutoRAI show in 2007. Though not quite yet a working car, the group presented technology demonstrator prototypes for the 2009 show.

Open Hardware Goes Mainstream

With so may pioneering new projects out there already, it shouldn't come as a huge surprise that some major companies have decided to join the bandwagon. In 2006, Sun Microsystems released the source code for their "UltraSPARC T1" and "UltraSPARC T2" multi-core microprocessors under the GPL. The resulting design is the OpenSPARC,[6] which has now grown a small hardware design community.

Although it is clear that open hardware has some special challenges, real projects succeed at overcoming them, and open hardware is clearly a growing phenomenon. The strongest areas have understandably been in the area of computer hardware, but there's no fundamental limit to what can be created by commons-based communities using free-licensed hardware designs. The same bazaar development rules apply to hardware as for software: both provide a smoother environment for collaboration on truly innovative designs.

Notes

1 LART multimedia computer
   http://www.lartmaker.nl/

2 Open Cores (chip design sharing site)
   http://www.opencores.org

3 OScar (Open Source Car project)
   http://www.theoscarproject.org

4 Open Source Green Vehicle (OSGV)
  `http://www.osgv.org`

5 C,mm,n (another open hardware car)
  `http://www.cmmn.org`

6 OpenSPARC (open hardware microprocessor based on Sun Microsystems design)
  `http://www.opensparc.net`

Impossible Thing #6:
Closing the
Digital Divide
OLPC & Sugar Labs

For many years, there has been a growing concern about the emergence of a **"digital divide"** between rich and poor. The idea is that people who don't meet a certain threshold income won't be able to afford the investment in computers and internet connectivity that makes further learning and development possible. They'll become trapped by their circumstances.

Under **proprietary commercial operating systems**, which impose a kind of plateau on the cost of computer systems, this may well be true. But GNU/Linux, continuously improving hardware, and a community commitment to bringing technology down to cost instead of just up to spec, has led to a new wave of ultra-low-cost computers, starting with the One Laptop Per Child's XO. These free-software-based computers will be the first introduction to computing for millions of new users, and that foretells a much freer future.

Myth #6:

"There simply aren't enough willing developers to do free development, and it only helps a tiny, privileged few"

Free culture is no longer a fringe phenomenon. It's a global phenomenon, and it is becoming accessible to more and more people, including many people that have been left behind by corporate proprietary culture and so have strong personal motivations to support it.

One Laptop Per Child

In 2005, Kofi Annan, former Secretary General of the United Nations, and Nicholas Negroponte, a professor from the MIT Media Lab, jointly announced a project to change the way that children around the world learn—using a constructivist learning solution: provide the children with a tool for "learning learning," based on the ideas of education expert Seymour Papert. The design selected is a "laptop" computer, though the term has to be used somewhat loosely, because the OLPC XO 1 is designed for a totally different mission than the typical business traveller's laptop. It is not like any prior design.[1]

One of its principle design criteria is that it must be very, very inexpensive. The target was US$100. The first units cost closer to US$200, though it is hoped that the cost will drop as the component prices come down and the design is further stabilized. The project has committed to lowering costs rather than increasing performance, since the whole point of the OLPC laptop is to create something that developing nations' education ministries can afford to purchase for the children in their countries.

It's not such a good idea to make a computer like this using proprietary software for several reasons. First of all, the usual per-computer licensing fee on a copy of Windows would cost more than the hardware! Second, presuming that subsidies were offered to make it affordable, the choice would introduce new constraints on the design as well as the brittleness intrinsic to any single-supplier system. Deep subsidies provided by a company offering their operating system at a loss would also raise serious questions of conflict-of-interest, since the company would have to make up that loss somehow. Finally, since the whole point is to help kids in exploration learning, it is counterproductive to hide the mechanism—access to the source code for the operating system is just another part of the learning experience.

So, it should be no surprise that the OLPC laptop runs Linux. In fact, the machines contain a complete free software system—right down to the **firmware BIOS**, which will be OpenFirmware,[2] written in the **Forth** programming language. Because of the complexity of shipping source code for all of the software on such tiny, storage-constrained computers, the team also decided to write a huge amount of the system in Python, an interpreted programming language that greatly simplifies the requirement of access to the code. With **Python**, the source is the working program, so there is only one thing to distribute; the source is particularly easy to read, even for grade schoolers; and no compiler or build system is required for them to modify and use the software on the computer. Changes are reflected immediately, at run time.

In fact, the OLPC laptops are designed to facilitate this kind of exploration as much as possible. Developing software is one of many "activities" which a child is invited to explore through the machine's **"Sugar" user interface**.[3] Every running program will (eventually, at least) allow the child to press a simple "view source" key to see the Python code behind it (just as most web browsers will let you view the HTML source of web pages, a feature which has made HTML highly accessible even to "non-programmers" around the world).

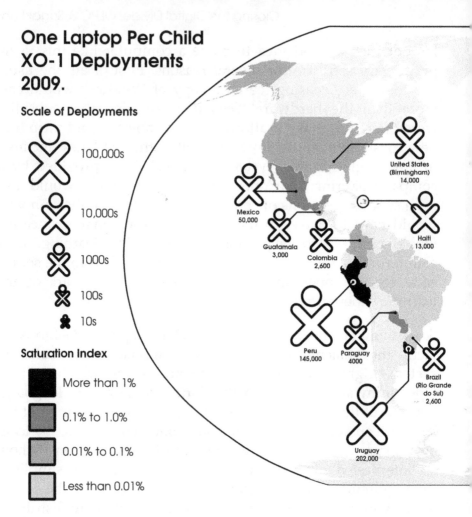

One Laptop Per Child XO-1 Deployments 2009.

Scale of Deployments

100,000s

10,000s

1000s

100s

10s

Saturation Index

More than 1%

0.1% to 1.0%

0.01% to 0.1%

Less than 0.01%

United States
(Birmingham)
14,000

Mexico
50,000

Guatamala
3,000

Colombia
2,600

Haiti
13,000

Peru
145,000

Paraguay
4000

Brazil
(Rio Grande
do Sul)
2,600

Uruguay
202,000

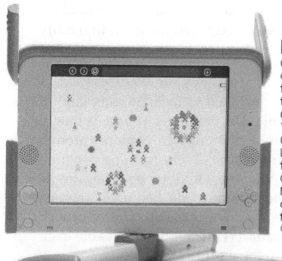

Figure 6.1:

(Above) Map of OLPC laptop deployments based on the status at the end of 2007, from information on the OLPC website and wiki.[1,4]
(Lower Left) The One Laptop Per Child "XO" computer.
(Lower Right, Clockwise from Upper Left) The very first laptops coming off the assembly line; teachers at an OLPC seminar; teachers in Ulaanbatar, Mongolia; and a Mongolian education official ceremonially handing out the first units

(Photos: OLPC Project / CC-By 2.5).

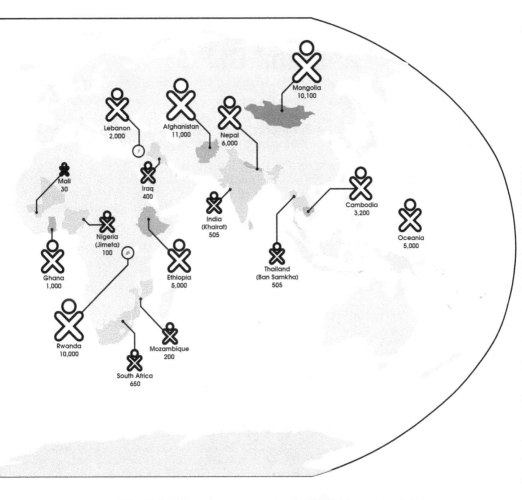

Mongolia
10,100

Lebanon
2,000

Afghanistan
11,000

Nepal
6,000

Mali
30

Iraq
400

India
(Khairat)
505

Cambodia
3,200

Nigeria
(Jimeta)
100

Oceania
5,000

Ghana
1,000

Ethiopia
5,000

Thailand
(Ban Samkha)
505

Rwanda
10,000

Mozambique
200

South Africa
650

Sugar Labs and OLPC

In 2008, OLPC found itself considerably short of its goals, and much finger pointing and acrimony ensued. It was probably inevitable that something like this would come up eventually. The OLPC project operates in one of the harshest political environments imaginable: not just education and not just the developing world, but both in one package!

The OLPC project compromised ideological purity by offering laptops with a **dual-boot** GNU/Linux and Windows XP system to those potential buyers who insisted on being able to run Windows. This may well have been the right decision, too, though it heartily annoyed some people in the free software community.

Tensions between industrial sponsors, the OLPC organizers, and the community of free software developers produced some sparks, and the result was a substantial reorganization. Sugar left the official OLPC project, becoming an independent project operated by Walter Bender and others as "Sugar Labs."[3] This was almost certainly the right move, since it put the community in charge of the community project, as well as increasing its visibility.

Nevertheless, the OLPC project—and now I am speaking of the whole movement surrounding the One Laptop Per Child mission, not just the organization that started the project—is getting back on track, and may do much better after this transition, though as of this writing in 2009, it's really too early to tell for sure).

Right now, the OLPC project stands at about half a million units either deployed, or in the process of being deployed worldwide. That's about 5% of the stated target for the end of 2007 (over a year ago), and only about 0.5% of the original stated objective of the OLPC project, which was closer to 100 million (about 1/60th of the population of Earth). Presumably the real target (every child on Earth) is an even higher figure. Clearly OLPC has fallen far short of its progress goals.

Nevertheless, a lot of good has been done, and it's likely that a lot more will be.

- OLPC's XO is still the freest thing going: free BIOS, free operating system, free window manager, free applications. That some of them will carry Windows as well is a detail: deploying free software is a lot more important than hurting Microsoft

- Sugar has broken away from the OLPC organization, taking Walter Bender and others with it, as a new entity called "Sugar Labs." It has its own independent online presence and community now. A series of more portable builds has been an outcome of this process.

- Nevertheless, we now have choices. The XO was popular enough in the developed world to spawn a raft of imitators: a whole new class of computer, popularly called "**netbooks**."

- Sugar runs on those imitators, on the XO, and on refurbished or new computers anywhere in the world. Whatever you might think of the XO as the deployment vector, Sugar is a free software tool that all free software advocates can support

- Sugar is 100% free software. Even the Squeak/Etoys package has gotten over whatever licensing quibbles it was encumbered with. Today, it's even being admitted into Debian main, although the administrative hurdles will take a few months to clear.

- OLPC is seeing bigger orders. Evidently, Negroponte's dual-boot gambit is working.

The break-up itself is somewhat enlightening for the purposes of this book. Note that the community needed to get better control of the software development effort in order to feel ownership of the project, and therefore more of a responsibility to update it. Note the tension created by the different cultures of the business and commons-based enterprised worlds. Finally, notice how the independence created by free licensing allowed the software project to migrate smoothly to community control, thus surviving what might have become a disastrous failure had the whole thing been managed as a proprietary enterprise.

OLPC XO laptops having their software updated as part of a recent deployment
(David Drake / CC By 2.0)

The consequences of this design decision are staggering and inspiring. Around the world, perhaps by 2020, there may be as many as 100 million children, ages six to ten, with a complete, easy-to-use Python programming environment and an operating system full of fun programs to tinker with. It's hard to imagine any child that wouldn't be drawn into that.

For the sake of argument, though, imagine that in fact only one child in a thousand genuinely gets involved and reaches a point where we would legitimately call them an "open source developer." That's 100,000 people. Remember: Debian GNU/Linux, which we've already seen (Impossible Thing #1) could be valued at $10 billion or more, was built by many fewer people.

Still, especially in light of the organizational problems that it experienced in 2008, some people fear that OLPC won't attain its lofty goals. But in the long run these are not very important considerations, because even if OLPC itself fails, the *idea* has been put forward, and it's the idea that matters. If not the XO, then some other ultra-low-cost machine will be deployed throughout the world to fill the same niche: several competitors have already entered the market. One of the advantages of the spin-off of the Sugar Labs project in 2008 into a separate, community-driven project, is greater independence for Sugar from any one type or brand of laptop.

A Whole New Kind of Computer Market

Enough people in the developed world have been impressed with the XO's design to make mainstream manufacturers and designers take notice. Clearly, there is demand for a $200 to $400 computer that does what the XO does. And since the production and distribution chain for the OLPC is hampered somewhat by the specifics of its mission, commercial developers are stepping in to close this market gap.

Figure 6.3:

(Facing Page) Kids exploring the technology. The OLPC, because of its free-software-based design, offers an unprecedented empowerment for new users around the world
(Photos: OLPC Project / CC-By 2.5)

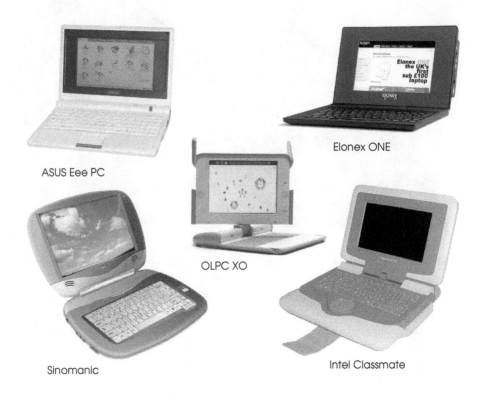

ASUS Eee PC

Elonex ONE

OLPC XO

Sinomanic

Intel Classmate

Sugar "Storybuilder" activity running on an Intel Classmate, using the "Sugar-on-a-Stick" distribution

A new array of low-end laptop computers, based on flash-memory, power-miser CPUs, extremely rugged design, and GNU/Linux operating systems are being built and marketed to supply the new demand.

Fortunately, these computers will have almost the same impact in richer countries that the XO will have in poor ones: millions and millions of people will be exposed to an out-of-the-box experience driven by GNU/Linux and free software. Such users won't ask "why should I switch to free software?", but "why would I ever switch to anything else?" The stick-with-what-you-know motivation is strong, and that advantage will now apply to free software.

But what's more interesting is that, with so many more people (and so many more kinds of people) exposed to it, the potential for new involvement, new ideas, and new software development also increases. With ten-fold more users, comes ten-fold more potential new developers. And, of course, every itch scratched serves ten times as many people: which means there's also a larger pool from which foundation activities can draw.

Pioneers and the New Wave

What this means, is that the present "free culture" may be no more than a "pilot project." The real social phenomenon is yet to come. And if the present array of free software developers, open hardware hackers, and free culture producers can shake the world as much as we have already seen that it has, then it's clear that this new wave—more than an order-of-magnitude larger—could quite simply *re-make the world*.

Figure 6.4:
(Facing Page) Although the OLPC is targeted to developing countries, it has scouted the marketplace and commercial competitors are rapidly closing the market gap
(Credits: OLPC Project / CC-By-2.5 (XO), S2RD2@Flickr/CC-By-2.0 (Classmate), Red@Wikipedia/CC-By-3.0 (Eee), Sinomanic and ONE are PR photos)

Notes

1 One Laptop Per Child (OLPC) is a project which intends to bring low-cost computers as well as access to the internet and free software to children all over the world.

`http://www.laptop.org`

2 OpenFirmware is a basic boot-up software which can launch several different operating systems including GNU/Linux.

`http://wiki.laptop.org/go/Open_Firmware`

3 Sugar is a graphical user interface system designed around an "activities" paradigm, specifically for kids.

`http://www.sugarlabs.org`

4 The "Saturation Index" included in figure 6.1 is an expedient but objective way to compare the progress of OLPC in various countries, which I calculated by simply dividing the number of laptops deployed into the number of children under the age of 14 in each country, based on data in the 2009 CIA World Fact Book. This is imperfect, because it includes more than the target group (which is children ages 6-10). It is a considerable improvement over dividing into the total population, though, and is available in a consistent way for all of the countries involved. The OLPC's goal of getting a computer to every grade school age child would probably represent a value of about 30% to 40% for this index for most of the countries in question, depending somewhat on the exact population distribution.

`https://www.cia.gov/library/publications/the-world-factbook`

`http://wiki.laptop.org/go/Deployments`

A New Paradigm

I've presented the empirical case for debunking six major myths on which our existing model of "intellectual property" and our existing belief that free development can only be a niche phenomenon are based:

- "Free development is only adequate for small scale projects"

- "Commons-based projects can't possibly compete with what corporations can do"

- "The service model limits free production to utilitarian, not aesthetic, works (so it can't work for art or music)"

- "Sometimes projects have to have money, and commons-based projects can't raise it"

- "Free development only works for pure information projects—so it can't work for hardware"

- "There simply aren't enough willing developers to do free development, and it only helps a tiny, privileged few"

Or, to invert, I've presented the empirical case for six "impossibilities" produced by peer production, in defiance of prior economic theory:

- Massive information products can be built using commons-based production

- In many cases, these products are larger than comparable corporate- or government-backed enterprises

- There is essentially no area of human endeavor that is off-limits to peer production, including software, science, technology, and art

- There are proven methods for peer communities to raise capital when it is needed

- Even for material production, design data can be developed by commons-based enterprises

- Already, peer production communities are large and powerful, but they are likely to increase by an order of magnitude in the coming decade, certainly by mid-century as the technology is made available to more and more people (a project which is important to many free culture proponents)

Now what? If we've crossed into the looking glass world where these six impossible things can be proven possible, then what shall we have for breakfast? Clearly we are looking at a new paradigm, but the next problem is to understand how that paradigm works and how best to make use of it.

Part II:
The Rules of the Game

The Rules of the Game

86

The Rules
of the Game

C learly, there must be new rules to learn if we want to be able to predict the existing successes (thus validating the theory), and to succeed with new, more ambitious projects. In order to get to the bottom of this, we'll have to take a much closer look at the mechanisms that drive existing peer production communities.

This is fundamentally a study of the behavior of people. In the peer production community, where the most important driving forces are volunteer and otherwise freely-contributed creative labor, the rules are much more complex than those of the proprietary economy.

Most of our existing economic theory (at least in the United States and other traditional bastions of capitalist philosophy) attempts to simplify the motivation problem by reducing the complex and subtle behavior of human psychology to that of a purely selfish and rational "economic automaton" (figure 7.1). Even though it is not accurate in detail, in the case of the monetary exchange economy, this model is frequently predictive of broad trends. So we have stuck with this model, even though we know it is an incredible oversimplification.

It has long been appreciated that social action: political parties, volunteerism, do-it-yourselfers, religion, charity, art, craft, and other forms of "altruistic" or "irrational" behavior create holes in the "economic automaton" model. However, for most of the matter economy, in most of the world, for most of history, these "higher motivations" provide nothing more than a slight perturbation to the basic assumption of selfish, unconsidered, economic motivation (which accounts for the bulk behavior of the economy).

We are not exclusively economic machines—at least not in the money-motivated sense we usually imagine when we talk about "economics"—and it is the step of dropping this simplifying assumption, that allows us to understand the workings of commons-based enterprises.

What has changed, is that free replication of information amplifies the higher motivations: tiny voluntary contributions which might otherwise be negligible in the matter economy can often accumulate or even synergize to form large effects (sometimes completely outperforming the system of "rational economic behavior"). Thus, if we do not take the time to understand these other effects, we will continue to be blindsided by massive, apparently unexplainable economic phenomena.

Intellectual Freedom versus Intellectual Property

The liberation of information has been going on for a long time: one might say for all of human history, as history itself is one of the oldest forms of information sharing. There are several major landmarks dotting that course, which I might point to: the invention of spoken language, of writing, of ink and paper, of block printing, movable type printing, digital typesetting, electronic distribution, and most recently, the internet (figure 7.2).

Each of these steps has produced an opening up in the exchange of information, resulting in more efficient technological progress, followed by additional steps in increasing our communications abilities. These steps have been associated closely with massive and rapid improvements in science, health, and standard of living, for most of human history. And, post-modernist angst notwithstanding, the reality is that there aren't many of us who would genuinely trade our present lifestyle for that of our ancestors: especially if we consider the additional pressures imposed by increased population.

Cheap computers, electronic data storage, and of course, the internet, have produced an unparalleled ease of information sharing. Today, we do better to think in terms of a sea of information into which our work is published, from which anyone can draw, rather than in terms of specific data exchanges. Just as we would never try to simulate or predict the behavior of an ocean by modelling its individual atoms, we'd be fools to try to manage the information economy in terms of tracking every individual exchange.

Trying to intelligently predict and control the transfers within this sea of information is at least as pointless (and procrustean) as trying to control the matter marketplace. The arguments for the "free market" also work as arguments for "intellectual freedom." "Intellectual property" has, as a result, become roughly as doomed an idea as the "planned economy" of twentieth century communist states.

Patents, copyrights, and other forms of "intellectual property" were created to protect certain kinds of business models, under the assumption that economic motivations are essential to production of information products. To some degree, this is no doubt true (even a perfectly altruistic creator must be fed, housed, and educated in order to continue contributing).

However, it is questionable whether the "intellectual property" model is the best method for solving the problem, especially as

Figure 7.1:
Existing economic models assume that all productive effort is unpleasant "work" which is only desirable because of the monetary reward. The joy of creation is often overlooked as a primary motivation—even though in reality this often outweighs all other considerations for doing the most valuable creative work
(Credit: Francisco de Goya y Lucientes, "La Forja"/PD, Amcaja@Wikipedia/CC-By-SA 2.5)

Figure 7.2:
Information has become increasingly freed from the limitations of matter
(Credits: cuneiform letter in dried clay/PD, ink-on-papyrus hieroglyphs/PD, movable type/Willi Heidelbach/CC-By 2.5, computer data in a text editor/Terry Hancock/CC-By-SA 2.5).

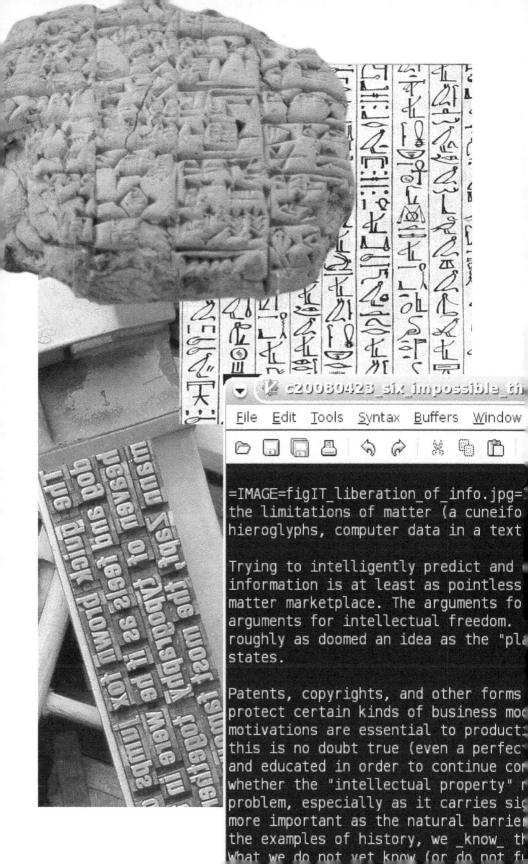

it carries significant social burdens, which become ever more important as the natural barriers to the mobility of information fall. From the examples of history, we know that sequestering information retards progress. What we do not yet know (or do not fully understand) is how to economically sustain the people who create intellectual works while simultaneously avoiding such obstacles to intellectual progress.

The Rules

As a society, though, we are learning—and the existing examples of commons-based peer production provide ample material to derive a basic understanding of how the commons-based enterprise must function, as well as pointing the way to problems that must be solved in order to fully enable this new form of organization and production.

Rule #1:

Hold On Loosely
Project Licensing

In the proprietary production world, what matters about a copyright is who owns it. In the free production world, however, who owns a copyright is relatively unimportant. What matters is what license it is offered under. There is a very simple rule of thumb about the best license to use: use a "free, copyleft license." Such licenses provide the ideal balance of freedom versus limitations, and projects that use them are overwhelmingly more successful than ones that don't.

The Culture of Innovation

The heritage of open source development stems largely from academia, where intellectual freedom is as fundamental an ideal as "democracy" or "freedom." It is this view of the concept which leads to the ideologically-based "Free Software Movement" and its preference for emphasizing user freedoms over developer process.

Rule #1: "Hold on Loosely"

Use a free, copyleft license

A free license provides everyone working on the project parity: they have an equal stake in the project's success, reap equal value from it, and do not feel they are losing the value of what they contribute to it to anyone else.

A copyleft license prevents any single entity from stealing value from the public by taking the project private (including the work of other participants).

The most popular license for software is unquestionably the **Gnu General Public License** (**GPL**).[1] However, that license is clearly written with computer programs in mind, so it is not really appropriate for all forms of information (this point is somewhat controversial, but there is no question that the GPL uses program-specific language in its text which may be ambiguous when applied to other works). Therefore, there are a number of other licenses, including the **Creative Commons Attribution-ShareAlike (CC-By-SA)** license,[2] which is optimized for creative content. No single license has emerged as appropriate for licensing open hardware, although the **TAPR Open Hardware License** (**TAPR OHL**) is a promising start.

While this approach is probably not so good as a method of persuasion, since it relies on cultural norms that do not apply broadly across all human societies or even across professions, it has a special importance to commons-based production: it is a core belief of the people who do the most work.

Whether you share this belief system or not, you cross it at your peril. Many people regard these ideas as moral imperatives and one of the first rules of the freedom game is learning not to offend the very people who are likely to be your most important asset in success. You cannot play the game half-heartedly, hoping to create a business advantage through appropriating publicly-created work, while holding back your own.

Intellectual Freedom

Intellectual freedom (IF) is a fundamental principle that underlies many of the beliefs shared by knowledge workers, particularly in academia, but also in a much broader area of complex engineering and scientific disciplines. Although it is often couched in ideological terms, the real point is that secrets are wasteful. Scientists learn from very early in their training the faults of suppressing information, perhaps most iconically in the person of Galileo Galilei, who published evidence supporting the Copernican theory that the planets orbited the Sun (primarily his observations of Jupiter's satellites), and was proscribed and forced to recant his beliefs by the Catholic Church.

Scientists view Galileo in heroic terms, and the Church's resistance to the Copernican theory was ultimately futile. Without the Copernican theory, we'd have never made it to the Moon. So it is fitting that Galileo's famous hammer and feather experiment was actually demonstrated by Cmdr. Dave Scott at the Apollo 15 landing site on the Moon (figure 8.1).

When scientists are free to share information and regard it as a duty, they fuel the process of science, which needs to check and recheck assumptions to reach an ever more accurate understanding of the world. Engineers and inventors also share information, so as to attain ever more refined improvements to the inventions that they develop. Software developers use this freedom to find bugs and refine their software as well as to improve upon what has been written before. All of them are using it to avoid wasting time re-inventing what has gone before.

Intellectual Property

The utilitarian argument for **intellectual property (IP)** is fairly simple: producing information costs time and effort of those who do the work, just as much as any other kind of production. Yet, unlike other forms of production, information can be freely

Figure 8.1:

Commander Dave Scott demonstrated Galileo's "hammer and feather" experiment on the surface of the Moon during the Apollo 15 mission
(Credit: NASA/PD)

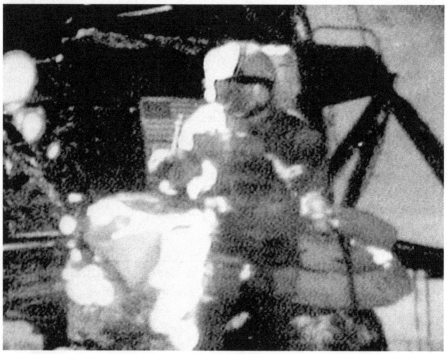

copied, so, in a completely free market, the monetary value per copy of an information product tends to be very nearly zero.

Intellectual property systems make it easier to recoup the development costs of information products via artificially inflating the cost of sales to cover the initial investment. This mimics the natural behavior of material products, where barriers to entry such as manufacturing tooling costs give the first entry into the market a chance to recoup its development costs so as to make a profit.

Of course, there are problems with the intellectual property idea. Perhaps the most obvious is that, taken to its logical conclusion, it's the just like the medieval guild system that locked Europe into a dark age for nearly a thousand years!

Suppressing the flow of information damns us to repeat the same mistakes over and over again, retarding technological progress and resulting in massive wastes of human capital. Only when inventors, authors, engineers, and scientists are able to build upon each others' works can civilization reap the renaissance rewards of a booming technological and intellectually creative society. Thus, even if and when intellectual property law is needed, it must always exist in tension against the long range benefits of preserving intellectual freedom.

An Unnecessary Evil?

Most serious creators of intellectual works in the United States know about the limited constitutional basis for intellectual property, but they still view it as a "necessary evil": a fictive arrangement we have to adopt in order to create intellectual works within our capitalist society. The free market, they argue, demands that we respect intellectual property as a tradable good, so that we can profit by producing intellectual works.

The experiences of free software and free culture, however, have empirically shown that IP is not essential to promote intellectual production. At the very least, we know that a free market society can produce intellectual works without the need to resort to the restrictiveness of conventional intellectual property laws. Free-licensing, which intentionally releases such works from these confines, produces more value from the free exchange of information than it loses to lost licensing sales and free rider problems.

In his essays, "The Cathedral and the Bazaar," "Homesteading the Noosphere," and "The Magic Cauldron," Eric Raymond illustrates the strategies that commercial entities have employed to defeat the conventional wisdom that locked-down "IP" is essential to business success.[3] His strategies are primarily described in terms of business reasoning, and are based on selling something ancillary to the intellectual work itself. Examples include selling services such as technical support in using the work, further modifications or customizations of an existing work, proprietary additional works (or content), convenient packaging of the work for easy use, products creating using the work, and so on.

Why Use a Copyleft?

There is one serious problem with all this freedom. If everyone is free to do what they want with the work, then one thing they can do with it in a society which has strong intellectual property laws is to claim it for themselves, appropriating all of the effort that has gone into the project.

Richard Stallman of the Free Software Foundation found a fairly simple way to deal with this problem, which has come to be known as a "copyleft." A **copyleft** is a clause which grants the license only on the condition that further distribution of the work and its derivatives be made under the same license. This prevents users of the work from adding a few minor changes to the work, then claiming the whole as their own (which can otherwise happen, as with works in the public domain). As more copyleft-licensed work is release, the desire to make use of that work creates an incentive for further works to be released under the same license.

Project Contributors

There is some evidence that copyleft is not so influential on users who make small contributions to projects (in that non-copyleft projects are generally as active as comparable copyleft ones[4] see figure 8.2). Indeed, the overall license choice has only a small effect on the activity rates for Sourceforge-hosted projects. Probably, such contributors simply follow suit on the license of the work they are contributing to.

Based on this alone, the use of a copyleft might not seem very important, and indeed if you have compelling reasons not to, the chances are that you will find enough like-minded contributors so that it doesn't really matter.

Project Founders

However, one thing that is clear is that **founders**, people who start new projects, overwhelmingly prefer the use of a copyleft license. This is illustrated by the overwhelming majority (80%) by which free-licensed project founders choose copyleft licenses (figure 8.3). These numbers include (indeed they are dominated by) small projects which rely on copyleft-licensed platforms, so

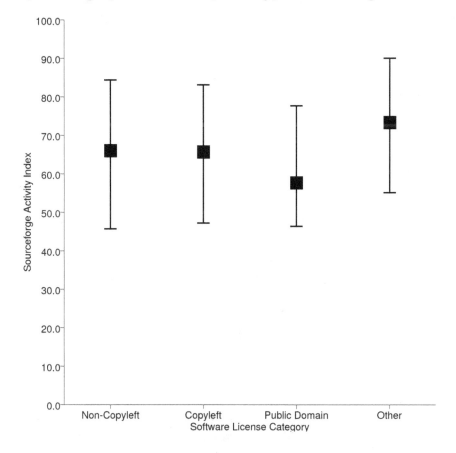

Figure 8.2:
Perhaps surprisingly, the activity level of projects on Sourceforge shows very little variation with respect to license category: non-copyleft projects are about as active as copyleft ones. The activity levels for public domain works and "other" licenses are shown as well, which show greater variations, although there are probably other effects folded into these. For example, the "other" category includes Creative Commons licenses, and therefore probably represents much more content than software (which may be easier to contribute). Meanwhile, public domain projects often represent releases of essentially mature software which may not require much maintenance.

Figure 8.3:

Over 80% of the software projects hosted on the Sourceforge free software project incubator use a copyleft license of some type

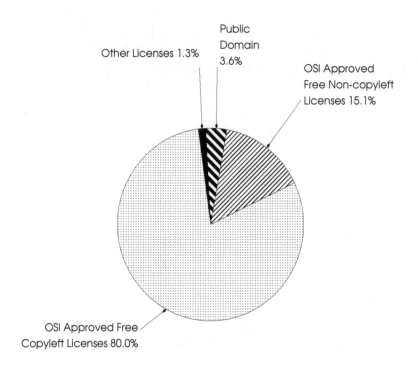

Other Licenses 1.3%

Public Domain 3.6%

OSI Approved Free Non-copyleft Licenses 15.1%

OSI Approved Free Copyleft Licenses 80.0%

"founder" also includes "contributions" of new separate projects relying on existing ones.

Why is this?

One need look no further than Apple Computer to see the answer. Apple's "OS X" operating system, which is used commercially on modern Apple Macintosh computers, is built on top of "Darwin" a particular distribution of BSD Unix.[5] OS X contains many, many improvements on Unix, and tools to make it easier to use. But of course, OS X is proprietary. As a result, the growth of the free project, OpenDarwin, was depressed, resulting in its eventual closure.[6]

This can happen because Darwin has no copyleft.

On the other hand, GNU/Linux, which is mostly licensed under the GNU **GPL** or **LGPL**, and therefore protected by copyleft limitations from this kind of hijacking of community effort, continues to boom in popularity.

In other words, people start free projects under the promise that they will stay free. Copyleft offers that promise.

The Four Freedoms

Use
The freedom to use the work and enjoy the benefits of using it.

Study
The freedom to study the work and to apply knowledge acquired from it.

Copy
The freedom to make and redistribute copies, in whole or in part, of the information or expression.

Improve
The freedom to make changes and improvements, and to distribute derivative works.

Figure 8.4:
The Free Software Definition introduced the idea that there are four fundamental freedoms needed for information works (traditionally numbered from 0 to 3, to reflect their origins among computer programmers). It originally specified these in very software-oriented ways. This version of the **four freedoms** is from FreedomDefined.org's definition of "Free Cultural Works"

"Copying" and "Use"

The term "use," when applied to intellectual works, can be treacherously ambiguous. After all, "copying" a work, "distributing" it, or "deriving" from it, are clearly ways of "using" the work in the English vernacular. Yet theorists talking about copyright or software freedom generally do not consider these uses to be included in the word "use."

Three of the four major definitions of software freedom that exist in the community include the requirement that a work must be "free to use for any purpose," and yet they also allow copyleft requirements to ensure that a work remains free by placing terms on "copying" and "distributing" it. These definitions include the **Debian Free Software Guidelines**[7] from the **Debian Project**,[8] the **Open Source Definition**[9] from the **Open Source Initiative**,[10] and the **Definition of Free Cultural Works**[11] from the **Freedom Defined**[12] wiki project).

The **Free Software Definition**[13] from the **Free Software Foundation**[14] and its **GNU Project**,[15] is less demanding: it says only that you must have the freedom to "run the program for any purpose." That's less vague, but of course, it also only makes sense for an executable program, which is why the other definitions opted for a broader expression.

The "free to use for any purpose" criterion has always contradicted copyleft terms if "copying," "distribution," and "derivation" are to be regarded as "use." The true ambiguities of this definition, however, only came to light with the introduction of **"digital rights management"** (**DRM**) and **"technological protection measures"** (**TPM**). These are both euphemistic names for encryption technologies designed to interfere with users' ability to copy and decode digital intellectual works.

It was argued by some that the right to *distribute* a work in such an encrypted file format, even when no key is made available to allow users to unlock the work, was a valid "use" (i.e. not an act of "copying" or "distribution," which might be subject to

Corollary:

Do not use a 'non-commercial' or any other 'restricted-use' license on a commons-based project!

Such licenses reserve commercial use to the original author, and therefore thwart the parity principle that links free licenses to commons-based production. As such, so-called "non-commercial" licenses are destructive to commons-based activities. So, even if the work is likely to be focused on "non-commercial" activities, it is a very bad idea to formally limit such uses through the licensing.

In practice, a copyleft will put a strong practical limit on the sorts of "exploitation" that most non-commercial authors are trying to protect themselves from with a "non-commercial" license clause.

copyleft restrictions). Some licenses, particularly those from the Creative Commons organization, do not permit encrypted distribution whenever it would interfere with users' legal rights under the license. A strong lobby was formed to try to convert Creative Commons' language over to an alternate form of protection against DRM-laden files, which relied on a requirement to provide a non-encrypted distribution of any file which was distributed in DRM format (an idea which seems logical based on the success of the GPL's requirement of a "source code" distribution along with any binary distribution).

However, some observers, notably Greg London, noticed an exploit which showed how this form of "protection" could fail to protect users' freedom to use and/or derive from encrypted works in a useful way.[16] As a result, the Creative Commons licenses retain the anti-DRM language, although the issue remains somewhat controversial.

Oops, Wrong License...

It's pretty much a no-brainer to use a free license for a free culture project, but there are a lot of situations in which you might find it difficult. For example, you may have created a software package you are willing to release under a free license, but made extensive use of non-free libraries. What then?

Occasionally, this can even happen with "free" licenses, when two incompatible copyleft licenses have been used.

Essentially, you have two choices:

Option #1: Re-licensing

Sometimes, the package you've relied on is under some sort of "semi-free" license (i.e. it's not a normal proprietary license, but it isn't a true free-license either. Or else, it might be under a free license, but one which isn't compatible with widely-used licenses like the GPL). In situations like this, it's probably a good idea to track down the copyright holder (usually, though not always, the author). Often, the use of this sort of license is a good sign that the author would be open to re-licensing the work if you ask nicely (or possibly, offer to pay for the change).

Occasionally, you'll find yourself having to sell them on the idea. Consider not only opening up about why you've decided to free your own code, but also engaging the user community to help you make the case for freeing the license.

Option #2: Re-writing

Free software now being fairly mature, there is a free software library to do just about anything you can find a proprietary library to do. Switching over will require some re-writing on your project, but maybe not as much as you would think. Often you can write a compatibility layer or simply modify the calls in your existing code, and free yourself of the burden of code that isn't compliant with your licensing goals.

If you get really stuck trying to convert your code, remember you can ask for help: freeing your code is a benefit to the whole community, so it may well be that you can find people who are interested enough to help make it happen.

Non-commercial licenses

A concept in competition with the idea of copyleft is the "**non-commercial**" license, which attempts to restrict the use of a work for "commercial" purposes. This is a somewhat compelling argument for aesthetic works, since for aesthetic works it is much harder to develop the kind of "service and support" models that have worked so well for free software.

Many people (wrongly) think of free software products as being "non-commercial" because you can't (or can't profitably) sell individual copies of the software. However, there are many other ways of using software "commercially" (such as providing support for it, using it as a promotional, delivering advertising with it, and so on). A "non-commercial" clause forbids them all.

Ironically, the only really rational use for a "non-commercial" license is when you want to operate commercially. If you are in the business of selling your work for commercial use, you can partially protect your monopoly, while still taking advantage of the fluid distribution and marketing provided by free internet file-sharing. However, the work never really enters the "commons" of free-licensed work unless you re-release it under a "free" license later (or until the copyright runs out, which takes practically forever under today's copyright laws).

So, while they may have other uses, for commons-based projects, "non-commercial" licenses are a dead end.

Copyleft Conflicts

It is extremely difficult to write a license which insists only that the intent of the licensing on derivatives is the same. It's much simpler and much more enforceable to require derivatives to be under the same license terms.

Even if you could interpret the copyleft as requiring only the same basic conditions, this will still invariably create obstacles. For example, the GPL insists that no "legal venue" be specified,

Figure 8.5:

Because copyleft licenses can conflict with each other, it's not good to have a lot of them. Over two-thirds of the projects on Sourceforge are simply licensed under the one "best practice" free software license: the GNU General Public License. Over 92% are "GPL compatible," meaning that derivatives based on them may be released under the GPL

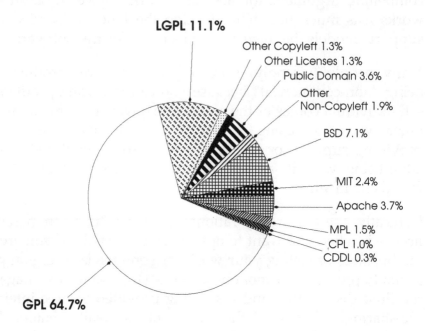

LGPL 11.1%

Other Copyleft 1.3%
Other Licenses 1.3%
Public Domain 3.6%
Other Non-Copyleft 1.9%
BSD 7.1%
MIT 2.4%
Apache 3.7%
MPL 1.5%
CPL 1.0%
CDDL 0.3%

GPL 64.7%

but some free licenses, like the original Python license insisted (as do many proprietary licenses) that court cases be held in a particular jurisdiction. As a result, the Python license was "GPL incompatible," even though it was otherwise "free," according to the Free Software Definition.

As a result, copyleft licenses are subject to incompatibilities which can make it impossible to publish a fusion between two packages with different free-copyleft licenses. Since this is obviously undesirable, there is a strong pressure in the community to stick with a very few copyleft licenses—the main one for software being the GPL—thus avoiding problems with license proliferation as it is called.

Note however, that proliferation is a much bigger problem for copyleft licenses than it is for non-copyleft licenses. This is why there is relatively little concern over the large number of non-copyleft licenses (such as the **BSD, MIT,** and **Apache** licenses[17-19]). These licenses can be combined into derivatives, and will even allow conversion to GPL, so they do not really interfere with user freedoms in the software. They still make the licensing more complex to read and understand, which is why (even for non-copyleft licensing) there are recommendations not to write your own license when one of the standard licenses will do.

Upgrade and Compatibility Clauses

One way to reduce problems with **license proliferation** is to provide a more flexible "upgrade" or "compatibility" clause. For example, some licenses simply have a clause explicitly allowing them to be converted to GPL licensing (overriding any otherwise conflicting terms). The Creative Commons started introducing a mechanism for forming cross-licensing agreements with its version 3.0 licenses. Upgrade clauses provide a mechanism for migrating from older versions of licenses to newer ones, so that old licensing problems can be fixed by new licenses (the GPL does this through a suggested voluntary statement in the license grant, while the Creative Commons licenses provide such a clause in the body of the licenses themselves).

Critics argue that such agreements would gradually erode the copyleft, leaving the works effectively little better off than if they were released under a non-copyleft license. However, if you're going to use another license, it's a very good idea to assure compatibility with the GPL (for software) or the CC By-SA (for aesthetic works).

The Problem with Hardware

Hardware licensing presents another special problem, since hardware manufacturing processes are generally not subject to copyright or **copyright-like protection** (with a few exceptions).

This means that hardware designs are in the position that software source code would be if there were no copyright protection for executable binaries.[20] Thus, it's apparent that an open hardware copyleft will probably require stronger rules in order to be effective.

Some hardware projects today use the GPL or BSD licenses, but it is likely that a strong copyleft license for hardware will emerge as an evolution of specific licenses like the **TAPR Open Hardware License**, which attempt to extend copyleft provisions to the physical products manufactured from the design.[21]

When Not to Use a Copyleft

There are obviously some negative effects to using a copyleft. Despite "Freedom Zero," there are a number of permitted limits to uses of copylefted software, and occasionally they get in the way. If you are interested in supporting commercial proprietary software development, or simply don't want the hassle of license compatibility issues, then a **non-copyleft license** may be more desirable.

Freedom, Copyleft, and the Commons

With proprietary projects, what matters is who owns an intellectual work. This is because such projects operate on a permissions basis, and so what you have to know is who to ask for permission. The overhead of managing this "**permissions culture**" is enormous. Our society, indeed, is practically being crushed by its costs. The most visible costs (such as lawsuits) are bad enough, but the worst damage happens when people simply give up and assume they can't get permission. It is this "**chilling effect**" that is most damaging to innovation in society, and the removal of that burden is the source of the success of the commons-based production movement.

With commons-based production, then, what matters is not who owns the work, but what freedoms you already have in the work. Thus, the nature of the public license granted in the work is of paramount importance. So, don't pick a bad one and don't write your own! At least not until you have reviewed all of the existing popular free software, free content, and open hardware licenses, and still can't find one that works.

The best and simplest choice is to simply use the **GNU General Public License** (**GPL**). It is quite versatile, and will work for many kinds of utilitarian works such as software or logic designs. You're in good company if you do this, as this is what about four out of five software developers will do.

If the work is not software, you may be looking at a more complicated choice. A good bet here is to stick with the **Creative Commons Attribution** (**CC By**) or **Creative Commons Attribution-ShareAlike** (**CC By-SA**) license, unless there is a clear and unambiguous definition of "source code" for the work you want to release. Appendix F includes some data to help you with this choice on specific projects, including the full text of some of the best licenses.

Notes:

1 Gnu General Public License (GPL)
   http://www.gnu.org/licenses/old-licenses/gpl-2.0.html

2 Creative Commons Attribution-ShareAlike (CC By-SA)
   http://creativecommons.org/licenses/by-sa/3.0

3 Eric Raymond; The Cathedral and the Bazaar, Homesteading the Noosphere, and The Magic Cauldron; 1997-2000. Also available in print as *The Cathedral & the Bazaar: Musings on Linux and Open Source by an Accidental Revolutionary* from O'Reilly books.
   http://www.catb.org/~esr/writings/cathedral-bazaar

   http://oreilly.com/catalog/9780596001087

4 Terry Hancock, "Copyleft has no impact on project activity?!" Statistics on project activity index were derived using features of the Trove search engine on Sourceforge for projects based on results from particular groups of licenses classified as "copyleft", "non-copyleft", "proprietary/other", and "public domain".
   http://www.freesoftwaremagazine.com/columns/
      copyleft_has_no_impact_project_activity

5 "PureDarwin" Project. A community-based continuation of the Darwin project.
   http://www.puredarwin.org

6 OpenDarwin Mirror. The final message describes the shutdown of the project due to the transfer of interest to the proprietary Mac OS X
   http://www.opendarwin.info/opendarwin.org/en

7 Debian Free Software Guidelines
  `http://www.debian.org/social_contract#guidelines`

8 Debian Project
  `http://www.debian.org`

9 Open Source Definition
  `http://opensource.org/docs/osd`

10 Open Source Initiative
  `http://opensource.org`

11 Definition of Free Cultural Works
  `http://freedomdefined.org/Definition`

12 Freedom Defined
  `http://freedomdefined.org`

13 Free Software Definition
  `http://www.gnu.org/philosophy/free-sw.html`

14 Free Software Foundation
  `http://www.fsf.org`

15 GNU Project
  `http://www.gnu.org`

16 An exploit, suggested by Greg London, shows how an unscrupulous party could use DRM to maintain a "platform monopoly" on rights which are granted by the license of a free-licensed work, even with a so-called "parallel distribution" requirement.
  `http://www.freesoftwaremagazine.com/columns/`
    `debian_and_the_creative_commons`

  `http://www.greglondon.com`

17 BSD license
  `http://opensource.org/licenses/bsd-license.php`

18 MIT license
  `http://opensource.org/licenses/mit-license.php`

19 Apache license
  `http://opensource.org/licenses/apache2.0.php`

20 See Appendix C: "What if copyright didn't apply to binary executables?"

21 TAPR Open Hardware License (TAPR stands for"Tucson Amateur Packet Radio", but today it is an international organization).
  `http://www.tapr.org/ohl.html`

Rule #2:

Create a Community
Project Hosting and Marketing

The "edge" free culture has over proprietary culture comes from volunteers, and they need to be treated right. When starting a project, you need to spend just as much effort on designing a comfortable and inviting project as you would on a store or restaurant: you may not be trying to convince customers to part with cash for your product, but you *are* asking volunteers to part with their *time* for your project (which may be harder).

Playing Tom Sawyer

Mark Twain's character Tom Sawyer, in a classic incident, avoided the chore of whitewashing (painting) a fence by convincing people that the job was a lot of fun. People eventually paid him for the privilege of doing his chore for him. Twain no doubt meant to characterize Sawyer as a bit of a huckster, but the truth is that if he could actually make the task fun through his marketing, then everybody would come out happier.

Rule #2: "Create a Community"

Create a community around your project that suits the people who will use it

Spend time to create a comfortable environment that is inviting to users, contributors, and developers alike around your project. Develop pathways that allow for smooth graded slopes between these groups of people—don't allow them to become isolated from each other.

Different projects have different users. Programmers, artists, engineers, and scientists tend to have different skills, interests, and temperaments. So don't assume the same cookie-cutter approach will work for all of them. Tailor the community facilities around your project to take advantage of the strengths of your users and allow them to contribute as much as possible to your product.

As a **founder** or **leader** of a **free-licensed open source** project, you are in much the same position. And you have a marketing job to do if you want people to help you out. You need to convince them that spending time on your project will be rewarding: in terms of a contribution to the community, personal accomplishment, a feeling of belonging to the group, and possibly other reasons. People are different, so you can't assume that the same motivations will apply to everyone.

More to the point, if you are somewhat familiar with the demographics and interests of your expected user base (the people you're trying to serve with your project), then you should be able to make some rough predictions about what sort of motivations will work for them. You should also be aware of what sort of barriers exist (e.g. many scientists can program, but are not up to serious software engineering tasks, and they may be particularly conservative about learning new programming languages).

So it stands to reason that you should give some thought to this marketing problem right at the beginning. Not marketing your end product, mind you—marketing the *project* to people who will help you with it. This could take the form of announcing the project in the sort of online "places" you expect to find your users, but before you can even start this, you need to create a place for them to go!

No matter how good a cook you are, would you start a restaurant without giving any thought to the location, decor, and dining environment that it provides? You shouldn't take starting a free software project any less seriously.

The standard comfort-level for volunteers on a free software project should be a lot higher than for professional developers working on proprietary software. People will go through a lot of pain to earn a paycheck. As such, commercial workflow software is often designed simply to minimize pain, maximize speed, and thus increase productivity. In other words, it tries to make it easier to get the job "over with."

But volunteers aren't there to earn a paycheck. They're there to have fun. And that means the process itself needs to be fulfilling, not just relatively painless. Contributors need to feel good about the work they're contributing. When there are unavoidable barriers to contribution, you need to make sure that these tasks are done by your most dedicated developers (possibly meaning you), who won't be stopped by the obstacles.

The simple approach

Community needs for a project vary over a huge range, depending on the skill-level and interests of the potential contributors to a project. Most can make do with very simple infrastructure.

Figure 9.1:

Decor and "atmosphere" are very important parts of the business plan for a new restaurant, and you should take just as seriously what sort of "atmosphere" your project will present to contributors and users

(Photo credits: dave_mcmt@Flickr/CC-By 2.0, avlxyz@Flickr/CC-By-SA 2.0, Megan Soh/CC-By 2.0, William Murphy/CC-By-SA 2.0)

Many of the free software projects now in existence run on a fairly "cookie-cutter" set of ready-made facilities:

- **Version control** (CVS or Subversion)
- A **mailing list**
- A **website** (often static)
- A **bug-tracking system**

For many small projects, this will be all you need. If you don't expect your project to require a whole lot of collaboration, or you only expect hardcore hackers will be capable of or interested in contributing, then there's nothing wrong with keeping things this simple. In fact, that's probably what those sort of contributors will be happiest with.

Figure 9.2:
How much time would you spend in a cubicle if you weren't paid to be there? Don't make the mistake of treating volunteers like paid employees
(Photo credit: Katy Warner / CC-By-SA 2.0)

Sourceforge

Features:
- Static webhosting (or can link to an outside page)
- Standard project page
- CVS or Subversion version control system
- News blog associated with each project (for announcements)
- Documentation server
- File download server
- Mailing list management
- Bug tracker

Advantages:
- High visibility (everyone knows to check Sourceforge for a project)
- Full range of features

Disadvantages:
- Requires approval for each project
- Often slow due to overload servers
- Interface is not very intuitive (though it has been improved gradually)
- Code for service is non-free (but there is gForge)

Google Code

Features:

- Wiki for homepage and documentation
- Subversion repository for code
- File download server for releases
- Bug tracker

Advantages:

- Fast
- Simple

Disadvantages:

- 100 MB limit on file downloads
- "Lifetime limit" of 10 projects
- Not a lot of features
- Code for service is non-free (but data is compatible with similar free software packages)

Figure 9.3:
Sourceforge (left) and Google (right) are among the most popular ready-made free software hosting sites. For software projects, one or the other will often be a good, low-maintenance choice

To get services like this for your project, your best bet is probably to just sign up on one of the existing free software incubators, like Sourceforge or Google Code. The price is certainly right: both services are free for free software projects (see figure 9.3).

Although the software for Sourceforge is now proprietary, it was originally a free software package. The original package, gForge, is still available, and has continued to be developed. It is deployed by a number of other, usually more specialized, software incubators: Savannah (run by the GNU project for gnu.org and non-gnu.org projects) and Blender.org are two examples. Other software is used on sites like Plone.org and Zope.org, to support development for those environments. You may find similar services related to any frameworks you might be using for development, and there are many smaller general-purpose hosting services out there, catering to different needs (figure 9.4).

Many projects will never need more than this, and can be hosted successfully on one of these sites. However, some projects will need to take a different approach.

Adapting the Technology to Your Community

If you are writing software intended for other developers, you probably don't have much to worry about—they are likely to enjoy messing with the tools as much as you do. But if your project targets other users—engineers, scientists, mechanics, or homemakers, for example—then the people who know the most about how well your package is working may need a more accommodating and less cluttered environment.

Don't fall into the trap of predicting your future community needs based only on your present community's skills and temperament. You may very well have a small group of people who excel at using the tools you have, but that's a selection effect! You may have those people only *because* those are the

Figure 9.4:

There are a wide range of other alternatives for hosting your project, ranging from highly-customized do-it-yourself sites, to minimalist and standardized database-driven sites

only people who will contribute under the present circumstances.

So, if your project is potentially of interest to people who aren't hard-core internet users, who don't feel totally comfortable in the all-text world that so many programmers gravitate to, then you might be doing yourself a disservice by not accommodating them—even if no one presently contributing to the project has a problem.

The further the free development envelope is extended into areas like textiles, graphics, multimedia, and engineering, the more and more we will encounter this problem: the people most familiar with the application domain will not be the ones familiar with the standard development tools. Yet, in order to serve that application domain, you need the expert help of people who know it well. Lourens Veen, a developer on the Open Graphics hardware project put it this way:

> *"Perhaps a key difference between hardware and software projects is that most hardware developers are not software developers, and the required tools mostly consist of software, not of hardware. If you give a programmer a buggy editor as well as its source, she will fix the editor. If you give a hardware developer a buggy schematic capture tool, he will find something else to work on. In a software project, creating the needed software tools is half the fun, in a hardware project it is a hurdle to be overcome"*
> —— *Lourens Veen*

Projects can only go so far relying on the few amphibious savants who happen to excel in both domains. At some point, you've got to start making accommodations to make the tools adaptable by and for the people who will use them.

Version control systems are generally pretty off-putting to anyone but programmers. Subversion does improve on CVS a lot, and there are other alternatives, but none of them is really comfortable for a non-programmer (which could include

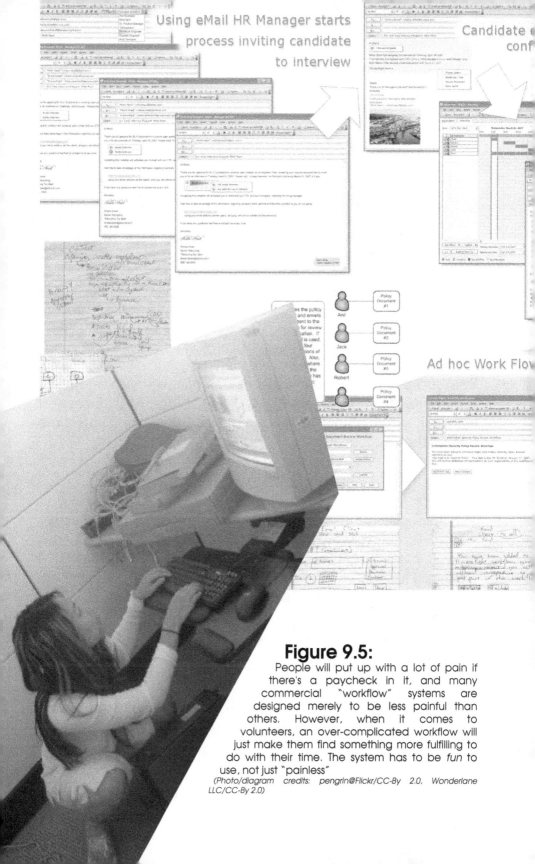

Using eMail HR Manager starts process inviting candidate to interview

Candidate confirms

Ad hoc Work Flow

Figure 9.5:
People will put up with a lot of pain if there's a paycheck in it, and many commercial "workflow" systems are designed merely to be less painful than others. However, when it comes to volunteers, an over-complicated workflow will just make them find something more fulfilling to do with their time. The system has to be *fun* to use, not just "painless"

someone who knows how to code, but doesn't self-identify as a programmer).

Mailing lists are pretty solid twentieth century technology, but they also present barriers to some people. Those of us who've been using these services for years have a range of lore about "trolls" and "flames" and other annoyances. Some of us may even enjoy the libertarian "Wild West" feel of unmoderated mailing lists. However, for people accustomed to a certain level of civility, they can be pretty irritating places to be. As a result some people find them more trouble than they are worth.

Static websites are okay in themselves, but they really don't do much to build a sense of community. You should consider using various kinds of interactive tools to make the website a useful and active hub for your project.

Bug tracking is good: but realize that not everyone is going to use it. One of the roles you'll want volunteers for is to convert informal complaints, feature requests, and problems into intelligible bug reports.

Productive Leisure

The ideal state of affairs for a project is a feeling of **productive leisure**. You probably felt this way when you started your project, and the best way to get others involved is to share that feeling. Think of how you feel in your favorite workshop, craftroom, sewing room, garage, machine shop, or home office. The tools you need are accessible. The work is clearly laid out. There's no interference from interlopers, and you are free to be creative.

That's the feeling that is ideal: a feeling of leisure, yes, but also of productivity and creativity. The sort of atmosphere that makes you want to do something.

Psychologists who study this kind of work sometimes refer to it as a **flow activity**: there is a great feeling of satisfaction for people when they are presented with work that is neither too

Figure 9.6:

The ideal setting is neither the pure leisure of a restaurant nor the austerity of a cubicle farm, but the feeling of creative energy you get in a workshop where you have peace and clarity of mind; easy access to your project; and all the tools you need to work on it
(Photo credits: daveseven@Flickr/CC-By-SA 2.0, Rachel Reynolds/CC-By 2.0, ladyada@Flickr/CC-By 2.0, Mike Terry/CC-By 2.0 Florian Groß/CC-By 2.0, Rossina Bossio Bossa/CC-By 2.0)

Filling an Empty Room

In my experience, community building is the biggest stumbling block for commercial developers trying to enter the free software community. It's a whole different way of thinking about the project. An effective community has to be (at least partly) under community control, so you have to be willing to step back and allow the community to grow, rather than trying to "manage" it all yourself.

At the same time, you can't just throw the project data out there and just hope it'll catch on. You need to remain engaged with the community you start. Here are a few practical ideas about how to do that:

• Take care in picking software for your community site. Make sure it has features that the community is willing and able to use (see Appendix A for some leads on free software packages for community building). Remember that a simple, easy-to-use site is going to be more important than one which either looks really glossy or has lots of features. A lot of mileage can be had by simply putting up a standard forum or wiki system.

• Minimize "gated entry." Every "buy-in" you force users to make in order to contribute to your project will cut down contributions significantly. Let people make at least some contributions anonymously (you'll need some mechanism to cut out spam, but vandalism isn't as much of a problem as you might imagine).

hard nor too easy, thus leading to neither frustration nor boredom. Indeed people can become quite fascinated and absorbed in this kind of work, and this is the role that most hobby activities (model building, machine work, knitting, sewing, amateur radio, etc) tend towards. In order to sustain this feeling as the hobbyist learns and improves, he or she will tend to take on successively more challenging projects.

Rarely will the hobbyist attempt to overcome enormous obstacles in difficulty. On the other hand, because of the fascination of the activity, the hobbyist will often stick with it longer, ultimately attaining greater heights of skill than

Some features might require a user account, but keep the overhead low: an email address and a password is enough for many sites. Don't hit new users with a survey form, no matter how much you'd like to know their demographics.

- Get involved in the community yourself. If you're coming from a company environment, then assign some work hours to knowledgeable people to get on the community site and interact with users. This includes programmers and engineers: people want to know that they are talking to the folks who can actually make a difference or can actually answer their questions, not just sales staff. If you have difficulty finding the skills in your own organization, then considering hiring a paid moderator or two from the community.

- One of the most common mistakes with both forums and wikis is to overspecialize, resulting in lots of little divisions with no content and no users in any given one. This makes your site boring and the few people who are there will start to leave. Instead, keep the environment really small at the beginning: everyone in one discussion forum or mailing list. For a wiki, create a "what's new" or other page that concentrates all the available content in one place. The smaller site will feel more crowded and active, and that will encourage further contributions. Remember, you can always divide up the site later, when it has grown large enough to need it.

professionals will attempt (since professionals are motivated primarily to do a "good enough" job and move on to the next one).

For amateur-driven projects, it is this progression of interest and skill that replaces the conventional promotion and chain-of-command hierarchy of the commercial setting. The challenge for the project manager is to create an environment that will encourage the natural behavior of contributors to self-organize.

In an ideal free-licensed collaborative project, the community should tend towards a kind of "onion model" (see figure 9.7) where the innermost leaders and core developers work directly on the code (or design), while successive outer layers: contributors, core users, and end users provide various degrees of feedback and contributed information.

Each layer in this model feeds information to the next layer inwards in a slightly more digested and organized form: general user satisfaction levels become specific feature requests and problem reports which in turn become patches or design concepts which in turn become usable code which then get built into the code or design itself. Likewise, information about the current state of the design or software matriculates outwards, in increasingly articulated and simplified ways: design documents become **developer documentation** which becomes **user documentation** which becomes application examples, tutorials, and how-tos.

The Role of Facilitators

Probably the least appreciated contributors to a project are the folks who simply hang out in the community, chatting on the mailing list or forum associated with it. Often it seems like these peope are just wasting time socializing, and some project leaders have gone as far as actively discouraging such behavior.

However, it's important to realize the value of such community members: just by chatting, they can be providing an important facilitation role for your project. If they are telling newcomers where to find more information, or even just repeating certain FAQs over and over again in their messages, they are preserving the layering order around your project. They may also serve a useful information-gathering role if they are also involved in other projects.

If they are also reminding people of previous ideas or posts, they are also moderating the exchange of information between the different layers of the project, and providing a kind of short-term memory for the project. They also encourage people to step across the various layer boundaries, thus blurring the

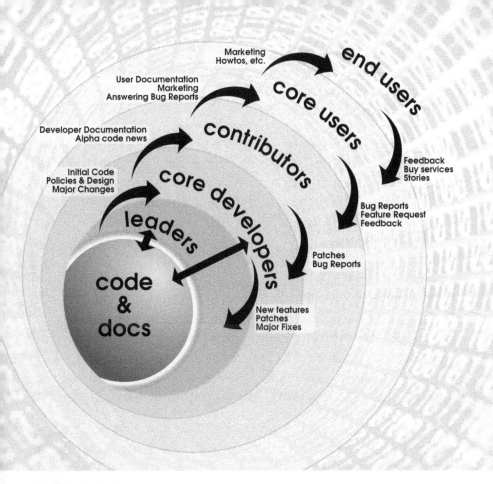

Marketing
Howtos, etc.

end users

User Documentation
Marketing
Answering Bug Reports

core users

Developer Documentation
Alpha code news

contributors

Initial Code
Policies & Design
Major Changes

core developers

leaders

**code
&
docs**

Feedback
Buy services
Stories

Bug Reports
Feature Request
Feedback

Patches
Bug Reports

New features
Patches
Major Fixes

Figure 9.7:

Like an information ramscoop, the ideal project will collect high-entropy information about user needs, and through the contributions of successive layers of interested parties, convert that into well-organized code contributions and documentation. In order for this to work, the lines of communication have to remain open, and ideally there is a very smooth transition between layers so that ultimately the boundaries become somewhat arbitrary, approaching a smooth graded slope from end user to core developer to project leadership

distinctions between "developers" and "users." In this way, they contribute to the creation of a "graded slope" between users and developers, with an ever-increasing level of skill and involvement (which is the ideal condition for motivated amateurs, since it allows each to attain an individualized, self-selected "flow" experience in contributing).

By merely being visible, such **facilitators** add their endorsement to the project, and create a feeling of activity and life in the project which will encourage others to contribute as well. So, they are also a means of marketing your community to newcomers, and therefore encouraging better retention of interested potential contributors.

Often such facilitators are not aware of their value to the community, and it can be useful to not only remind them of that value, but also to guide them in maximizing it, through pointing out how these particular activities benefit your community. In other words, don't just shoo them away, learn how to make use of them.

If You Build It, They Will Come...

Don't give up too easily! Spend the time it takes to market your project. You may find that it finds supporters if you can approach them in a way that is comfortable for them. It doesn't take a lot of usability issues to make someone who's just there for fun decide that it isn't any, but on the other hand, it doesn't take that much effort to be fun, either.

Creating the right atmosphere of productive leisure may be a challenge for some projects, but it will be worth it. So spend some time to understand who you're trying to serve with your project and also who's likely to be in a position to contribute. Make it as easy as possible for them to do so.

As we push the envelope on what free development and commons based peer production can accomplish, we will need to pay closer attention to how communities are created and maintained. We will also need to adapt our techniques to suit a broader audience of potential contributors.

Figure 9.8:
People need a comfortable but energizing environment to turn creativity into action, and this is one of the challenges of creating a community around a free development project
(Photo credits: Ilpo's Sojourn@Flickr/CC-By 2.0)

Notes:

1 See the Wikipedia article on flow activity for more about this subject
   `http://en.wikipedia.org/wiki/Flow_%28psychology%29`

Rule #3:
Divide and Conquer
Design Structure

A consistant pattern in the corporate environment is the gathering of resources, but with the free exchange of information inherent in commons-based projects, the pattern of choice is the *dispersal* of resources. This presents certain design challenges, which manifest themselves in the Unix-style **"small sharp tools"** approach to specialization; encourage **"bottom-up design"**; and most importantly, require easy-to-obtain, shared, free standards for data interchange between programs. When every train car is to be made by a separate builder, it is essential that the rail gauge is constant and known.

Deconstructing "GNU/Linux"

When I tried to compare the size in "source lines of code" (SLOC) between "Debian GNU/Linux 'Sarge'" and "Windows Vista," the first problem to arise was that there really is no direct free software analog to the "Windows operating system." Instead of one single monolithic development project, the free

Rule #3: "Divide and Conquer"

For large projects, establish a platform and interface standard, making it easy to contribute small, independent, pluggable elements

Concentrate on just one of these elements yourself

Community-based project participants only tolerate very limited "buy-in" to platforms and standards and thus seek systems that will let them work more or less independently, with only the minimal interface requirements being placed on them by the platform.

Whatever interface requirements do exist must be explained succinctly and clearly so as to make the barrier to the platform as low as possible.

As much as possible, all new platforms should take advantage of existing interface standards, both to allow direct use of existing design resources targeted for those standards, and to minimize the learning curve of new standards as they arise.

Single projects should try to do just one thing very well, rather than trying to provide lots of features. This promotes use of the package as well as the platform it is built on, and encourages other features to be contributed by others.

community produces a swarm of smaller projects. However, by choosing a popular selection of projects, it's possible to build an "equivalent function" alternative to Windows, as presented in figure 10.1.

This figure certainly dispels the notion that Windows code might be smaller than Debian because of inefficiency in the free software code (indeed it suggests the opposite might be true), but what it also shows is a pattern of specialization wherein functionality is separated as much as technically possible and each functional unit is provided by separately-managed projects. Instead of one "operating system" project (for an ever-expanding definition of "operating system") like the proprietary "Windows Vista," the equivalent free software functionality is a **stack** of several completely-independent projects, each with a more narrowly-defined range of functionality.

One thing figure 10.1 does *not* show is the range of choice that is also possible. This particular stack (glibc + Linux + GNU utilities + X.org + KDE + Mozilla) is only one popular choice out of many. This choice is made possible by the fact that each

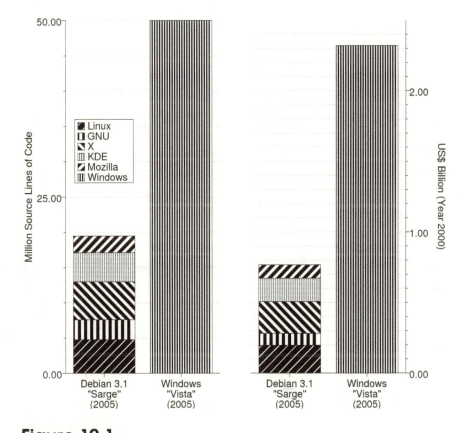

Figure 10.1:

A comparison of the source lines of code and COCOMO-estimated equivalent cost of an equivalent stack of free software to what ships with Windows Vista
(Repetition of Figure 1.3)

layer in the stack adheres closely to published interface standards. With relatively few problems, any of the stack layers can be swapped out with alternative programs providing similar functionality. Figure 10.2 shows an assortment of the options available. Even though this not a complete list of the available choices, the number of possible combinations (over 2000) is staggering!

Some of the combinations shown (e.g. BSD libc + HURD + Xvfb + Kwin + XFCE + Nautilus) are pretty unlikely to be in actual use and therefore may be very buggy, but they should be possible. The greatest bottleneck is actually the X Windows system, since all of the examples given here are really forks or parts of the same project. Of course, given that these are free-licensed projects, one might wonder why anyone bothers creating "duplicate" functionality.

The truth is, though, that as with programming languages or word processors, there are a lot of fine differences which affect personal preferences among users, and there are fundamental differences in design philosophy and tools among developers. Additionally, there are disagreements about which licenses are "free enough" for certain parties' interests (e.g. there probably wouldn't have been a separate BSD libc, except for the desire of BSD developers to avoid dependencies on GPL software).

The use of smaller, more highly specialized programs ("small sharp tools"), rather than big **"flagship applications,"** is of course a long-standing Unix environment tradition (even for proprietary Unix). It represents good engineering design in any context. But the pressures of expediency near the end of release cycles in the commercial proprietary software world tend to cause a breakdown in this engineering discipline. At the same time, the distributed and relatively disorganized community development environment, lacking any formal command structure, cannot sustain much in the way of large-scale coordination efforts. Thus, the community's very nature tends to reinforce the important engineering design principle of **"separation of concerns."**

"Too Many Cooks Spoil the Broth"

The wisdom of capitalist/corporate industry is to gather resources and put them under the control of one strong leader. Regimented control of the entire industrial process is thought to be essential to avoid conflict and waste when many people are trying to work together. Our capitalist economic system is designed to support this idea by providing means to

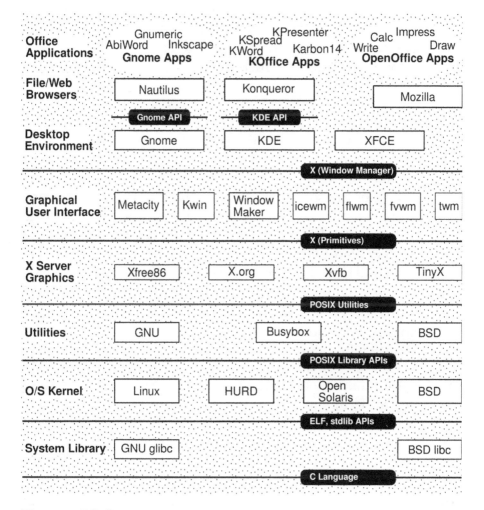

Figure 10.2:

Alternate choices are available for each layer in the free software stack that represents the same functionality as Microsoft's single "Windows operating system." Although some combinations are unlikely, these options represent 2×4×3×4×7×3 or 2016 possible "complete operating system stacks." This is a staggering combinatorial explosion of user options—made possible by adherence to standard interfaces

concentrate wealth in the hands of those who are perceived as having the best chance of using the resources successfully and beneficially for society. Indeed, the system is named after this practice of "gathering capital."

In addition of course, the system is competitive, creating a situation where corporate entities with sufficient capital often reproduce the same basic effort and the redundant products compete for market share. The theory is that the one that wins the competition will be a better product, thus encouraging corporate entities to put in their best effort and the public is provided with superior products.

Unfortunately, this depends on the public being able to tell when one product is genuinely better than another, and with things as complex as software, the comparison process can be extremely difficult. As a result, various proxies and superficial comparisons become more important than the core functionality of the software, and maintaining the extra burden of "feature wars" detracts from the engineering effort to produce good code and concentrate on the features which are most needed. Perceived value also relies heavily on "psychic value" established through advertising and on "network effects" after a winner begins to emerge. Thus a product may emerge quickly on the basis of a completely irrational value proposition, then hold that position due to the need for compatibility with others who are already sold on it.

The most familiar example is probably the Microsoft Windows operating system, but there are many others. This is not a peculiarity of bad business practices from just one company, but rather a broad systemic fault caused by the incentive system and poor metrics available to the consumer—simply because the product is so complex and its inner workings are so secret that it is really impossible for a buyer to make an intelligent decision about which system to buy into.

In software, this approach leads to enormous flagship software applications with highly complex internal structure, great

Figure 10.3:

The commercial/proprietary way of creating information products relies heavily on centralized control
(Image Credit: Scott Maxwell I http://www.lumaxart.com / CC By-SA 2.0)

difficulty of maintenance, and poor **interoperability** with competitors (probably by design).

"Many Hands Make Light Work"

The wisdom of commons-based peer production is to require few common resources and make the ones that are needed as publicly-documented as possible and as available as possible to as many people as possible. This eliminates barriers to entry and participation on projects—which, without a strong profit motive (lost because copy sales are not profitable for free-licensed information products), is essential to the success of community-based projects.

Money can be made by users of a free licensed product, but they have limited ability to profiteer from it because they cannot exclude others from competition in order to maintain the limited monopoly position required to raise prices and thus offset their capital investment in the product. Instead, the contribution of individual participants in a free design project has to be regarded as part of their simple "overhead" costs, and

Figure 10.4:

In the community development model, individual, finely-chosen pieces of the overall problem are picked and worked on in isolation by very small development teams (the most common size is one lone developer). The clear, complete, and simple specification of interfaces becomes very important in this model, because there is little opportunity to challenge, revise, or query them for unwritten details once the actual development process begins

(Image Credit: Modified from works by Scott Maxwell | http://www.lumaxart.com / CC By-SA 2.0)

thus, each individual can only afford a much smaller investment.

This makes it essential both to contain the effort required so that it does not undermine the participant and also to leverage that effort as highly as possible by exploiting the contributions of others. By contrast, competitive advantage in the design serves little purpose since it has already been given away. As a result, the participants are motivated to minimize their collective redundant effort and maximize interoperability and extensibility of their contributions.

This makes it critical to divide projects up into small manageable chunks; to make those chunks independent enough to allow development by unaffiliated parties; and to make all remaining interdependencies readily-available public knowledge. These requirements impose strict engineering disciplines of "**separation of concerns**" and "**design by contract**" in project designs.

Even in the case of "competing" packages like KDE and Gnome, which do essentially the same thing, there is communication of ideas. If something works well enough in Gnome, it will tend to be borrowed into KDE. Thus while competition does serve a positive role in allowing different ideas to be tried, and in serving different users with different needs and preferences, it does not lead to the negativity of a "zero sum game." Instead, a new "competitive advantage" may simply be ported from one package to another (as a quick example, look how quickly "window tabs" spread among major free software applications).

Common Gauges

Standards-based interface design and high levels of component-ization mean that projects which might otherwise be seen as single very large projects deconstruct into dozens or even thousands of tiny projects. Ideally each such project falls within the capability of a single independent developer (in reality

Figure 10.5:

Any system that must interact with other systems has to follow an interface, just as trains must run on tracks of a particular shape and size (called a "gauge"). The existance of many different railroad gauges in the world occasions some serious design problems. The tracks above are designed to support two different gauges, while the picture below shows the wheels of a train being changed with passengers aboard, as must happen when crossing some European borders. There are many more such design adaptations in the world of software, even if they are less visible to the end user. Much of the work of developers is simply getting around such obstacles
(Photo Credits: Les Chatfield/CC By 2.0, Mark Tristan/CC By-SA 2.0)

some engineering problems are hard to break down, and small formal or informal teams are needed).

Of course this imposes a kind of design discipline which is extremely beneficial to the long-term engineering stability of the systems so-designed, and which is nevertheless extraordinarily rare in the products of corporate industry. It is this design discipline which is largely responsible for the perception of engineering superiority and practical robustness of open source software designs: systems of many interacting, interchangeable parts are much more fault-tolerant than "brittle" systems designed as monolithic pieces with high levels of interdependence between separately developed components.

As a result, the free software community is largely organized around data standards (like XML, HTML, SVG, ATOM, JSON, or ODT etc) rather than individual software packages (like MS Word or Adobe Illustrator). To hide such a standard or obfuscate it any way is seen as obstructionist and unconscionable (an attitude which is unfortunately not so prevalent in other engineering disciplines where standards are often only available for purchase—and are sometimes very expensive, effectively shutting-out small-scale developers).

Putting It All Together

It has been said that the structure of programs mirrors the structure of the organizations that created them, and this is just as true of free software as proprietary. A loose aggregation of developers with different interests and needs and very limited individual resources naturally tends to produce a large collection of narrowly-focused programs. A practical necessity of this structure is the use of well-defined, freely-available, and easy-to-implement standards.

These two patterns of design, imposed by the natural structure of commons-based development, happen to coincide with important principles of good engineering design (particularly the separation of concerns and well-defined interfaces) which

Refactoring for Modularity

Especially if you come from a systems-engineering background, you may have thought of your project as one giant machine to be built. Dividing the problem up into functional blocks is something you usually think of as an internal engineering problem.

Unfortunately, such projects require a lot of "buy-in" from potential developers. They have to overcome the learning curve before they can begin to contribute to your project (or even use it). This puts off a lot of potential contributors who might really support your project if they could try it a little piece at a time.

Spend some time brainstorming about the various pieces of your project. What else can these things do? Try to break the project up into a lot of smaller, multi-purpose tools; make them as independent as possible; and present each of these to the community as a separate project (this kind of reorganization is called re-factoring).

It's okay to describe your "master plan" somewhere, but keep the emphasis on the individual components. Other people will contribute to them for their own reasons.

By far, my own most successful projects have been "spin-off" projects like this: ideas I developed because I needed them as components, but which could be re-used by others.

can be hard to enforce in a commercial environment where time-pressure and expediency of communication can put short-term gains ahead of long-term stability.

With such a chaotic sea of unaffiliated project development, though, how is it that large scale structures (such as entire operating systems and distributions) arise in free software?

In the commercial environment, organization comes first: A "manager" sets goals, makes guesses about the difficulty of implementation, and assigns various "teams" to overcome them. By contrast, in the community environment, organization comes last: vague goals are suggested (often by high-profile community opinion leaders), self-selected **developers** choose to solve some of the intervening problems, and then finally **packagers** search for already existing packages; test and ensure interoperability with other packages according to selected standards and policies; and then build a **distribution** or **stack** which combines them into a working whole.

Figure 10.6:

When common standards are used, separate development groups produce pieces that can be assembled into a larger whole by "packagers" (an important role with free software) after the fact, rather than before creating the elements
(Image Credit: Scott Maxwell | http://www.lumaxart.com / By-SA 2.0)

As hard as this is in practice, what is more remarkable is that it is generally feasible. So long as the individual pieces have been designed against good interface specifications and tested against good implementations of them, the chance of fitting the pieces together into compiled, consistent, and functional code is quite high. Clearly some software-writing must happen in this adaptation task, and occasionally requests get back to the original developers, but for the most part the integration process is kept simple.

Packagers, like the people of the Debian Project, are in a way, the greatest heroes of the free software movement, because they are the ones who make the system "just work," despite its patchwork origins.

Rule #4:

Grow, Don't Build

Design Process

S ince free software and other free culture products are formed by an incremental, organic process, they tend to be highly organic in their design as well. Free software is not so much built as it is grown. Thus, when considering a new project, you must think not about how to break it down into implementable chunks that can be assembled into a working product, but rather about how the project can organically grow—moving from working product to working product as it does so—becoming progressively more useful as it is developed.

In the world of proprietary software, big, highly-engineered packages are the norm. There is a defined "product life-cycle" for a piece of software: it is imagined, broken down into manageable chunks, which are then assigned to teams, with appropriate concern for interacting with other teams; the product is marketed; and then the engineering team has to produce the best result they can by the promised release date. This system usually has somewhat mixed results, since

Rule #4: "Grow, Don't Build"

Create a tiny seed of working code that can grow into what you want

Successful projects evolve like living, growing things, through a series of tiny changes forming a continuum of "constant release," as opposed to an engineered machine built from pieces which come together into a single "product."

Don't try to engineer a "perfect" solution and then get people to cooperate with you on developing it. In practice, very few people will contribute to a project that has no working code. The critical phase for a project is the single-developer phase when one person has to get the program to do something that other people will find useful. Once people find it useful, they'll find it worth their while to make it more useful.

When starting a project, you aren't engineering a complete solution, you are planting a seed for later success and growth.

engineers and programmers are often overly optimistic about what they can achieve and salesmen are quick to promise the moon when they know they don't have to deliver it.

For free software, though, this approach doesn't work so well.

With free software, things are much more organic. Someone has an idea, and they try it out, usually on something small. Someone else sees that idea, adds one of their own, and builds an incrementally more functional version (or adds on a package to extend the first so that both are needed).

What programs can do is determined as much by what people are willing to implement as by any plan to achieve certain design goals. Usually, developers are quite limited in the amount of time each can devote, and there are few promises to bind teams together, so programs progress in tiny increments.

Although individuals working on free software projects do think in engineering terms about their contributions, there is a very high premium on time, so developers tend to stay focused on their particular needs. It's extraordinarily rare for a free software project to be organized with a group of people actively trying to create a complex program from scratch.

Instead, most projects are about adapting or extending the functionality of some already working piece of software. Tell someone that you have an "idea" or worse yet, a top-down engineering plan for the software you want, and you'll usually face a lot of disbelief, cynicism, and (frequently) contempt. Most free software developers are highly distrustful of such a structured approach to creating software, and they want to see working code as proof that you know what you are talking about. And unlike, proprietary software management, you (usually) can't afford to pay them to swallow their doubts and follow your plan.

The "Exceptions" That Prove the Rule

Most of the "counter-examples" in the free software world—big flagship packages like Open Office, Mozilla, or Zope—did not start out as free software programs! Instead, they were developed by companies, either as a product to be sold, or as a product to be used in commercial production. Either way, the company did not share the source code to their project until much later when the early engineering and integration phase was completed.

Another important trend is the tendency of such monolithic applications to splinter into components after they have gone over to free software licensing. Netscape's monolithic internet browsing tool, for example, spawned not just the Mozilla series

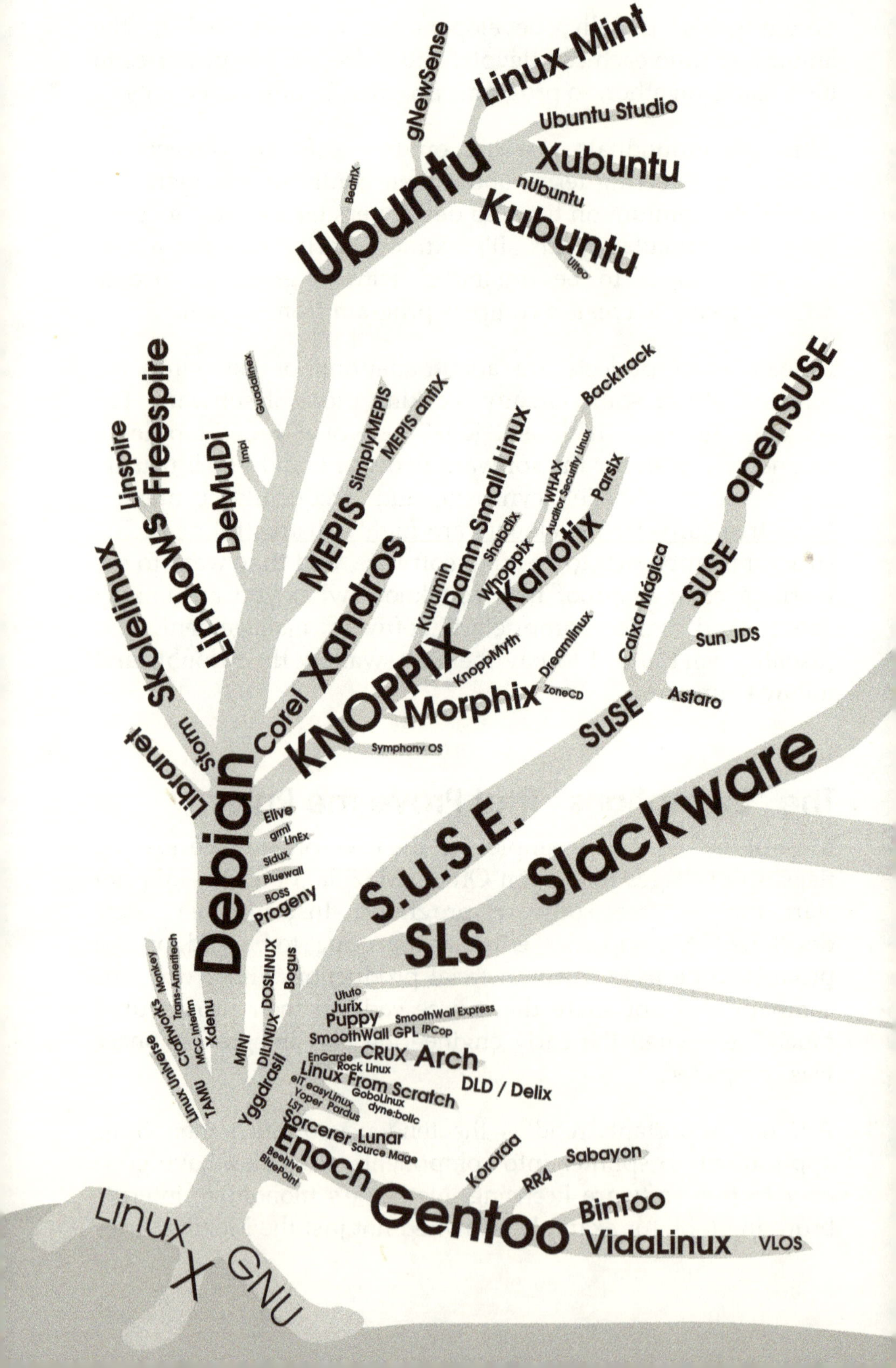

gNewSense
Linux Mint
Ubuntu Studio
Xubuntu
nUbuntu
Kubuntu
Ulteo
BeatriX
Ubuntu
Guadalinex
Impi
Freespire
Linspire
DeMuDi
Lindows
Skolelinux
SimplyMEPIS
MEPIS antiX
MEPIS
Backtrack
Damn Small Linux
WHAX
Auditor Security Linux
Parsix
Shabdix
Whoppix
Kanotix
Kurumin
Xandros
opensUSE
SUSE
Caixa Mágica
Sun JDS
Dreamlinux
KnoppMyth
KNOPPIX
Morphix
ZoneCD
Astaro
Corel
Storm
Libranet
Symphony OS
SuSE
Debian
Elive
grml
LinEx
Sidux
Bluewall
BOSS
Progeny
S.u.S.E.
Slackware
SLS
Monkey
Trans-Ameritech
Craftworks
MCC Interim
Xdenu
Linux Universe
TAMU
DOSLINUX
Bogus
MINI
DILINUX
Yggdrasil
Ututo
Jurix
Puppy
SmoothWall Express
SmoothWall GPL
IPCop
EnGarde
Rock Linux
CRUX
Arch
Linux From Scratch
DLD / Delix
eiT easyLinux
GoboLinux
Yoper
Pardus
dyne:bolic
LST
Sorcerer
Lunar
Source Mage
Enoch
Beehive
BluePoint
Kororaa
Sabayon
RR4
Gentoo
BinToo
VidaLinux
VLOS
Linux
X
GNU

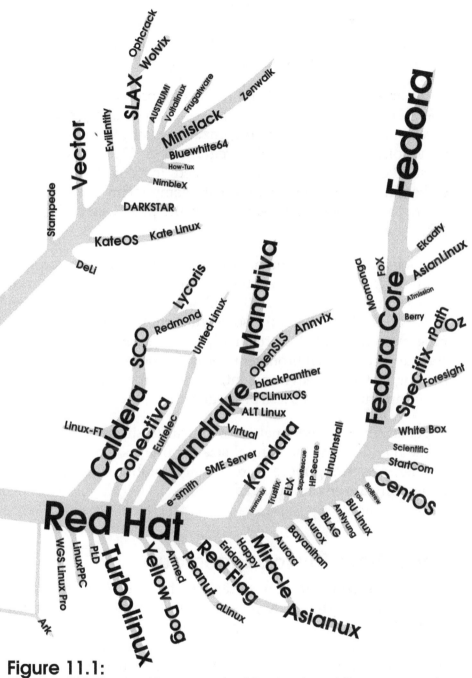

Figure 11.1:

GNU/Linux distributions provide an example of the organic evolution encouraged by free-licensing. Distributions freely branch, recombine, and evolve to meet the needs of various user communities—much more readily than do proprietary distributions which have artificial gate-keepers between users and the development process (Data from Wikipedia[1])

of web browsers, but also separate email clients and composition tools. Likewise, Zope, with the Zope 3 project, moved to a component model with greater and greater separation of concerns introduced into its design.

In the absence of financial and marketing pressures to maintain one marketable product, these projects have simply started to revert to a more natural organization from an' engineering standpoint. The continued integration of OpenOffice.org is most likely due both to a real need for object-linking and embedding technology between its components and also the desire to compete head-to-head with the proprietary Microsoft Office suite.

Blender remains fairly monolithic (with the possible exception of the game engine runtime), but its role has moved increasingly to that of a "platform," with tools written to run on it. This probably reflects the somewhat demanding needs of 3D programming and the relatively little support for it that standard desktop environments provide (perhaps in a truly 3D paradigm desktop environment, the need for a specialized 3D environment would be less pronounced).

Together, these exceptional cases appear to support rather than refute the idea that the natural size for free software projects is smaller, permitting more incremental evolution and branching of the software environment as a whole.

Linux: From Toy to Juggernaut

By contrast, software that started in the free software milieu was invariably started as a small, but functioning, product, within the capabilities of one person to create. Consider Linux, originally written by a single student, Linus Torvalds. At its outset in the early 1990s, it was little more than a toy: a slightly more functional variation on Minix (an operating system created to teach the theory of operating system design, but not seriously intended for production use).

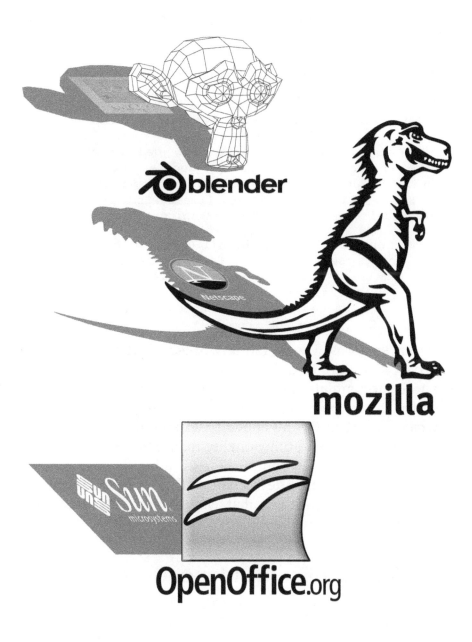

Figure 11.2:
The few existing free software flagship applications didn't start out as free software, but migrated to new licensing after being developed in private. Their monolithic structure is primarily a relic of their proprietary origins
(Drawing elements are trademarks of their respective companies and projects, used to refer to those companies)

Announcing it, Torvalds (figure 11.3) wrote this innocuous looking post:

```
Hello everybody out there using minix -

I'm doing a (free) operating system (just a
hobby, won't be big and professional like gnu)
for 386(486) AT clones. This has been brewing
since april, and is starting to get ready. I'd
like any feedback on things people like/dislike
in minix, as my OS resembles it somewhat (same
physical layout of the file-system (due to
practical reasons) among other things).

I've currently ported bash(1.08) and gcc(1.40),
and things seem to work. This implies that I'll
get something practical within a few months, and
I'd like to know what features most people would
want. Any suggestions are welcome, but I won't
promise I'll implement them :-)²
```

However, small as it was, Linux worked. And as such, there were people willing to tinker with it and use it. As a result, it began to accumulate more functionality and that in turn interested more people, and so on. These projects tend to snowball, and it is the functional packages that are the ones that people want to add functionality to, not the ones that aren't functional yet. Today, of course, Linux is a big flagship project, with hundreds of active developers and a rapid development cycle. But it didn't start out that way: it grew into that role, starting from a very tiny seed.

GNU: From Shelter to Independence

The "big and professional" project, "GNU," also started out pretty small. Though Richard Stallman had big ideas, the things he and his colleagues at the Free Software Foundation started with were pretty small components: an editor, a compiler, various Unix utilities, and so on. Even though some of these projects later grew into massively complex programs in their own right, the early releases of these packages were small enough for one person to manage.

Figure 11.3:

Linus Torvalds started with a very tiny seed when he started Linux
(Photo Credit: Alex_Dawson/CC By-SA 2.0)

Of course, all large projects start out with something small, but the difference here is that each of the small things that was made was not just an otherwise useless piece of code that needed to be part of a larger whole to be meaningful. No, each piece of software developed by the GNU project was a useful, working piece of software in itself.

For a long time, using GNU meant using a collection of free software tools on non-free operating systems (typically one of the many commercial or ambiguously-licensed versions of Unix available in the late 1980s). In a sense, the proprietary Unix environment of that era acted as a testing rig for the GNU programs, incubating their development.

Don't Over-design

The key point here is that it's a mistake to try to design something top-down with lots of elements that must be independently developed and then integrated in order to work at all. Doing things that way requires a managed effort in order to succeed, because no one is going to contribute time and effort to a project that may or may not produce any fruit at all (at least not unless you are paying them for their time).

Instead, break the project up into independently useful components: that way each part will be of enough interest to attract development effort on its own merits. If it happens to also be part of a grander scheme, that's fine, but don't expect that to motivate contributors. Or, as Linus Torvalds put it:

> "Nobody should start to undertake a large project. You start with a small trivial project, and you should never expect it to get large. If you do, you'll just over-design and generally think it is more important than it likely is at that stage. Or worse, you might be scared away by the sheer size of the work you envision. So start small, and think about the details. Don't think about some big picture and fancy design. If it doesn't solve some fairly immediate need, it's almost certainly over-designed. And don't expect people to jump in and help you. That's not how these things work. You need to get something half-way useful first, and then others will say 'Hey, that almost works for me,' and they'll get involved in the project."

Release Early, Release Often

The mantra of the "bazaar" development process is to "release early and release often." This is also called "continuous release" (see figure 11.4). The idea here is that in order for users to

Don't Over Specify

It might seem funny to even list this as a rule: what exactly does it mean to "Grow, Don't Build," after all? Isn't it pretty much the same as "Divide and Conquer"? Well, sort of...

As an engineer or a manager, the temptation to over-design is extreme. You have to learn to overcome it. Your project will acquire a life of its own, but only if you let it breathe. Other people will have different reasons for contributing, and you need to let your project serve their needs as well as yours.

So don't push too hard on specific design concepts. Let the design evolve to do what it needs to do. When you find you do need some specific functionality, then focus your own resources on solving that problem. Leave other areas of the design as open as possible.

Some other useful tips:

- Let others claim territory in your project. Create a "platform" on which others can build. If they found their own projects, they'll be more attentive to them.

- Keep the code working. Avoid major overhauls and re-writes as much as possible. Instead, make incremental changes. This will ensure that the code keeps being used, so it stays relevant, so people will keep contributing to making it better.

- Don't mind forks. They can be constructive. Related projects can still share information, and occasionally the other fork will turn out to be a better solution. If so, don't fight it. Just adopt the solution that works best and move forward.

- Figure on "toughing through" the initial phase of any project: it takes a lot of work to get a working or useful product, but it's unlikely that you'll see contributions before you reach that point. This is a fact of life with free culture projects. People generally contribute to make useful things more useful, not to create useful things out of nothing.

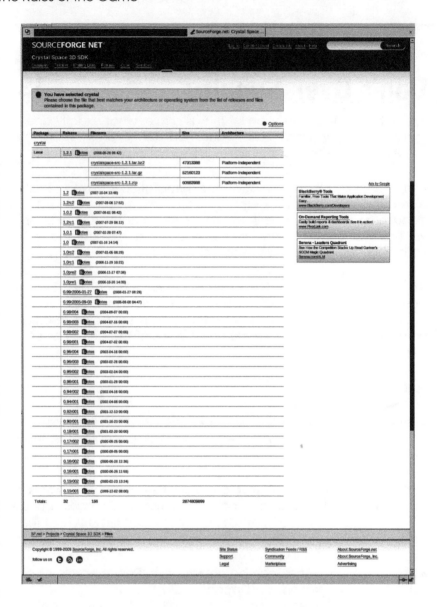

Figure 11.4:

For an actively-developed free software project (such as the Crystal Space library, shown here), dozens of releases are often available to the community, facilitating frequent testing of up-to-date code

contribute significantly to your project, they have to be using a very up-to-date version of your code. Otherwise, what they are testing is old news: the bugs they report are very likely to be ones you've already fixed—which wastes effort.

The mind-set of users in thinking about free software packages is intriguingly different than the mind-set of users of proprietary software: they speak in terms of the software's current status, not the last released status. Thus, Linux users do not think of themselves as using "Linux ME" or "Linux 2000" (nor even "Linux 2.6.18"). They instead think of themselves as using "Linux." Any discrepancy between what they are using and what is already developed is simply a gap to be corrected at the next opportunity, not a question of migration to a new product. Thus, the user actually perceives the improvement in the program as if it were actively changing while they use it, growing into a (usually) better fit with their needs and expectations.

In this sense, too, the user experience of a free software program is of an organic living thing, rather than a cut-and-dried released product which can only be appreciated for what it was, rather than for what it is.

This can happen, of course, because downloading and installing the new version is easy and costs nothing (both facts facilitated by the free licensing of the software).

But of course, tracking the development version of a piece of software is a very dynamic process. From the developer's perspective this relationship places some additional limitations on the development process: with very few exceptions, it is highly desirable not to ever "break" the code. Each change should move the code from one working version to another in tiny increments.

This need to work on the code in a "live" state imposes yet another good engineering discipline: constant testing. Since the code for each release needs to work, the modification of the software tends to progress through tiny changes to small parts

of the program. Making that feasible, in turn, brings us back to the "separation of concerns" and also "**don't repeat yourself**" (whenever you do repeat code in a project, changing one instance results in an inconsistency—thus it's a lot better to design the code so that a single instance is used in both places rather than to copy and paste code from one system to another).

Nurturing the Living Code

The practical consequence of all of these factors is that a free culture project grows (and evolves) like a living thing. It's a mistake to think of it in static terms as a machine to be built (even if, as with real living things, there are significant architectural parallels). A free software program, like a living organism, is a watch without a watchmaker. There is no overriding management process to ensure that the gears mesh, the system must instead self-organize into a functioning whole through the actions of the many participants in the development process.

The would-be **maintainer** (or **founder**) of a free culture project is not so much like an engineer as like a gardener: planting the seed of an idea (perhaps with visions of what it might become, but no certain knowledge), and nurturing it with the water, soil, and light it needs to flourish. The problem is one of establishing the right conditions for natural processes to take over, not to try to force the project along a pre-ordained track.

Notes

1 Data taken from the GNU/Linux Distribution Timeline.
  `http://futurist.se/gldt`

2 Linus Torvalds and the announcement of the Linux project.
  `http://www.linux.org/info/linus.html`

Figure 11.5:

(Facing Page) You can't engineer a tree, but you can tend it and take care of it. So it is with free-licensed projects
(Photo Credit: "Tony the Misfit"@Flickr/CC By 2.0)

Rule #5:

Be Bold!

Setting Inspiring Goals

One of the hardest rules that entrepreneurs have to learn is that investors don't like revolutionary new ideas. Even when they work, the reasoning goes, they won't make you any money. Instead, investors want to see "innovative" ideas: ideas that push the existing envelope a little further, but don't totally change the map.

With free culture projects, however, the situation is precisely inverted: people don't get as excited about contributing to merely "innovative" projects, they want to make "revolutionary" change in the world. High ambitions attract good company, and free licensed projects will do better not to set their sights too low.

This last rule is of course, a popular slogan for Wikipedia, but in a broader sense, it applies to all free culture projects. Timidity can be a slow but sure death for a project if it fails to inspire enough people to give it the resources and interest it needs to stay alive. In order to get finished and supported, a project needs to be seen as a vital need, a fascinating original

---

Rule #5: "Be Bold!"

Think big; set your sights high; and don't be afraid to say what you're after!

Merely "innovative" ideas attract capital investment (when there is any to be had), but "revolutionary" ideas attract followers. On a free culture project, it is usually helping hands rather than cash that wins the day.

Many perfectly good commercial ideas simply fail to capture the imagination of potential amateur developers, and as a result languish in a zone of half-measures, sustained by the minimum cost-effective effort of the handful of people who develop the project because they need it for work.

Amateurs are the soul of the free culture movement, and they need a goal they can be proud of.

---

solution, or in some way fundamentally fun in order to get finished.

After all, writing code, drawing diagrams, or copy-editing text are no-fun jobs on their own. With no paycheck at the end of the tunnel, we do these tedious tasks because we are driven to see the result, and we want that result to matter.

Manifestos, Meaning, and Motivations

Richard Stallman could've told the world he wanted to create a collection of free utilities and libraries for the Unix operating system. After all, that's what the GNU project on its own accomplished.

But that's not what he did. Stallman exposed his real vision: a world without proprietary software, with an operating system made entirely from free software. That was a revolutionary

Figure 12.1:
"Be bold!" is a popular slogan on Wikipedia, where it means that you should just go
ahead and make changes rather than asking for permission
(Drawing credit: Eric Piercing/CC By-SA 2.0)

idea, and he knew it. Why else would he write a "manifesto"?
Stallman articulated his dream in a way that is not common
outside of ideological revolutionary documents. Consider these
excerpts:

> *"Once GNU is written, everyone will be able to obtain good
> system software free, just like air."*

Richard Stallman, at Wikimania (*left*) and as "St. Ignucious" (*right*)

Figure 12.2:
Strong personalities and ideologies have an appeal which many project founders use to court public (and developer) interest in their projects
(Photo Credits: Thomas Bresson / CC By-SA 2.0, Elke Wetzig / CC By-SA 2.0, Martin Schmitt / CC By 2.0, Loco85@Wikipedia / CC By-SA 2.5)

Mark Shuttleworth

Jimbo Wales being interviewed by Rosario Lufrano for an Argentinian news program

Bruce Perens

Lawrence Lessig

Linus Torvalds

Ian Murdock

Figure 12.3:

Ideology is not the only way to be bold. Bruce Perens promoted free software to business as **open source**; Lawrence Lessig's vision was to bring the success of free software to aesthetic works; Linus Torvalds inspires mainly through appeals to technical excellence; Ian Murdock's goal was to make GNU/Linux more user friendly. Donald Knuth started TeX in order to typeset mathematics "beautifully"

(Photo credits: PR Photo, Ed Schipul/CC By-SA 2.0, Paul Fenwick/CC By-SA 2.0, Ilya Schurov (Computerra Weekly)/CC By-SA 2.0, Jacob Appelbaum/CC By-SA 2.5)

Donald Knuth

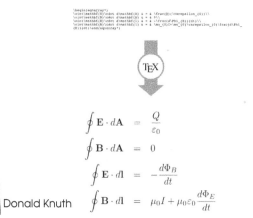

> *"Complete system sources will be available to everyone. As a result, a user who needs changes in the system will always be free to make them himself, or hire any available programmer or company to make them for him. Users will no longer be at the mercy of one programmer or company which owns the sources and is in sole position to make changes."*

> *"Finally, the overhead of considering who owns the system software and what one is or is not entitled to do with it will be lifted."*

Perhaps the most stirring text, though, is the preamble which is found in every copy of the GNU General Public License, a document as critical as a national constitution to the advocates of free culture. In part, it reads:

> *"The licenses for most software are designed to take away your freedom to share and change it. By contrast, the GNU General Public License is intended to guarantee your freedom to share and change free software—to make sure the software is free for all its users."*

Stallman didn't just try to create a "product," he created a "cause." That kind of bravado attracted followers who were inspired by the vision he depicted. It turns out that there are plenty of talented and capable people out there who don't have a cause, but want one.

Other successful projects have been just as bold in their visions. Jimbo Wales (figure 12.4) expressed the purpose of Wikipedia thus:

> *"Imagine a world in which every single person on the planet is given free access to the sum of all human knowledge."*

Nicholas Negroponte also managed to capture some of the revolutionary spirit of free culture early in promoting the One Laptop Per Child (OLPC) project:

> *"One laptop per child: Children are your most precious resource, and they can do a lot of self-learning and peer-to-peer teaching. Bingo. End of story."*

Today, the OLPC website continues to carry a mission statement for which the term "bold" is almost inadequate:

> *"To create educational opportunities for the world's poorest children by providing each child with a rugged, low-cost, low-power, connected laptop with content and software designed for collaborative, joyful, self-empowered learning. When children have access to this type of tool they get engaged in their own education. They learn, share, create, and collaborate. They become connected to each other, to the world and to a brighter future."*

Of course, most marketing strives to make products *seem* bold and revolutionary, but the difference here is that these projects' goals actually are as revolutionary as they claim to be.

Figure 12.5:
The OLPC is an ideal example of a "bold" project, and its marketing appeals to high ideals
(Screen capture from OLPC website)

The Cult of Personality

Do you have to be a "character" to run a free culture project? Well, a strong personality certainly does seem to help. But there's a lot of leeway in just what sort of personality you have. What is really required is just self-confidence.

The more you violate the previous two rules, the more you'll have to rely on this one: as projects get bigger and more complex, the need for charismatic leadership grows. You'll need to work harder to attract people to your goal, because they have to overcome a bigger "buy-in" in order to join you.

And so you should present it as a cause: "I want to do this, and this is why I want to do it." Write a manifesto if you need to, or even just a vision statement. Make people understand why the world will be a better place if you can achieve your goal.

Trust in your own personality, and don't try to make one up. Not everybody was meant to be an ideologue like Richard Stallman or a public speaker like Lawrence Lessig. But there are just as many "quiet" leaders like Donald Knuth, who simply wanted to make a really good typesetting engine or Linus Torvalds, who started out just having fun, but later wanted to focus on real technical quality in the Linux kernel. Those kinds of goals attract followers too.

The main thing to remember is to do something good. Communicate how good it is, and others will want to help you do it. Sincere vision really matters.

Mind you, not all such revolutions are political or even social. Some are founded on an appeal to artistic aesthetics or to craftsmanship—like Donald Knuth's TeX, which he proposed would simply typeset text beautifully, or Matthias Ettrich (of KDE) who proposed simply to create a consistent and usable interface:

"So one of the major goals is to provide a modern and common look and feel for all the applications. And this is exactly the reason why this project is different from elder attempts"

The need to be doing something new is important: after all, if it's been done before, what's the point in doing it again? So, when you express what you're doing, don't shoot yourself in the foot by trying to minimize what it means or the problems it presents. Hard problems are what developers live for.

Community projects' success in fully achieving their goals may well vary: OLPC's disagreements in 2008, which could be characterized as tension between government and business investors' timidity about such a bold mission and community contributors' impatience with that timidity shows one extreme. At the other extreme, GNU and Wikipedia are both clearly successful projects. The success of TeX at its aesthetic goals has made it the standard for its own academic market. A sense of *mission*, however, consistently bolsters all of these projects within their supporting communities.

Think Big, Start Small

At first, this rule might seem to contrast sharply with the previous "grow, don't build" rule, which counsels you to start really small. But in fact both are compatible—because even mighty oaks are grown from tiny acorns. The main point here is to have a higher goal in mind when you start and to share that inspirational vision with potential contributors.

There is however, a degree to which these rules balance each other. The less you follow the previous two rules (by dividing your project up into small components, each to be grown as an independently useful project), the more you are going to be stuck with a big and difficult to manage project. Running that larger project is going to require you to capture the imagination of potential helpers, and that's where having bold goals can help you get the help you need.

Fortunately, there is not just one model or personality type for bold leadership of a project. Many different people have managed to get their thoughts across in many different ways, ranging from the friendly academic humor of Donald Knuth to the revolutionary fervor of Richard Stallman. There's enough room for you to find your own pace and style.

Doing the Impossible

T here is no "magic" to commons-based peer production. Most of the techniques that have brought free culture products ranging from software to art to electronic hardware have been in play for hundreds or thousands of years. But they do run counter to the patterns of commercial proprietary industry. Due to the massive improvements in communications and authoring technology, we have reached a point where we can be more productive in our "leisure" than we are in our "work." And any labor of love is almost always going to be superior to labor alone.

The Impossible

In this series, I've presented six phenomena—Free Software (GNU/Linux), Free Knowledge (Wikipedia & Project Gutenberg), Free Arts (Creative Commons), Collective Financing (Blender Application & Open Movies), Open Hardware (LART & Open Graphics Project), and Closing the

Digital Divide (One Laptop Per Child)—which are succeeding despite the fact that our conventional understanding of society and economics says they shouldn't.

These phenomena therefore represent a fundamental challenge to our understanding, and force a re-evaluation of how the world works, and how it can work. All of these are examples of various applications of "commons based peer production" (CBPP), and have been made possible primarily by the huge gains in the fluidity of information provided by the wide availability of internet access.

Based on experience with successful projects and a little bit of analytical thought, it's possible to infer some important rules for how to make such projects succeed. Of course, many of the rules that you might come across are unsurprising, but I've selected five that really stand out as "counter-intuitive" in that they violate the assumptions that many people coming from an entrepreneurial, corporate, or government project background might make. These are:

- "Hold on loosely": Use a free license

- "Create a community": Focus on community before conceptualizing a product

- "Divide and conquer": Divide projects down to a very fine scale before implementing

- "Grow, don't build": CBPP projects are living, organic things, don't try to pin them down or you'll kill them

- "Be Bold!": Don't shy away from "revolutionary" ideas, they are paradoxically easier to create because they will attract more talent

In my experience, most failures of projects created by newcomers to the CBPP way of doing things can be traced to ignoring one or more of these rules. That's why I selected them as the ones to focus on in this series.

A New and More Joyful Paradigm

The corporations and government were the two great powers of the twentieth century—the engines of human production that conventional wisdom led us to fear and hold in awe as the sole mechanisms by which great human endeavors could be achieved.

Yet, the commons-based organization of the community, as exemplified by Wikipedia, shows up their productivity. GNU and Linux easily exceed their quality standards. Free arts may well exceed their artistic scope. In a few short years, the commons-based enterprise has out-produced centuries of corporate and government production.

These facts compel a new conventional wisdom: that commons-based enterprise may well become the most powerful creative force on Earth if it isn't already.

The community works so successfully because it harnesses the joy of human endeavor, not the fear of human limitations. How could we imagine that the pittance of human endeavor that can be forcibly extracted under the whips of wage slavery, where workers merely do what they must to evade starvation, can ever compete with a joyful labor of love created by fully actualized human beings, doing what they really want to do? *That's* the "secret", the one rule that lies behind all the others: joy.

Though still in its infancy, commons-based enterprise has already seriously challenged the supremacy of corporate and even government enterprise. Certainly it is ready to stand alongside them as an important method for organizing large human endeavors, with its own unique and powerful capabilities.

Appendices

Appendices

Appendices
Improving the Process

O f course, no system is perfect. There are a number of problems which, to my knowledge, have not been adequately solved.

However, every one of them is being attacked by one or more interested parties today, and solutions may arise over the next several years. I do not pretend to know with any certainty what the solutions will be, but I have contributed several of my own ideas for addressing some of these problems as articles or columns in Free Software Magazine.[1-7]

Five of these articles are included as appendices A to E in this book. They do not address all of the dimensions of each issue, but should offer some helpful advice. A few other articles worth reading are included in the notes at the end of this section.[8-10]

Tools for Non-Software Production

There are extremely well developed free software tools for software development, but in all other areas of engineering and creative arts, there remains a lot to be accomplished. This means that many potential CBPP opportunities are limited due to the availability of proprietary tools which many casual developers could not afford. Since the people most capable of writing these tools are not in these development communities, there is a skill/interest mismatch which retards development in those areas.

Appendix A, "Tools for Community Building," presents some networking software that might be used to help solve part of this problem by making the development process more accessible to people who are not programmers.

The Gender Gap

Less than 2% of free software developers are women! At this point, there is little more than speculation as to the causes of and possible solutions to this problem.

Appendix B, "Ten Easy Ways to Attract Women to your Project," presents some simple ideas about making projects more comfortable for women (although many of these changes will help some men too).

Hardware Licensing

Open Hardware remains pretty marginal, partly due to the fund raising problem, but there are other problems relating to the licensing, because hardware manufacturing is not legally a "copy" and therefore not regulated by copyright law. This makes pure copyright license protection awkward and incomplete at best.

Appendix C describes a way that copyleft can be extended to hardware designs, by considering "What if Copyright Didn't Apply to Binaries?"

Unfair Competition

I don't think it's nearly as much of a threat as many people fear, but there is no doubt that certain threatened corporate and government bodies have attempted to retaliate against CBPP projects and products through various marketing and legal means. Appendix D, "Marketshare or Sharing?", offers a perspective on why this might not be as dire a situation as some people fear.

Fund Raising

Though the Blender example is promising, it still falls about an order-of-magnitude short of where it needs to be to give corporate financing a run for its money. There are also limited examples of viable business models for certain kinds of free-licensed works. Future collaboration systems should attempt to solve this problem, but it is incredibly tricky (people can get much crazier when money is involved).

Appendix E, "CC+ and Buying for the Commons," presents an idea for a simple fundraising tool based on a Creative Commons protocol.

Licensing

Finally, since free licenses are so important to project success, Appendix F provides some information on best practices for choosing a license for a commons-based project, including a comparison table and the full text of a few selected licenses.

Notes:

Some Free Software Magazine articles on improving both the efficiency and the scope of the commons based enterprise:

1 Terry Hancock; "Free software tools for designing productive community sites"; 2008 (Included as Appendix A).
   http://www.freesoftwaremagazine.com/columns/
      free_software_tools_for_designing_productive_community_sites

Appendices

2 Terry Hancock; "Ten easy ways to attract women to your free software project"; 2008 (Included as Appendix B).

```
http://www.freesoftwaremagazine.com/columns/
    ten_easy_ways_attract_women_your_free_software_project
```

3 Terry Hancock; "What if copyright didn't apply to binary executables?"; 2008 (Included as Appendix C).

```
http://www.freesoftwaremagazine.com/columns/
    what_if_copyright_didnt_apply_binary_executables
```

4 Terry Hancock; "Why sharing matters more than marketshare to GNU/Linux"; 2008 (Included as Appendix D).

```
http://www.freesoftwaremagazine.com/columns/
    sharing_matters_more_than_market_share_linux
```

5 Terry Hancock; "Deploying CC+ for the common good: Buy4Commons"; 2008 (Included as Appendix E).

```
http://www.freesoftwaremagazine.com/columns/
    deploying_cc_common_good_buy4commons
```

6 Terry Hancock; "Group interview: a graphic view of the open hardware movement"; Part 1: "Motivations" and Part 2: "Technical and Social Issues"; 2008. A collection of first-hand observations on a major Open Hardware project.

```
http://www.freesoftwaremagazine.com/articles/
    group_interview_graphic_view_open_hardware_movement
    _part_1_motivations
```

```
http://www.freesoftwaremagazine.com/articles/
    group_interview_graphic_view_open_hardware_movement
    _part_2_technical_and_social_issues
```

7 Terry Hancock; "Towards a Free Matter Economy"; Part 1: "Information as Matter, Matter as Information", Part 2: "The Passing of the Shade Tree Mechanic", Part 3: "Designing the Narya Bazaar", Part 4: "Tools of the Trade", Part 5: "Discovering the Future, Recovering the Past", Part 6: "Legal Landmines", and Part 7: "A Free Future in Space"; 2005-2006. Explores the development challenges involved in developing a commons based enterprise for development of technology in support of space development and settlement.

```
http://www.freesoftwaremagazine.com/articles/free_matter_economy
```

```
http://www.freesoftwaremagazine.com/articles/free_matter_economy_2
```

```
http://www.freesoftwaremagazine.com/articles/free_matter_economy_3
```

```
http://www.freesoftwaremagazine.com/articles/free_matter_economy_4
```

```
http://www.freesoftwaremagazine.com/articles/free_matter_economy_5
```

```
http://www.freesoftwaremagazine.com/articles/free_matter_economy_6
```

```
http://www.freesoftwaremagazine.com/articles/free_matter_economy_7
```

8 John Calcote; "Running a free software project"; 2007.

```
http://www.freesoftwaremagazine.com/articles/
    running_a_free_software_project
```

9 David Horton; "How to get people to work for free: Attracting volunteers to your free software project"; 2005.

```
http://www.freesoftwaremagazine.com/articles/recruting_people
```

10 John Locke; "What's a Wiki? A survey of content management systems"; 2005.

```
http://www.freesoftwaremagazine.com/articles/whats_a_wiki
```

Appendix A:
Tools for Community Building

These days there's a lot of buzz about "Web 2.0" and making websites more interactive, but what's really going on is a reconnection to the community nature of the internet. Collaboration, cooperation, and the information commons are all ideas that pre-dated the world wide web in the form of older internet technologies. In today's distributed computing environment, though, these technologies have really flourished. Here's a guide to eight that you should consider making use of in building a community around an information commons project of any kind, from multimedia, to hardware, to software.

Community-Building Tools

The early twenty-first century has brought us some excellent tools for building more sophisticated and responsive communities around peer production projects. Few projects need to deploy more than one or two of these technologies.

However, a greater consideration of the community atmosphere and electronic landscape can make a huge difference in the success of your project.

Free software has played an important part in this technical revolution. As a result, there are free software tools for every one of these categories. In many cases, in fact, the free software tools lead the market. Which particular package you use will depend on what sort of content management system, portal, or hosting you have available to you.

I can't possibly hope to be comprehensive in listing packages to provide these services, but I have tried to present a reasonable sampling of some of the most popular and/or interesting tools that I could find. For the web-based tools, I've included information on LAMP-based (Linux-Apache-MySQL-PHP) packages, Drupal (a PHP-based CMS, on which Free Software Magazine is based), Plone (a Python/Zope-based CMS that we use at Anansi Spaceworks), and a selection of others (based on C, Perl, Ruby, Java, and others). I've also listed sites that provide these features as hosted services, which gives you the option of not having to install anything on your own server.

Certain technologies—particularly synchronous or visualization tools—rely on alternative client/server technologies. For those, I've listed clients, servers, and infrastructure information (including protocols and libraries) that may be of use.

Regarding tools for installation on your own server and/or client software to be used by visitors or contributors, I have restricted this list to free-licensed open source software only. However, in the column "Services," I have relaxed this requirement: where there are widely-used, market-leading proprietary software based services, I have included them. This includes services like SecondLife and Yahoo Groups, both of which have been used extensively to promote free software or free content projects.

Building an Online Community

Within the free software and free culture communities, there are plenty of reasons to build community sites, so as to involve visitors. Some of these can contribute a lot to the production, sharing, and understanding of free software, designs, and art.

I've tried to assemble the resources needed here, along with some ideas of how to use them. No doubt some would disagree with this particular breakdown, and I've probably omitted some important technologies, but I think these are eight that anyone setting about to design a community site should think about in their design.

Private Messages
Private Conversations & Mail

Private Communications: Email and Instant Messaging

The most basic communications technologies are those that provide simple one-to-one communication. Email is the traditional way to do this in the free software community, but for a given project, conversations can also happen through forum "private message" (PM) communications or, if immediacy is also desired, through instant messaging technology (and don't forget, there's always the telephone!).

Email software is ubiquitous of course. Private messaging is usually a feature of "forums" (see the next section). Synchronous "chat" systems are fundamentally different from a technical perspective, though they serve much the same purpose.

There are a few cases of chat "applets" which can run from within a browser window, which can bring chat into the web browsing experience. There are also a number of "webmail" applications that can be embedded in a website, though I didn't attempt to list these below.

(Photo credit: Daria Radota Rasmussen/CC-By 2.0)

		Packages	References and Notes
Low-Tech		E-mail	`http://en.wikipedia.org/wiki/E-mail`
Web	LAMP	CoolSmile	`http://www.coolsmile.net/`
	Drupal	Forummail	`http://drupal.org/node/61445`
	Plone	qi.LiveChat	`http://plone.org/products/qi-livechat`
		MailNode	`http://plone.org/products/mailnode`
		PloneFormGen	`http://plone.org/products/ploneformgen`
		SignupSheet	`http://plone.org/products/signupsheet`
	Other		There are many 'web mail' packages available which allow emails to be sent from a web server via an online form.
			Private messaging is also a common feature in many forum packages (next table).
	Services	Google Mail	`http://www.google.com/mail`
		Yahoo Mail	`http://www.yahoo.com/mail`
Chat	Clients	ChatZilla	`http://chatzilla.hacksrus.com`
		Konversation	`http://konversation.kde.org`
		XChat	`http://www.xchat.org`
		BitchX	`http://www.bitchx.org`
		Other IRC	`http://en.wikipedia.org/wiki/` `Comparison_of_Internet_Relay_Chat_clients`
		Kopete	`http://kopete.kde.org`
		Pidgin	`http://sourceforge.net/projects/pidgin`
		Other IM	`http://en.wikipedia.org/wiki/` `Comparison_of_instant_messaging_clients`
	Servers	IRCd	`http://www.irc.org/tech_docs/ircnet/faq.html`
		EIRC	`http://eirc.sourceforge.net` (Java)
		Other IRC	`http://en.wikipedia.org/wiki/` `Comparison_of_IRC_daemons`
	Protocols	IRC	`http://en.wikipedia.org/wiki/Internet_Relay_Chat`
		Other Protocols	`http://en.wikipedia.org/wiki/` `Comparison_of_instant_messaging_protocols`
	Services	OFTC	`http://www.oftc.net`
		freenode	`http://www.freenode.net`
		EFnet	`http://www.efnet.org`
		Undernet	`http://www.undernet.org`

Forums

Public Conversation & Consensus

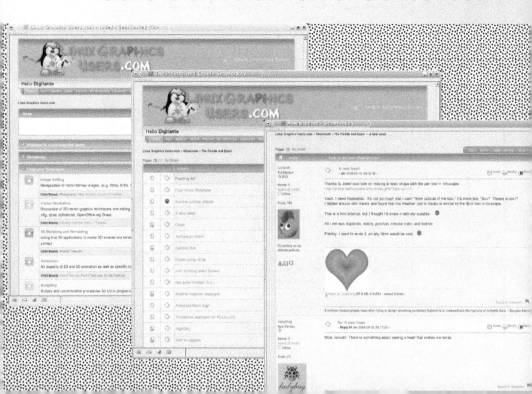

Forums

The next step up is a web-based "forum". These are the evolution of the "bulletin board systems" (BBSs) of the 1980s and 1990s, adapted for use on the world wide web. They are accessible for most users, even ones who might have trouble with email. More importantly, they provide a lot of moderation options which gives you more ability to keep trolls and flames and other bad conduct out of your project. Doing so will encourage more people to stay on with your project.

If you want to stay low-tech, of course, the preferred technology nowadays is the electronic mailing list. Most of the newer email list servers, however, have some form of web-based subscription system. There are also the Google and Yahoo "Groups", which have nearly the same functionality as usenet newsgroups, but are accessible via both a web interface and email.

(Photo credit: laffy4k@Flickr / CC By 2.0)

		Packages	References and Notes
Low-Tech		Mailing Lists Newsgroups	`http://en.wikipedia.org/wiki/Electronic_mailing_list` `http://en.wikipedia.org/wiki/Newsgroup`

Web	LAMP	PHP BB
		Phorum
		FluxBB
		XMB
		Others
			`http://www.phpbb.com`
			`http://www.phorum.org`
			`http://fluxbb.org`
			`http://forums.xmbforum.com`
			`http://en.wikipedia.org/wiki/`
			    `Comparison_of_Internet_forum_software_(PHP)`

	Drupal	Forum
		Advanced Forum
		flatforum
		Forum Thread
		Democracy
		+PHP BB
		+Phorum
			`http://drupal.org/handbook/modules/forum`
			`http://drupal.org/project/advanced_forum`
			`http://drupal.org/project/flatforum`
			`http://drupal.org/project/forumthread`
			`http://drupal.org/project/democracy_forum`
			`http://drupal.org/project/phpbbforum`
			`http://drupal.org/project/phorum_integrate`

	Plone	Ploneboard
		SimpleForum
		zForum
		TIForum
		Gossip
		EasyForums
		NunBB
		PloneMailList
		Listen
			`http://plone.org/products/ploneboard)`
			`http://plone.org/products/simpleforum`
			`http://plone.org/products/zforum`
			`http://plone.org/products/tiforum`
			`http://plone.org/products/plonegossip`
			`http://plone.org/products/easyforums`
			`http://plone.org/products/nunbb`
			`http://plone.org/products/plonemaillist`
			`http://plone.org/products/listen`

	Other	JForum
		Beast
		Others
			`http://www.jforum.net`
			`http://beast.caboo.se`
			`http://en.wikipedia.org/wiki/`
			    `Comparison_of_internet_forum_software_(other)`

	Services	Google Groups
		Yahoo Groups
		Simple Machines
			`http://groups.google.com`
			`http://groups.yahoo.com`
			`http://www.simplemachines.org`

Blogs

News & Opinion

Terry Hancock

- Invite your friends
- My account
- My posts
- My subscriptions
- Own blog entries in moderation
- Your Referrals
- Create content
- Pending articles
- Log out

Looking for Linux hosting, reviews, coupons, etc.? See out user-voted list

1. Dreamhost (reviews, coupons)
2. HostPapa (reviews, coupons)
3. Hostmonster (reviews, coupons)
4. InMotion (reviews, coupons)
5. DollsHosting (reviews, coupons)
6. FastDomain (reviews, coupons)
7. StartLogic (reviews, coupons)

Community posts

Free Software and the State of the World

Rob Strover   2008-09-05   1

 Write a full post in response to this!

Today I want to talk about free and open source software in connection with the them and us feeling that I believe is widely felt all over the world.

Initially you might think that these two topics have nothing to do with each other but hopefully by the end of this post you will understand that these two topics are actually connected in many complex ways.

 Rob Strover's posts   Add new comment Read more   168 reads   Subscribe user's posts   Subscribe post

Skegness Grammar School, using GNU/Linux and thin-clients across the school

Richard Rothwell   2008-08-21   3

 Write a full post in response to this!

Gerry Saddington is ICT co-ordinator at Skegness Grammar School. It is a specialist sports college and a specialist maths and computing college with nearly 800 pupils, and has a boarding provision for around 60. Alistair Crust is responsible for serving the technology needs of the Skegness Grammar School community. All the school's 180 curriculum computers run GNU/Linux.

 Richard Rothwell's posts   Add new comment Read more   2509 reads

Buzz authors

Laurie Langham

Terry Hancock

Tony Mobily

Anthony Taylor

Rosalyn Hunter

Other sites

The Top 10 Everything (Dave). The good, the bad and the ugly

Free Software news (Dave & Bridget). All about free software – free as in freedom!

Book Reviews: illiterarty (Bridget). Book reviews, blogs, and short stories.

Hot topics - last 60 days

Blogs and Online Contents

Maintaining an up-to-date website, by directly editing static HTML is a major chore. So "content management systems" (CMS) were invented to simplify the task. One of the most popular types today is the "web log" or "blog". There are dedicated standalone blog packages, but there are also blog modules for most of the major content management systems (including Drupal and Plone).

(Photo credits: Antony Mayfield / CC By 2.0, freddie_boy@Flickr / CC By-SA 2.0)

		Packages	References and Notes
Low-Tech		Static Webpage	For many projects, a simple static HTML webpage which is updated frequently enough will serve for this purpose.

Web	LAMP	Wordpress
		b2evolution
		LifeType
		Serendipity
		Nucleus CMS
		FlatPress
		Others
			`http://wordpress.org`
			`http://b2evolution.net`
			`http://lifetype.net/blog`
			`http://www.s9y.org`
			`http://nucleuscms.org`
			`http://www.flatpress.org/home`
			`http://www.weblogmatrix.org`

	Drupal	Blog
		Single-User Blog
		Blog List
		Mini Blog
		Blogroll
		Blogger
		DrupalMU
			`http://drupal.org/handbook/modules/blog`
			`http://drupal.org/project/single_user_blog`
			`http://drupal.org/project/blog_list`
			`http://drupal.org/project/mini_blog`
			`http://drupal.org/project/blogroll`
			`http://drupal.org/project/blogger`
			`http://drupal.org/project/drupalmu`

	Plone	COREBlog2
		Quills
		SimpleBlog
		q Plone Blog
		bda.blogview
		PloneWorkflows
		ReactiveWorkflow
		Press Room
		Slideshow Folder
		Plumi
			`http://plone.org/products/coreblog2`
			`http://plone.org/products/quills`
			`http://plone.org/products/simpleblog`
			`http://plone.org/products/qploneblog`
			`http://plone.org/products/bda-blogview`
			`http://plone.org/products/ploneworkflows`
			`http://plone.org/products/reactiveworkflow`
			`http://plone.org/products/pressroom`
			`http://plone.org/products/slideshowfolder`
			`http://plone.org/products/plumi`

	Other	Typo	`http://typosphere.org/projects/show/typo`
	Services	Wordpress Others	`http://wordpress.com` `http://en.wikipedia.org/wiki/Category:Blog_hosting_services`

Wikis & Version Control

Collaboration & Change
Management

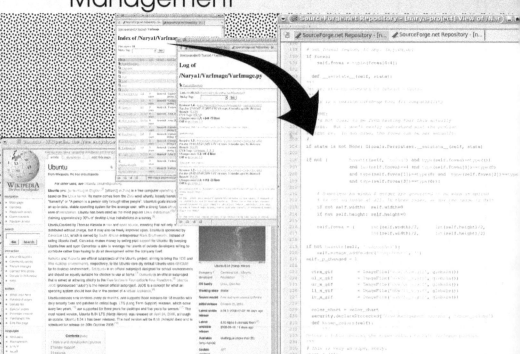

Wikis and Version Control Systems

It may seem a little strange to lump wikis and version control systems together, but the truth is that they do much the same task. A wiki is a kind of lightweight version control system combined with viewing and editing directly in your browser. Wikis usually present a much shallower learning curve than do tools to manage CVS or Subversion, although there are some nice integration packages available.

A wiki is just a quick, easily marked-up web site generation system, with simple shortcuts for creating new pages as well as rendering them to HTML (and sometimes other formats as well).

Version control systems are based on a different kind of mental model: one in which the package is downloaded (or "checked out") entirely by one user who then makes changes which must be "checked in". This is a much heavier solution than the wiki, and there are typically access limits which result in a more complicated workflow. Formal version control systems are preferred for handling program source code, though. There are a lot more version control systems available, but I've listed Subversion here because it contains a web-accessible browsing system (ViewVC and Trac provide this for some other version control systems, including CVS, which was the standard for free software for many years).

(Photo credits: Lars Plougmann/CC-By-SA 2.0, Ralph Bijker/CC-By 2.0, Kevin Quinn/CC-By 2.0, Ellie Van Houtte/CC-By 2.0)

		Packages	References and Notes
Low-Tech		Static Webpage	For many projects, a simple static HTML webpage which is updated frequently enough will serve for this purpose.
Web	LAMP	MediaWiki TikiWiki DokuWiki) Others	http://www.mediawiki.org http://www.tikiwiki.org http://www.dokuwiki.org/dokuwiki http://en.wikipedia.org/wiki/Comparison_of_wiki_software
	Drupal	Drupal Wiki interwiki Wikitools	http://drupal.org/project/drupal_wiki http://drupal.org/project/interwiki http://drupal.org/project/wikitools
	Plone	ZWiki ZWikiFolder Wicked Cuic pages ViewVC++	http://plone.org/products/zwiki http://plone.org/products/zwikifolder http://plone.org/products/wicked http://plone.org/products/cuic-pages http://plone.org/products/viewvc
	Other	Moin Moin JAMWiki Instiki ViewVC Subversion Trac	http://moinmo.in http://jamwiki.org http://www.instiki.org http://www.viewvc.org http://subversion.tigris.org http://trac.edgewall.org
	Services	Wikia Wikibooks Other Wikis Sourceforge Google Code Other Incubators	http://en.wikipedia.org/wiki/Wikia http://www.wikibooks.org http://en.wikipedia.org/wiki/Comparison_of_wiki_farms http://sourceforge.net http://code.google.net http://en.wikipedia.org/wiki/Comparison_of_free_software_hosting_facilities

Social Nets

Finding Friends & Contacts

Social Networking Software

Social networking software is primarily about getting to meet and greet individual people. Typical features include "friends" and "favorites", which provide connections to various other projects. A similar application is a "social bookmarking" system, in which the favorites are links to other websites, possibly with an excerpt (making it into a kind of news system as well).

(Photo credit: xt0ph3r@Flickr/CC-By-SA 2.0)

		Packages	References and Notes
Low-Tech		Link lists Web rings	Static webpages can be used to link to related material or projects.
Web	LAMP	Elgg	`http://elgg.org`

	Drupal	Profile
		OpenID
		Drigg
			`http://drupal.org/handbook/modules/profile`
			`http://drupal.org/handbook/modules/openid`
			`http://drupal.org/project/drigg`

	Plone	Org. Profile
		My Address Book
		mxm Contacts
		ExpertPool
		Plonelicious
		Tasty Bookmarks
		Content Ratings
		TagCloud
		PloneWorldKit
			`http://plone.org/products/organizational-profile`
			`http://plone.org/products/myaddressbook`
			`http://plone.org/products/mxmcontacts`
			`http://plone.org/products/expertpool`
			`http://plone.org/products/plonelicious`
			`http://plone.org/products/atbookmarks`
			`http://plone.org/products/contentratings`
			`http://plone.org/products/tagcloud`
			`http://plone.org/products/ploneworldkit`

	Services	MySpace
		Facebook
		LinkedIn
		Ning
		Other Networking
		
		Digg
		Other Bookmarking
			`http://www.myspace.com`
			`http://www.new.facebook.com`
			`http://www.linkedin.com`
			`http://www.ning.com`
			`http://en.wikipedia.org/wiki/`
			    `List_of_social_networking_websites`
			
			`http://digg.com`
			`http://en.wikipedia.org/wiki/`
			    `List_of_social_software#Social_bookmarking`

Protocols		OpenSocial Shindig	`http://www.opensocial.org` `http://incubator.apache.org/shindig/`

Virtual Reality
Presentations, Meetings, 3D Visualizations, & More

Virtual Reality

Virtual reality used to be all the rage among futurists. In practice, it provides a very literal community experience online, but may not be as efficient at some of the most important tasks. There are things that can *only* be done in a 3D interactive environment, though

This technology has come a long way in the past few years. With OpenSimulator and the Second Life Viewer, there is now a complete free software virtual world system available for hosting your own virtual realities. There are also, of course more general-purpose 3D viewing and serving systems based on X3D (the successor to VRML).

(Photo credit: Vanessa Tan/CC-By 2.0)

		Packages	References and Notes
Low-Tech		Renderings Scene Files	For users without access to virtual reality clients, 3D content can be pre-rendered and displayed as images or the original scene files can be provided for viewing with an offline viewer.

VR	Clients	SecondLife Viewer †
		FreeWRL
		Xj3D
		Collada Loader
		WorldForge
		Planeshift
			`http://secondlifegrid.net/programs/open_source/code`
			`http://freewrl.sourceforge.net`
			`http://www.xj3d.org`
			`http://sourceforge.net/projects/colladaloader`
			`http://www.worldforge.org`
			`http://sourceforge.net/projects/planeshift`

	Servers	OpenSimulator †
		WorldForge ‡
		PlaneShift ‡
			`http://opensimulator.org`
			`http://www.worldforge.org`
			`http://sourceforge.net/projects/planeshift`

	Protocols	CrystalSpace
		
		VOS
		X3D
		U3D
		
		COLLADA
			`http://www.crystalspace3d.org`
			`http://en.wikipedia.org/wiki/Crystal_Space`
			`http://interreality.org`
			`http://www.web3d.org/x3d`
			`http://sourceforge.net/projects/u3d`
			`http://en.wikipedia.org/wiki/U3D`
			`http://www.ecma-international.org/publications/`
			`  standards/Ecma-363.htm`
			`http://www.khronos.org/collada`
			`http://en.wikipedia.org/wiki/COLLADA`

	Services	Second Life Other Grids	`http://secondlife.com` `http://en.wikipedia.org/wiki/OpenSimulator`

† OpenSimulator is compatible with the SecondLife Viewer. Together, they now provide a complete free software virtual world system.

‡ WorldForge and PlaneShift servers are included with the client in the source code packages.

Downloads
Managing Large Packages

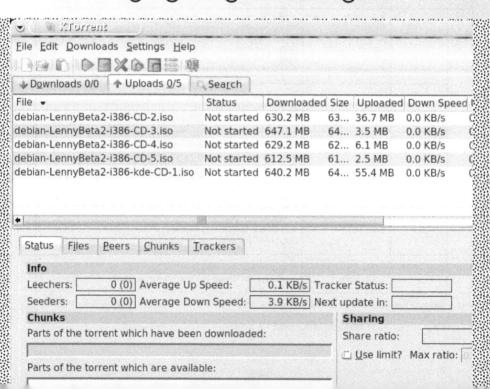

Delivering Large Downloads

A major problem for multimedia content, design, or software projects is how to deliver the end product. Downloads of a few megabytes are common, and some things, like entire GNU/Linux distributions or feature-length motion pictures, can be multiple gigabytes in size. Most people can't afford to pay for this kind of download service on their own server, especially when the download is offered at no cost.

Fortunately, there are plenty of service providers who will carry most kinds of content you might create for HTTP or FTP download. Additionally, there is a relatively new technology, called a "swarming" download system which combines internet file-sharing technology with conventional hosting. The most successful such technology is Bit Torrent. These swarming download systems take load off of your server, allowing much of the work to be shared among the clients requesting the download, and they are particularly useful for high-volume, large-size, and very popular downloads.

To host such content on your own site, you'll need only to provide the "torrent" file (which is a kind of index to the download), a "seed" of the original file, and a "tracker" to help coordinate the download process among clients. There are even free services providing the tracker and seed system, so that you don't have to handle them.

(Photo credit: FaceMePLS@Flickr/CC-By 2.0)

		Packages	References and Notes
Low-Tech		FTP HTTP	The old-fashioned way to deliver files is to simply make them available via an FTP (File Transfer Protocol) or HTTP (Hyper-Text Transfer Protocol) server (better known today as a "web server").
Web	Drupal	BitTorrent Filebrowser	`http://drupal.org/project/bittorrent` `http://drupal.org/project/filebrowser`

	Plone	Railroad
		ARFilePreview
		PublicationProduct
		PloneFilesZip
		PloneForge
		Software project
			`http://plone.org/products/railroad`
			`http://plone.org/products/arfilepreview`
			`http://plone.org/products/ploneformgen`
			`http://plone.org/products/plonefileszip`
			`http://plone.org/products/ploneforge`
			`http://plone.org/products/software-project`

	Services	Sourceforge
		Google Code
		Other Incubators
			`http://sourceforge.net`
			`http://code.google.net`
			`http://en.wikipedia.org/wiki/`
			`    Comparison_of_free_software_hosting_facilities`

Torrent	Clients	BitTorrent
		Other Torrent
		
		Other File Sharing
			`http://www.bittorrent.com`
			`http://en.wikipedia.org/wiki/`
			`    Comparison_of_BitTorrent_Clients`
			`http://sourceforge.net/softwaremap/`
			`    trove_list.php?form_cat=251`

	Servers	mod_bt PHPBTTracker+	`http://www.crackerjack.net/mod_bt` `http://phpbttrkplus.sourceforge.net`
	Protocol	torrents	`http://en.wikipedia.org/wiki/BitTorrent_(protocol)`

	Services	LinuxTracker
		TuxDistro
		TLMP
		Undernet
		Other Torrent
			`http://linuxtracker.org`
			`http://www.tuxdistro.com`
			`http://tlm-project.org/public/distributions`
			`http://www.undernet.org`
			`http://bittorrent.wikia.com/wiki/`
			`    Comparison_of_BitTorrent_sites`

e-Commerce
Fundraising & Commercial Trade

E-Commerce

You might not think of internet stores as "social" software, but in many ways they are. Amazon's marketplace provides a way for smaller suppliers to compete. Ideas about "collective patronage" for free-licensed works, will require both basic payment processing, and also simplification of fund-raising through collective fund-raising systems.

In a commons-oriented world, monetary trade is still very important. The conventional "store" infrastructure can be used in unconventional ways, and adding things like collective patronage and fund-raising systems can turn commercial tools into important community support systems (see also Appendix E).

There are also a number of services related to both payment processing and collective funding.

(Photo credits: The Consumerist/CC-By 2.0, Tinou Bao/CC-By 2.0)

		Packages	References and Notes

Web	LAMP	osCommerce
		ZenCart
		ECSCS
		Others
			`http://www.oscommerce.com`
			`http://www.zencart.com`
			`http://www.ecommerceshoppingcartsoftware.org`
			`http://en.wikipedia.org/wiki/`
			   `Comparison_of_shopping_cart_software`

	Drupal	Ubercart
		e-Commerce
		osCommerce
			`http://www.ubercart.org`
			`http://drupal.org/project/ecommerce`
			`http://drupal.org/project/oscommerce`

	Plone	PloneMall
		Simple Cart Item
		EasyShop
		GetPaid with Plone
		PFG Payment Field
		LetsPay
		FlexPortlets
			`http://plone.org/products/plonemall`
			`http://plone.org/products/simplecartitem`
			`http://code.google.com/p/easyshop-for-plone`
			`http://plone.org/products/getpaid`
			`http://plone.org/products/pfgpaymentfield`
			`http://plone.org/products/letspay`
			`http://plone.org/products/flexportlets`

	Other	JadaSite
		Other Carts
			`http://www.jadasite.com`
			`http://www.dmoz.org/Computers/Software/Business/`
			   `E-Commerce/Shopping_Carts`

	Services	ZenCart Hosting
		
		PayPal
		Authorize.net
		Registered Commons †
		Fundable
		PledgeBank
			`http://www.zen-cart.com/`
			   `index.php?main_page=infopages&pages_id=10`
			`http://www.paypal.com`
			`http://authorize.net`
			`http://www.registeredcommons.org`
			`https://www.fundable.org`
			`http://www.pledgebank.com`

Protocols		CC+
		SPP
		RSPP
			`http://wiki.creativecommons.org/CCPlus`
			`http://en.wikipedia.org/wiki/Street_Performer_Protocol`
			`http://logarithmic.net/pfh/rspp`

†Registered Commons recently implemented a CC+ protocol for re-licensing works from various Creative Commons licenses for money.

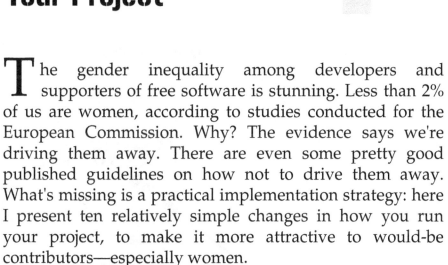

Appendix B:
Ten Easy Ways to Attract Women to Your Project

T he gender inequality among developers and supporters of free software is stunning. Less than 2% of us are women, according to studies conducted for the European Commission. Why? The evidence says we're driving them away. There are even some pretty good published guidelines on how not to drive them away. What's missing is a practical implementation strategy: here I present ten relatively simple changes in how you run your project, to make it more attractive to would-be contributors—especially women.

There's a lot of research on this subject, and if you are interested in a deeper understanding of the problem, then you'll want to go and read some of the notes. The FLOSSPOLS[1] study is particularly informative, and although long, it is well structured, and has good summaries. Val Henson wrote an excellent HOWTO[2] on the behavioral issues, which I highly recommend you read. A lot has been written about how big the problem is, the factors that are probably contributing to the problem, and even some broad social and political ideas about solutions.

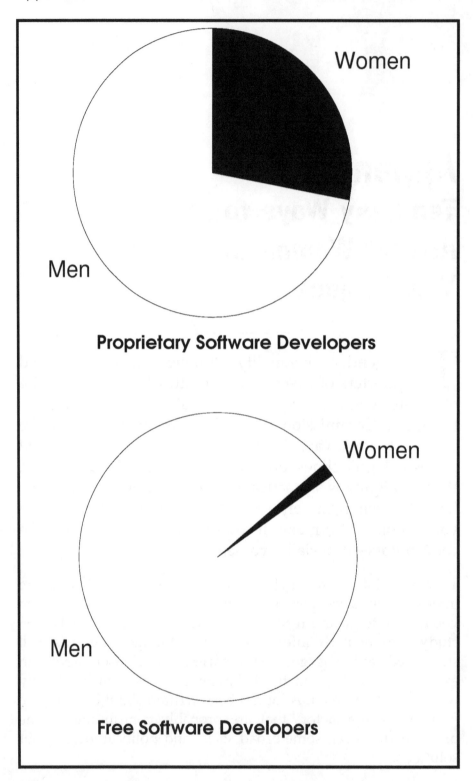

Proprietary Software Developers

Free Software Developers

To put it very briefly, the studies conclude that there is no dearth of women interested in computer science, nor women capable of doing it well, and there are excellent reasons why women should be involved for their own benefit and for the benefit of the community.[1] But the community's process is exceedingly male-centric and hostile to anyone who doesn't fit that mold—a problem confirmed by the few pioneering women who do participate.[2-9] The recommended solutions primarily involve intentional cultural changes that need to happen to avoid the hostility and make the field more accessible.[1-2]

I'm going to assume that you're already sold on the value of inviting more women into our community, or at least committed to stopping the things that drive them away. But what are you going to do about it? As a free software project leader or founder, you make a lot of fundamental design decisions about how you're going to run your project. And that's where I think that change needs to start: make one project friendlier. Then another, and so on.

In my opinion, the key is the technology problem. Online society is a product of its participants, but also of the landscape artificially created by the software that we use in our production process. That toolchain has been crafted almost entirely by men, and unconsciously, *for* men and their social needs. Women's needs have been ignored, if not actively derided. And surprise, surprise... they don't show.

It's time to fix that. Here's a list of ten not-so-difficult process decisions to make in laying out a new project, or to adopt in an existing one. Nine of these ten suggestions do not involve any special treatment for women (the tenth does, but only in a trivial way). Making your project friendlier and more open to new contributors will attract some men as well as women. But it is (probably) women who will benefit the most from these particular changes.[10]

Facing Page:
Yes, there is a problem[1]

Pages: [1] Go Down   Reply Notify of replies Mark Unread Send this topic Print

Author   Topic: Just thinking about flowers..... (Read 173 times)

MeeMaw   Just thinking about flowers.....
Full Member   « on: 2008-09-14, 18:22:12 »   Reply with quote
★★★

Cookies: 8   I did the rose a long time ago and I started with some clipart and
[give] [take]   "morphed" it - so I thought I might start with Inkscape and make
🖥 Offline   something..... and I haven't put in any details yet.......

Posts: 242

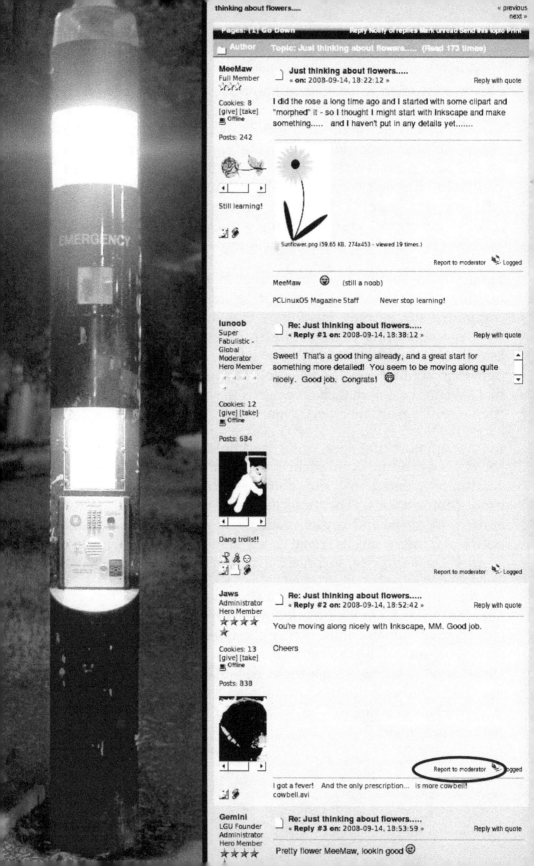

Still learning!

◄   ►

🗑 Sunflower.png (59.65 KB, 274x453 - viewed 19 times.)

                                                  Report to moderator 🖥 Logged

MeeMaw   😊   (still a noob)

PCLinuxOS Magazine Staff   Never stop learning!

lunoob   Re: Just thinking about flowers.....
Super   « Reply #1 on: 2008-09-14, 18:38:12 »   Reply with quote
Fabulistic -
Global   Sweet! That's a good thing already, and a great start for
Moderator   something more detailed! You seem to be moving along quite
Hero Member   nicely. Good job. Congrats! 😊
★ ★ ★ ★

Cookies: 12
[give] [take]
🖥 Offline

Posts: 684

Dang trolls!!

🧑👤😊
🖥🗑

                                                  Report to moderator 🖥 Logged

Jaws   Re: Just thinking about flowers.....
Administrator   « Reply #2 on: 2008-09-14, 18:52:42 »   Reply with quote
Hero Member
★ ★ ★   You're moving along nicely with Inkscape, MM. Good job.
★

Cookies: 13   Cheers
[give] [take]
🖥 Offline

Posts: 838

◄   ►
                                                  Report to moderator 🖥 Logged
🖥🗑
                 I got a fever! And the only prescription... is more cowbell!
                 cowbell.avi

Gemini   Re: Just thinking about flowers.....
LGU Founder   « Reply #3 on: 2008-09-14, 18:53:59 »   Reply with quote
Administrator
Hero Member
★ ★ ★   Pretty flower MeeMaw, lookin good 😊

1 Use forums instead of mailing lists

"When asked about the large gender imbalance in FLOSS [free software] development, many women relate stories about harassment or other inappropriate treatment at a FLOSS meeting or in a FLOSS newsgroup. Since most FLOSS projects aren't affiliated with a company, university or other accountable body, civilized behavior isn't enforced."

—— *Michelle Levesque/Greg Wilson*[5]

"Just knowing that there is one other person in the group who is willing to publicly disagree with the 'bad apple' will help immensely, and will make women more willing to stay."

—— *Val Henson*[2]

Reasons

• Community standards are easier to maintain

• Avatars create a face-to-face-like feeling that encourages "more human" behavior

• Badges and ranks afford a better understanding of how representative any poster is

• Signatures and avatars provide a form of graphical self-expression more comfortable for women than the sorts of posturing and crowing behaviors that fill this role for men

• Out of channel communications allow "meta" conversations to happen without disrupting the forum: you don't have to post to counter a flame, you just vote it down or report it to a moderator

• Things like gender status and dating information can be communicated in profiles, by those who want them, and ignored by those who don't, eliminating the motivation for talking about it in a thread

The absolute number one problem with women joining free software projects is that, from square one, they have to put up with jerks. If you're on the job, you put up with jerks, because you have to. But would you do that to yourself, just for fun? No. And most potential contributors—especially the new ones and the ones you most want—are here for the fun.

Val Henson's "HOWTO Encourage Women in Linux"[2] pretty much covers the behavioral issues and what needs to change, but it says little about how to make these changes happen. As a leader, you need a way to set community standards and enforce them. Despite a certain "Wild West" charm some of us feel about the libertarian environment of internet text forums, no one seriously needs to tolerate flame wars. They are not constructive, and you can always argue the same points in a civilized tone.

So ban the jerks and put the fun back in for everyone. Mailing list software is lousy at moderation options, so don't use it! Set up a web forum in your CMS, on your server,

Facing Page:
A web-based forum typically provides much better ability to moderate and maintain community behavioral standards. Like a campus security phone, the mere existence of a "Report to moderator" link deters most serious abuses, and other features create a friendly and inviting atmosphere which encourages good behavior
(Credits: Brian Schulman/CC-By-SA 2.0, Terry Hancock/CC-By-SA 3.0)

or use a paid or free forum hosting service. Have the conversations there: for users and developers.

Forums are a lot of fun once you get used to them, and women like them for other reasons besides the feeling of a "safe haven". They also promote more camaraderie and social behavior than do mailing lists, contributing to a greater feeling of "constructive leisure". Women often collaborate on projects in order to socialize, so this is a good way to encourage more serious contributions.

It goes without saying, of course, that you need to have forum behavior guidelines and you need to enforce them. Empower moderators to take on that job (and women often will volunteer for this kind of job if you ask them nicely).

2 Use flat conversation rather than deep-threads: focus on "who" not just "what"

"While it is possible for a programmer to be relatively successful while being actively anti-social and programming does tend to attract people less comfortable with human interaction, computing is as social as you make it. [...] For me, programming by myself is less fun or creative than it is when I have people around to talk to about my program."

—— *Val Henson*[2]

Reasons:

- Flat threading environments encourage a simpler "logic of conversation" that is more like a face-to-face discussion

- It is easier to track who is talking, not just what they are talking about, and this is likely to matter more to women, for whom individual relationships in the community are generally more important than just mining it for information

- Flat threading encourages smaller, more focused conversations with intentional topic-setting, these are likely to be easier for all newcomers to follow, not just women

This is a much more subtle and less obvious point. When confronted with the observation that women often prefer flat-threading to deeply-nested topical threading, some people leap to the conclusion that this is a product of limited experience with the technology. However, I'm convinced that it's more than that.

The key is the nature of the information and the psychological needs of the participant: if you are there primarily just to grab some information and go, then deep threading serves you by categorizing information. But if your reason to be there is largely social—you want to be in the company of like-minded people discussing a subject you love—then flat threading serves you by providing a better conversational context.

Facing Page:
Women are much more likely than men to communicate for the sake of communication and for the bonding value. Men often grudgingly communicate in order to solve a problem (though sometimes that's a act)

(Credits: Henri Bergius/CC-By-SA 2.0, Pingu1963@Flickr/CC-By 2.0, Terry Hancock/CC-By-SA 3.0)

Women feel a stronger commitment to contribute when they are surrounded and depended-upon by people they consider friends. So ironically, these behaviors, which may sound counter-productive, will result in greater productivity.

In the same way, I recommend keeping IRC sessions small and intimate, with "teams" targeted to solve particular problems. Make arrangements for online "sprints" in this way, so that people with "lives" (which a lot of women do have) can work these projects into their time. But don't try to run continuous massive IRC sessions which you would have to dedicate your life to in order to follow.

3 As much as possible, use wikis instead of version controlled archives

"Being good at computing is considered to be an activity that requires spending nearly all your waking hours either using a computer or learning about them. While this is another misperception, women generally are less willing to obsess on one topic, preferring to lead a more balanced life. Women often believe that if they enter computing, they will inexorably lose that balance, and avoid the field altogether instead."

—— *Val Henson*[2]

Reasons:

• Women like working cooperatively, they don't just tolerate it

• The "reputation game" is much less important to women than is "belonging" to the group

• Everybody has a browser, but women may have less control over what equipment and software they use, especially as beginners

• Even if women do have the control they need to install development environments, they generally don't want to waste as much time "fiddling with the tools," and want fewer obstacles to simply getting the job done

• Women are more likely to want to discuss or seek approval for their changes, owing largely to confidence issues

Wikipedia has a much more representative group of contributors than does free software in general. One reason is that it doesn't take much "buy in" (time risked) to participate. You see something wrong with an entry, then you punch "edit" and fix it—there's no big barrier to overcome, so you don't have to be as extremely motivated to overcome it.

It's too bad that there's not yet any good way to implement source code version control via a wiki-like environment (how would you test the changes?), but it's

Facing Page:
If you look at the traditional ways women collaborate on projects, you'll see a much lighter-weight process with lots of give and take, and contributions made in lots of small ways in parallel, rather than "rewrites" or "versions" made in large blocks. For women, the higher social interaction this requires is part of the payoff
(Credit: claygrl@Flickr/CC-By 2.0)

absolutely feasible for everything else in a project: documentation, textual and graphical resources, and so on.

4 Use very-high-level languages (Perl, Python, Ruby, etc)

"Another important point is that Free Software development is often done as a hobby, just for fun, and in one's spare time. Where is a woman's spare time? After their working day, most of them still have the second working journey, which is at home, taking care of the home, the children and her husband. If the men can have the privilege of doing Free Software in their spare time, sitting in front of the computer and having some fun coding what they want, women in general don't have this privilege."

—— *Fernanda Weiden*[9]

"It matters when you have kids, it really does"

—— *Mitchell Baker*[9]

"So I set out to come up with a language that made programmers more productive, and if that meant that the programs would run a bit slower, well, that was an acceptable trade-off. Through my work on implementing ABC I had a lot of good ideas on how to do this."

—— *Guido van Rossum (on his motivation for writing the Python programming language).*

Reasons

• Women have less time for buy-in to the technology.

• Time often comes in smaller chunks, as it must be fit in around responsibilities like support and care-giving roles in their families

• Unexpected interruptions and the resulting uncertainty of time intervals spent programming is an even bigger issue: you never know whether you're going to have time to put back together what you just took apart

• For reasons of low confidence and a later start in programming, many women today will simply lack the faith that they can fight through to the end on a large, complex problem in a language that doesn't make it easy

• Modern Very High Level (VHL) programming languages like Python, Perl, and Ruby can often condense out the busy work of programming, providing a better use of the time available

• A language that emphasizes readability, like Python, can make recovering from an interruption easier, and less time is wasted as a result

This one was a deeply-personal revelation. For years during high school and college, I programmed in BASIC, then FORTRAN, and then C and C++. I felt pretty good

Facing Page:
Women often find themselves in various support and care-giving roles. These are interrupt-driven lifestyles in which the large blocks of time required by traditional programming methodologies are hard to come by. But modern very high level programming languages can make shorter sessions productive
(Credit: LizaWasHere@Flickr/CC-By-SA 2.0)

about it, and like most hackers, I put in some long late night sessions of programming.

Then, sometime after college, we had our first child. After that, I found I couldn't program any more. Seriously. There were just too many interruptions. As soon as I got back "up to speed" with the software I was working on and "recovered state" enough to make the next logical step, I would get another interruption, and the program would go back on the back burner. Later, I'd find myself having to puzzle out what I had written a day, a week, or even a month in the past.

When I finally did get back into programming, it was through free software, and someone on my first project recommended I try Python. It was amazing. I could get stuff done again. That's both because Python code is more compact and because it is more readable.

Now the kids are school age, and I have more time, but I'm too hooked on the rapid productivity of Python to go back now.

5 Embrace "extreme programming"

"Like any other discipline, computer science is easier to learn when you have friends and mentors to ask questions of and form a community with. However, for various reasons, men usually tend to mentor and become friends with other men. When the gender imbalance is as large as it is in computer science, women find themselves with few or no other women to share their interests with."

—— *Val Henson*[2]

Reasons:

- Test-driven development turns long-delayed gratification into lots of little wins, each one a confidence-building victory which women, who often lack confidence in their technical abilities, need to see

- Pairs programming is a very "feminine" way to work, in close-knit teams, observing the code together. Two sets of eyeballs find more bugs, and there is no better time to find a bug than right after (or even before) you make the mistake

- Getting rid of the male "power-world" of hierarchical programming teams is a definite win for women, who prefer flatter "peer" structures

One wonderful trend, largely motivated by free software development is so-called "**Extreme Programming**" (**XP**). In my opinion, it's actually a very "feminine" way to work, and in any case, it directly confronts some of the obstacles that women face with programming. There are plenty of other reasons to use XP methods, but attracting women developers is a good one.

One issue that may be a problem is that women may not easily be able to find partners for pair programming sessions. It may be desirable to try to simulate this experience with small (tiny) IRC chat sessions and some means of viewing the same code as it is being worked on.

Facing Page:

Pair programming is so "girlie" it ought to giggle. Seriously. Extreme programming plays to women's strengths and mitigates their weaknesses. And it works pretty well for men too

♥Thank You♥

GREAT
WORK

6 Replace pecking-orders with affirmation processes

"Interestingly, rude responses are often given by people who are in the process of gaining a reputation. It is often as if lower ranking participants try to build their reputation by either responding rudely and thereby implying impatience with the ignorant, or by showing off the extensiveness of their knowledge, instead of providing an uncomplicated answer."

—— FLOSSPOLS[1]

"Often, the only reward (or the major reward) for writing code is status and the approval of your peers. Far more often, the 'reward' is a scathing flame, or worse yet, no response at all."

—— Val Henson[2]

Reasons:

- The cult of personality is all about glory and honor, things that matter a lot to men, but are usually of secondary interest to women

- Macho superiority contests are generally boring to women, and let's face it, they're dumb

- Women don't like to "blow their own horns," but they love to be appreciated, and they'll do more work when they are

- Subjective reputation is often flat-out wrong and very, very biased. Objective measures are useful to see what the score really is, especially when the players are not equally forthright

- Explicit acceptance rituals encourage a feeling of "belonging" that is more important to women than it is to men, and more important than a competitive desire to "lead the pack"

- It builds confidence and encourages people to contribute if they get tangible feedback and recognition for what they do

It's important to realize that flame wars and other male dominance contests *do* serve a social function. They are a very primitive way of evaluating the importance and value of individuals in the group. Knowing "who's in charge" is something that makes it much easier (especially for men) to cooperate. Men, either instinctively or through childhood experiences, know how to play this game, and they do it unconsciously.

Women's methods of achieving the same goals are very different. They revolve around higher levels of cooperation, less competition, and much more careful attention to affirming other people in the group. Women care more about "belonging" than about "winning." They don't care so much about "glory", but they care a lot about being "appreciated."

Facing Page:

How hard is it to say those two little words, "Thank you"? Men often won't care (but some will). Women often will care, and the cold shoulder of not responding to a contribution with some kind of acknowledgment is truly unacceptable

So concentrate on positive reinforcement of good behavior and good contributions. When someone does something helpful for the project, recognize them for it. Give them more responsibility. And—on the forum—give them some token (a label or avatar) that recognizes what they've done. That way, there isn't the necessity to crow about it. People will be able to tell in an instant who has made real contributions.

Women, because of shyness, low confidence, or social admonitions against "putting themselves forward," generally won't take these titles for themselves. They have to be given them by others, or they don't feel that they count. Being "appreciated" or "useful" was the point of the contribution.

All too often, that just doesn't happen in the free software process. People spend hundreds of hours writing and/or improving code, and what do they get for their trouble? Often not much.

Spend some time lurking on a female-dominated forum or mailing list if you want to see what I'm talking about. Women actually do this amazing thing of encouraging and complimenting each other. Above all, they remember to say 'thank you' when somebody does something good for their community.

7 Don't discount what women do

"Opening up our definition of hackerdom to include such traditionally female concepts as user interface and psychology, written and verbal communications, group interactions (both electronic and face to face), et cetera, may be a valid alternative to requiring women to fit the existing hacker mold. Additionally, it may result in communities and processes which are even more powerful than our current models."

—— *Kirrily "Skud" Robert*[6]

Reasons:

- Good software is a lot more than just "code"

- Documentation is no easier to write than code (unless you do it very badly)

- Marketing, graphics, logos, icons, and just generally helping people are also important

- Given a safe and affirming environment, women will do a lot of the stuff that men don't want to do on a project, and which is absolutely essential for the project's success

- Artificial distinctions like "Turing-completeness" are a silly way to divide the world: HTML, SVG, XML, and SQL are no easier to write than C, Java, or Python, and just as important to many projects

- Systematically undervaluing women's work is a holdover from archaic and sexist gender politics, it's just a way of perpetuating them

There is a pattern (in all of society, not just in computing) of systematically trying to devalue anything that is done by women as somehow less important or less difficult

Facing Page:

Women do important things, but gender politics often lead to 'women's work' being degraded or discounted. Don't fall into this trap!

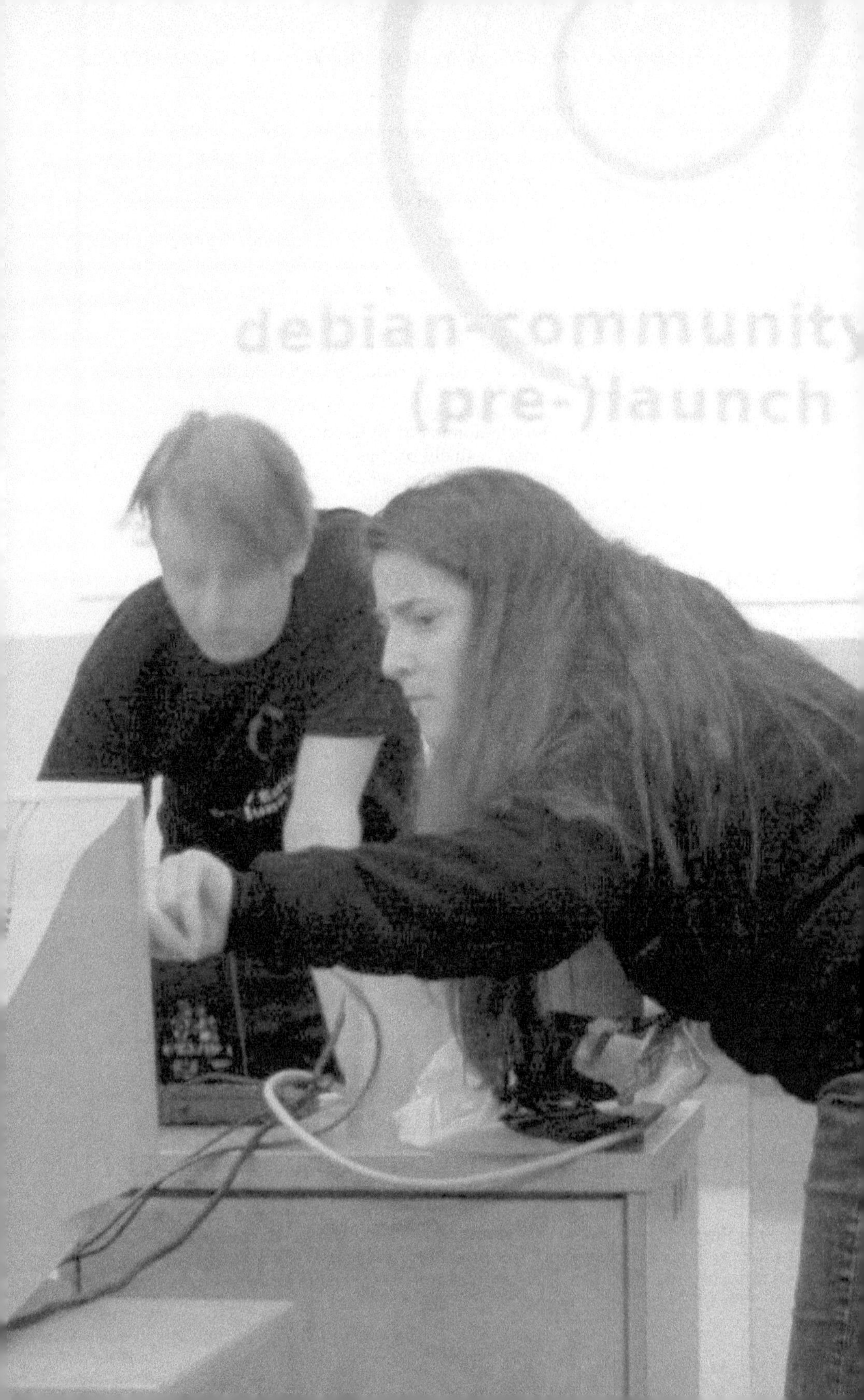
debian community
(pre-)launch

Women, of course, tend to gravitate much more to support roles than men do. Yet they receive very little acknowledgement for this. See anything weird? Yes, that's right, the women are doing the big money work. So why is there so little appreciation of this fact?

9 Create a formal mentoring and induction processes

"LinuxChix started as a space for women who worked as techies to come together and get support. Generally when these women joined us they felt happy and surprised that there was a group of women discussing technology and that they were not alone."

—— Sulamita Garcia[7]

Reasons:

• Women have fewer opportunities for apprenticeship

• Informal apprenticeships with men may be awkward (Is she your "apprentice" or your "girlfriend"?)

• Women may have missed out on early training opportunities due to sexism earlier in their lives

Ultimately, learning to program tends to be an apprenticeship process. You can learn quite a bit through formal classes or by reading. You can even learn by spending enormous amounts of time bashing your head against the wall while trying to make something work on your own. But the best way is to be able to ask for help—even at the beginning when you need to ask the really, really dumb questions.

Facing Page:
Programming, like sewing, is largely a "tacit" skill, which is best learned by doing and by watching others

Grace Hopper
First High-Level
Compiler

Ada Lovelace
First Computer
Programs

Frances Allen
Optimizing
Compilers

ENIAC Programmers (USA)

Mary Lou Jepsen
OLPC XO
Hardware
Platform

Rosalind Picard
Affective
Computing

Colossus Programmers (UK)

Mitchell Baker
Mozilla
Foundation

10 Make the existing women in your project visible

"I encourage all women in computing to be as visible as possible—accept all interviews, take credit publicly—even when you don't want to. You may be embarrassed, but by allowing yourself to be publicized or promoted, you might change a young girl's life."

—— Val Henson[2]

Reasons:

• There are pioneering women in free software who can act as role models for young women in seeking careers and vocations, but they are "lost in the noise" of all the men in the field

• Role models can be powerful motivators for everyone, but especially for younger people who may not be very certain they can really follow a certain vocational path

• Often, we act like free software forums are 100% male-only, when they are really more like 90%-95%. Making the minority of women visible now makes it easier for men and women to adjust to the reality and leaves room for that minority to grow

• Many women lurk more than they post, for many of the reasons described. Seeing visible women accepted by the community —will stir more of them to participate

While it's a hard road to be a pioneer, the presence of women will encourage more women to join in. It will also make it clear to the men in your project that they are in "mixed company" and this by itself will curtail some of the worst behaviors.

Of course, it requires that the pioneering women who do work on free software projects be willing to expose themselves to a bit more scrutiny than might be comfortable. You certainly should not try to force recognition onto them, but you should ask them if they're willing to stand up and be counted.

Facing Page:
The evidence of history proves that women have what it takes to do programming even at the most advanced levels. After all, the very idea of programming was invented by one woman (Ada Lovelace[11]) and the idea of compilers and high-level languages was invented by another (Grace Hopper[12]). A few women like Frances Allen[13] and Rosalind Picard[14] continue to innovate at the very highest levels. Other women, like Mitchell Baker[15] and Mary Lou Jepsen[16] have contributed in equally important ways to the success of free software. In the early days, programming computers was primarily "women's work" as these photos of ENIAC[17] and Colossus[18] programmers show
(Credits: US Navy Photos, UK Government Photos, Rama@Wikipedia/CC By-SA 2.0/fr, James Duncan Davidson/O'Reilly Media/CC By 2.0, David Bruce/CC By-SA 2.0)

Diversity is Strength

"People write software to meet their needs, to make software do what they want. If women don't participate in writing code and writing documentation, they will never have the results and the answer for their needs. That's how it is. Those who merely watch have no influence on driving development, and the consequence is not having software that [does] precisely what you want it to do."

—— *Fernanda Weiden*[9]

I hope the benefits of having more women participate in free software are obvious. We write software to serve the needs of people, but we can only clearly see our own needs. A greater diversity of those involved means more perspectives on every problem, a better understanding of the problems that need to be solved, and better solutions for solving them.

Many of the "stereotypically female" contributions: interface design, documentation, and even marketing are areas in which free software is sadly lacking. It should be fairly obvious that if this is what women want to contribute, we should darned well make it easy for them to do so.

There's a lot to be gained by bringing women into free software, and the best way for you to help make it happen is to start with your project and the projects that you contribute to.

Notes

1 Dawn Nafus, James Leach, Bernhard Krieger; "Free/Libre and Open Source Software:Policy Support" (FLOSSPOLS), D16 – Gender: Integrated Report of Findings; 2006-3/1
   `http://flosspols.org/deliverables/`
      `FLOSSPOLS-D16-Gender_Integrated_Report_of_Findings.pdf`

2 Val Henson; "HOWTO Encourage Women in Linux"; The Linux Documentation Project; 2002-10/29
   `http://www.tldp.org/HOWTO/Encourage-Women-Linux-HOWTO`

3 Emma Jane Hogbin; "Form an Orderly Queue Ladies"; OSCON 2008
   `http://geekfeminism.wikia.com/wiki/Form_an_Orderly_Queue_Ladies`

4 Whitney Butts; "OMG Girlz Don't Exist on teh Intarweb!!!!1"; The Escapist; 2001-11/1
   `http://www.escapistmagazine.com/articles/view/issues/issue_17/`
      `109-OMG-Girlz-Don-t-Exist-on-teh-Intarweb-1`

5 Michelle Levesque, Greg Wilson; "Open Source, Cold Shoulder"; Dr. Dobb's Journal; 2004-11/01

`http://www.ddj.com/architect/184415216`

6 Kirrily "Skud" Robert; "Geek Chicks: Second thoughts"; Freshmeat; 2000-02/05

`http://freshmeat.net/articles/view/145`

7 Graciela Selaimen; "Women developing FLOSS – freedom for knowlege free from prejudice"; GenderIT.org; 2006-02/10 (Interview with Sulamita Garcia)

`http://www.genderit.org/en/index.shtml?w=a&x=91693`

8 Elizabeth Bevilacqua; "Women in Free/Open Source Software"; MontcoLUG meeting, Royersford, PA USA, 2007-1/15

`http://princessleia.com/presentations/montcolug_women_in_foss`

9 Fernanda G. Weiden; "Women in Free Software"; Groklaw; 2005-09/11

`http://www.groklaw.net/article.php?story=20050911153013536`

10 Throughout this article I make a lot of generalizations about how "men" and "women" behave. Obviously men and women are not monolithic groups, and there's a lot of variation, so this is just short hand. There are some important differences that apply in the real world, though, whether because of nature or nurture. Indeed, in writing this article, I have taken the assumption that many of the issues are really just manifestations of lifestyle differences, and it's largely because of lifestyle issues that I feel I can identify with many of the problems that women face when dealing with "hacker culture" in general and "free software" in particular.

11 Wikipedia Biography: Ada Lovelace

`http://en.wikipedia.org/wiki/Ada_Lovelace`

12 Wikipedia Biography: Grace Hopper

`http://en.wikipedia.org/wiki/Grace_Hopper`

13 Wikipedia Biography: Frances Allen

`http://en.wikipedia.org/wiki/Frances_E._Allen`

14 Wikipedia Biography: Rosalind Picard

`http://en.wikipedia.org/wiki/Rosalind_Picard`

15 Wikipedia Biography: Mitchell Baker

`http://en.wikipedia.org/wiki/Mitchell_Baker`

16 Wikipedia Biography: Mary Lou Jepsen

`http://en.wikipedia.org/wiki/Mary_Lou_Jepsen`

17 Wikipedia: ENIAC

`http://en.wikipedia.org/wiki/ENIAC`

18 Wikipedia: Colossus

`http://en.wikipedia.org/wiki/Colossus_computer`

Appendices

Appendix C:
What If Copyright Didn't Apply to Binaries?

L ogically, copyright really shouldn't apply to **binary executables**, because they are purely "functional" (not "expressive") works. The decision to extend copyright to **binaries** was an economically-motivated anomaly, and that choice has some counter-intuitive and detrimental side-effects. What would things in the free software world look like if the courts had decided otherwise? For one thing, the implementation of copyleft would have to be completely different.

Hypothetical? Academic? Not if you're a hardware developer! Because this is exactly what the law does look like for designs for physical hardware (where the product is not protected by copyright).

Expression and Function

One of the fundamental limits in copyright law, at least in the USA, is that copyright can only be applied to fixed, tangible representations of particular expressions of ideas, not to the ideas themselves. Thus Anne Rice has a protected monopoly over the novel *Interview with the Vampire*, but no monopoly on the idea of "interviewing a vampire." You are free to write your own novels in which journalists interrogate the undead, and while critics may well find your work "derivative," copyright law will not.

Similarly, while copyrighting a recipe for stew may give you a monopoly over printing the recipe, it gives you no power over the distribution of the stew itself. More significantly, it doesn't give you power over equivalent recipes for stew—that is to say, recipes with exactly the same physical components, quantities, and procedures. In fact, it's very likely that a recipe, which is usually quite minimal in expression, will not be subject to copyright protection at all, simply because there is so little "expressive" content.

Instead, the major content of a recipe is said to be "functional": conveying only that information which is strictly necessary to communicate the composition of the stew.

As a way of further illustrating this distinction, imagine that two different cooks watch a third prepare the stew, and they take notes. Then, each is asked to write their notes up as a recipe, without copying or looking at each other's work. Now, assuming that they are both perfectly attentive observers, they will produce functionally identical works, although their expressive content can be expected to differ.

In practice, because this is a recipe, the two will be nearly identical, because a recipe is fundamentally functional. The residual amount of expression is likely to be so small, that it is not worthy of copyright, simply because of its trivial length.

Figure C.1:

(*Facing Page*) The difference between "functional" and "expressive" works: Two cooks will produce essentially the same work, when trying to communicate a recipe, while two poets will produce quite different expressive works. Copyright is meant to only cover "expression," not "function," although actual court cases have lead to some anomalies, such as executable binary software
(Art: Ryan Cartwright / CC-By-SA)

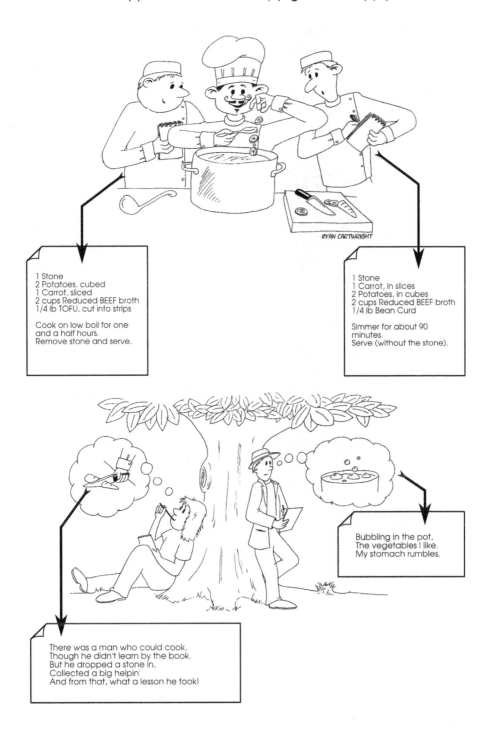

If, however, two poets observe the same events, and are each encouraged to write a poem expressing their impressions, they are likely to create two quite different works. These are likely to be even shorter than the recipes, but they will be almost entirely expressive, with very little (if any) functional content (Figure C.1).

Software is Copyrightable

It wasn't always clear that software of any form should be copyrightable, since it is primarily directed towards accomplishing functional goals. But, software—at least source code—is more like an instruction manual or a set of blueprints than it is like a recipe. It is complex and there are many ways of formulating it which involve much human creativity. Thus, it has significant (and therefore copyrightable) expressive content.

But what of binary code? Almost no one ever directly writes binary code. It is usually generated by programs, based on human-authored source code. This is true even of code which is designed in an assembly language!

We have historically defined "creativity" as "something only humans can do," regarding the evidence that a machine can do a job as proof that it requires no creativity. Thus, the fact that compilers exist, which convert source code into binary code with minimal human intervention is enough to prove that binaries are not created by human creativity, but are only the functional end-product of following the "recipe" represented by the source code.

Windows, ReactOS, and the Clean Room

An interesting illustration of these principals, the legal fuzziness surrounding them, and the industry's response, is the case of ReactOS[1] (Figure C.2). ReactOS is supposed to be an exact, work-alike clone of the Windows operating system (it is closely linked with the much better known Wine project which emulates a Windows environment on top of the GNU/Linux/X operating system[2]).

Figure C.2:

ReactOS is a free, clean room re-implemented drop-in replacement for Windows
(ReactOS project)

Unlike GNU/Linux which is happy to remain a separate platform, requiring specially-compiled binary packages, ReactOS aims to run actual Windows binary executable programs. This means that ReactOS must implement the entire Windows environment. Functions must do exactly what their Windows counterparts would do. In other words, like our notional parallel stew recipes, ReactOS and Windows should be functionally identical.

In order to avoid copyright prosecution, though, ReactOS must be expressively completely distinct and non-derivative from Windows. This is a careful tightrope walk!

So, consider this, especially regarding extremely simple library calls: is it legal for ReactOS to produce identical binary code to Windows? In many cases, it would be extremely hard to come up with code that did the same job, but was in any way different. This becomes even more true when the original code contains bugs, which later software came to depend upon. This sort of "bug compatible" code must often be bit-for-bit identical!

If the binary code were regarded as "functional" (and therefore not subject to copyright, just like our fictional recipes), then there'd be no problem: we wouldn't care what the outcome of compilation were, because that wouldn't be "copying" or "deriving from" source code, it'd just be "using" it.

Though the legal necessity of it remains unclear, the industry has adopted a litigation-proof mechanism for making functional (but not expressive) copies of software: it's called the "clean room implementation." In this approach, the functionality of the original software (in this case, Windows) is reverse-engineered by one group of people, who create a "specification document," which contains only functional information about the software. Then, a different group of people attempts to write new software to the same specification.

This gets around the problem of the original software having no published specification, as well as eliminating any cause for believing that the implementors have copied any expressive information from the original work (since they got everything they need from the published specification).

But in the case of Windows, where some of the functions being implemented are essentially BIOS calls consisting of only 10 to 15 machine instructions, the specification is often sufficient to nail the code down to the same 10 to 15 machine instructions. And in the one-to-one simplicity of machine language, the source code is likely to be nearly identical as well (mere differences in the names of variables or labels, while clearly expressive, have not been regarded as sufficient to differentiate two piece of source code from each other for copyright purposes).

So it may well be that creating a "functionally equivalent" operating system to Windows—a true drop-in replacement—will result in a system for which much of the binary executable code is actually identical, even though none of it was copied.

If binary code were treated as intrinsically functional, and therefore non-copyrightable, this would be no problem: two bowls of identical soup made from different recipes.

Why copyright binaries?

So why'd they do it? Well, the short answer is because the copyright office listened to software publishers, and they wanted binaries protected by copyright so they could sell them that way. The only other alternatives were to rely on patents (which the patent office had rejected at the time, and which were not a very popular idea in the industry back then), or to simply rely on the obfuscation which comes naturally to binary code (which is not optimized for human readability).

Consider what would've happened if binaries weren't copyrightable. Then, a software company, which distributed binaries would have no copyright protection for what they sold. And, like manufacturers of household appliances, they would have no legal recourse against people reverse engineering their products and designing replacements for them. Nor could they bind people into an **End User License Agreement (EULA)**, any more than people who sell hammers can. Proprietary source code, would of course, still be kept a closely-guarded secret, just as it is under the current scheme.

What would copyleft look like in a world without copyrighted binaries?

Of course, if the copyright lawyers had taken that route, then the legal landscape that Stallman and Moglen faced in fashioning the GNU General Public License would've been quite different. Assuming no change in the ideology of the "four freedoms," then the "copyleft hack" would've been a bit trickier.

GPL as Written

If binaries were not copyrightable, the GPL copyleft would be ineffective. Since the production of binaries from the code wouldn't be a copyright privilege, doing so would not invoke any agreement. Thus no source code requirement could be enforced.

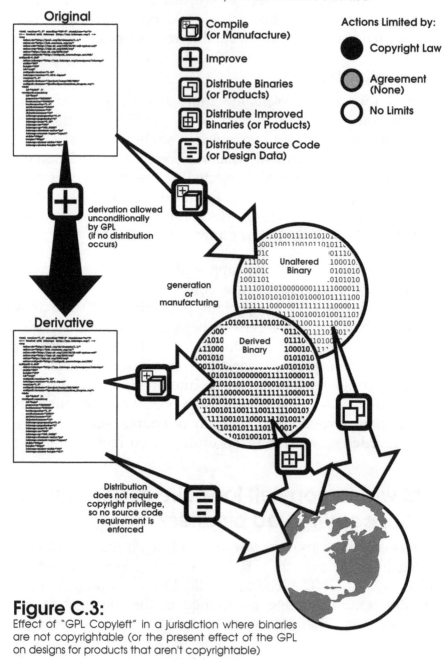

Original

Compile
(or Manufacture)

Improve

Distribute Binaries
(or Products)

Distribute Improved
Binaries (or Products)

Distribute Source Code
(or Design Data)

Actions Limited by:

Copyright Law

Agreement
(None)

No Limits

derivation allowed
unconditionally
by GPL
(if no distribution
occurs)

generation
or
manufacturing

Unaltered
Binary

Derived
Binary

Derivative

Distribution
does not require
copyright privilege,
so no source code
requirement is
enforced

Figure C.3:

Effect of "GPL Copyleft" in a jurisdiction where binaries are not copyrightable (or the present effect of the GPL on designs for products that aren't copyrightable)

So what would the options have been?

Option 1: Copyleft only applies to source code, binary distribution is unrestricted

The first option (Figure C.3) would be to apply copyleft only to source code. In this scenario, the GPL would've been essentially identical to the Creative Commons Attribution-ShareAlike license: it would require you not to restrict derivatives of the work, but it would have no true "source code" requirement (because only the source code itself would be covered).

This would mean that copyleft would only affect those who received source code in the first place. Users who received only binaries, would have essentially no right to know how their software worked. Companies could opt to build on GPL-copylefted software, but never release the source code, only the binaries. Since they never release, they never become subject to copyleft requirements, and the result is essentially no change from the same-old proprietary software publishing game.

Note that this is essentially the effect of the present day GPL if applied in a such a (hypothetical) legal jurisdiction. It is also roughly equivalent to the behavior of the Creative Commons "Attribution-ShareAlike" license in real copyright jurisdictions.

Option 2: Structure copyleft as a contract enforced through a EULA

In this "EULA Copyleft" (Figure C.4), the license becomes a contract (an "end user license agreement" or EULA[3]) for anyone who receives the source code. It's really quite restrictive, and might very well fail Stallman's idea for "Freedom 0," since use of the source code imposes possibly expensive requirements.

There is also the question of how to enforce the contract: many jurisdictions won't recognize a two-party contractual relationship (one in which you agree to give up freedoms you would otherwise have), unless there is a clear "signing ceremony" and possibly even money changing hands.

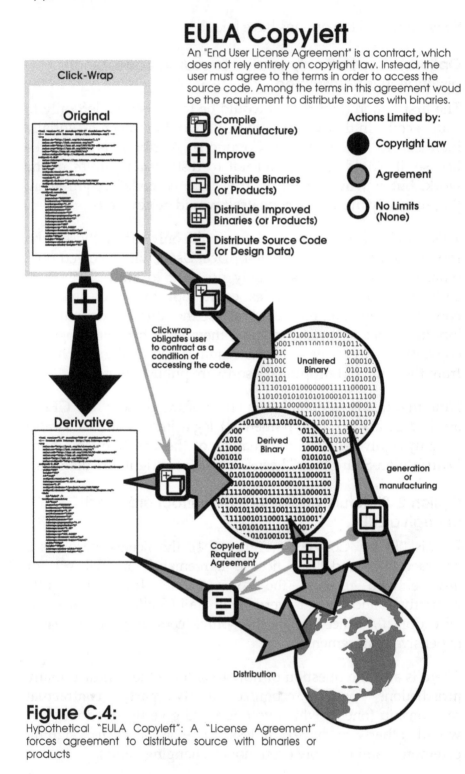

EULA Copyleft

An "End User License Agreement" is a contract, which does not rely entirely on copyright law. Instead, the user must agree to the terms in order to access the source code. Among the terms in this agreement woud be the requirement to distribute sources with binaries.

Compile
(or Manufacture)

Improve

Distribute Binaries
(or Products)

Distribute Improved
Binaries (or Products)

Distribute Source Code
(or Design Data)

Actions Limited by:

Copyright Law

Agreement

No Limits
(None)

Click-Wrap

Original

Clickwrap
obligates user
to contract as a
condition of
accessing the code.

Unaltered
Binary

Derivative

Derived
Binary

generation
or
manufacturing

Copyleft
Required by
Agreement

Distribution

Figure C.4:

Hypothetical "EULA Copyleft": A "License Agreement" forces agreement to distribute source with binaries or products

Proprietary software has managed to get around this with the EULA, using a "click-wrap" approach in which you supposedly are bound to the contract by the action of clicking on a button during the installation process. But of course, with open source code, you can probably remove the click-wrap before running the installation, so it's questionable whether this would really make sense.

Remember that, even in this scenario, only manufacturers (people who compile the software) are subject to the EULA.

Option 3: Leave as a license, but make derivation trigger copyleft agreement

This "Production Copyleft" license (Figure C.5) takes advantage of a another somewhat controversial aspect of copyright. "Copyright" is a monopoly right to copy, not to distribute. You violate copyright not when you sell 300 bootleg copies of a CD, but when you actually made the copies! In fact, the law is written to forbid copying, except for certain "fair uses" (For example, "fair use" includes making a backup copy, by the way—but not making copies for your friends).

Furthermore, you also must have copyright privileges in a work to legally create a derivative of it. This is significant for the publisher described above, who takes a free software, builds upon it, and then sells the result as a proprietary binary.

Had they only made binaries from the original work, they could theoretically have never copied it (using only the copy that was provided to them—or copies made entirely within the bounds of "fair use" exemptions). However, once they make a derivative, there is definite proof that they made a copy. As such, they are bound by the license.

If the license then carries a clause saying that products made from the design (the binaries) must include the source code, or access to get the source code, then the copyleft can be effectively enforced.

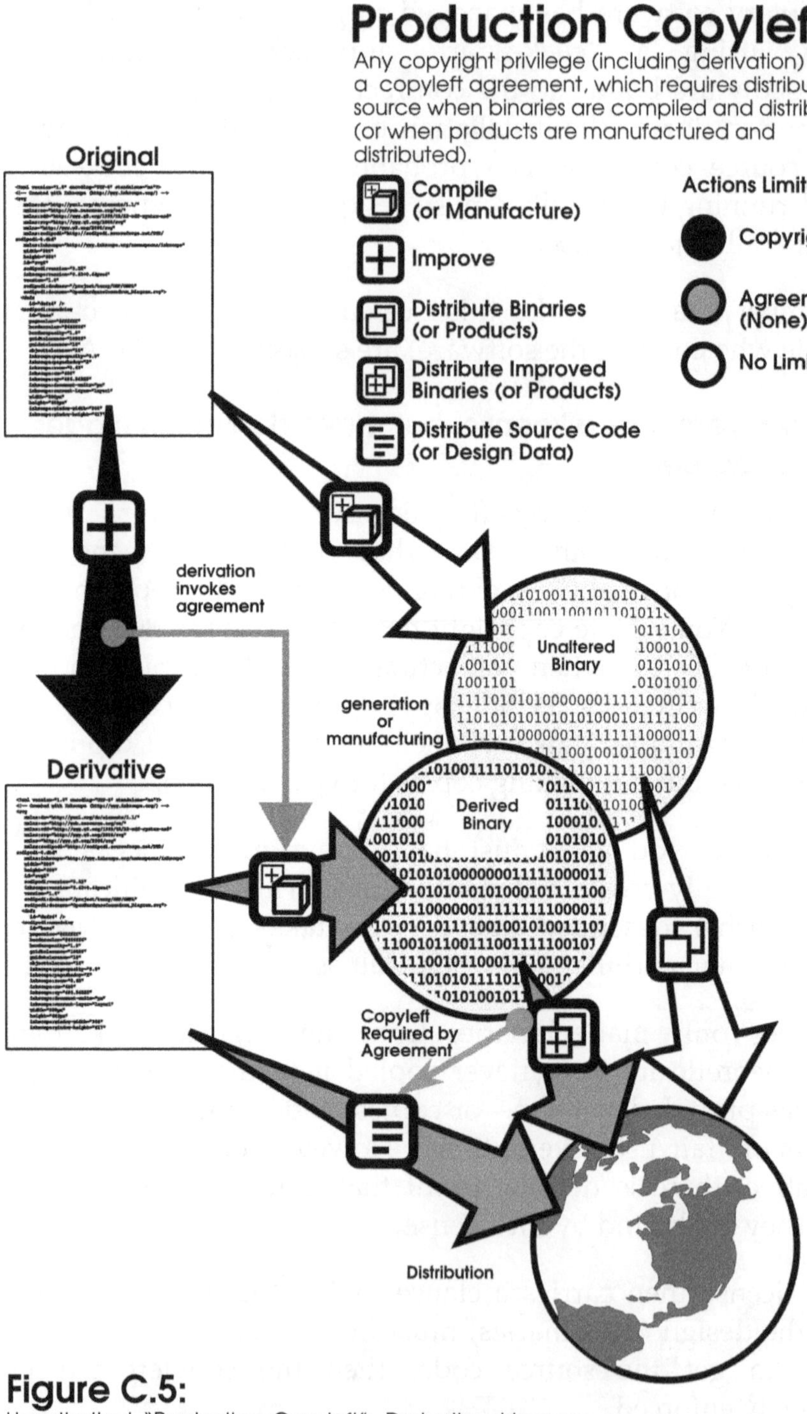

Production Copyleft

Any copyright privilege (including derivation) invokes a copyleft agreement, which requires distribution of source when binaries are compiled and distributed (or when products are manufactured and distributed).

Compile (or Manufacture)

Improve

Distribute Binaries (or Products)

Distribute Improved Binaries (or Products)

Distribute Source Code (or Design Data)

Actions Limited by:

Copyright Law

Agreement (None)

No Limits

Original

Derivative

derivation invokes agreement

generation or manufacturing

Unaltered Binary

Derived Binary

Copyleft Required by Agreement

Distribution

Figure C.5:

Hypothetical "Production Copyleft": Derivation triggers copyright agreement, and imposes a requirement to publish sources with binaries or products

Hypothetical? Not for hardware!

This may all seem rather dry and academic: after all, the courts did decide to make binary software copyrightable. Thus, under present-day law, compiling source code to binary is "making a derivative," and distributing that binary is "distributing a derived copy of the original work." Both actions clearly require copyright privileges, and thus there is no problem with requiring source code to be made available to recipients of binaries.

But there are many other cases where an information product (a design, schematic, or Computer-Aided Design/Computer-Aided Manufacturing (CAD/CAM) file) is used to drive production of products which are not covered by copyright. The distribution of these products does not trigger any sort of copyleft clause, because manufacturing parts to a design is mere use, and not copying, under the present-day copyright laws.

There are a few exceptions: for example, in the semiconductor industry in the USA, there is a "mask right," which is a "copyright-like law" restricting the copying and distribution of the mask data used to create semiconductor chips. No such law exists for printed circuit boards, though. Nor for automotive engines or other devices. Indeed, we probably don't want such laws!

Most open hardware designers today use the unmodified GNU GPL to license their work. Many appear to believe that building products from their designs is *equivalent to compiling a source code into binary*.[4] From a technical perspective this is sensible. Legally, however, it is not correct!

Using the GPL for hardware designs allows a company to create a monopoly on a derivative design, which they never publish, but only use to manufacture products (Figure C.6). In other words, its effect on hardware designs is equivalent to my "GPL Copyleft" case described above. The only real protection you get from the requirement on providing source code is for

Figure C.6:

Many aspects of open hardware projects are not subject to copyright in their manufactured form, which also means they don't have an effective copyleft if only licensed under the GNU GPL. This image is a composite of circuit traces created for the Open Graphics project. The copyleft loophole would allow an unscrupulous company to manufacture and sell an improved version without releasing the plans for the improvements, since the *plans* are never "distributed" according the terms of the GPL. This defeats the intended *quid pro quo* of the GPL's copyleft terms
(Credit: Open Graphics Project)

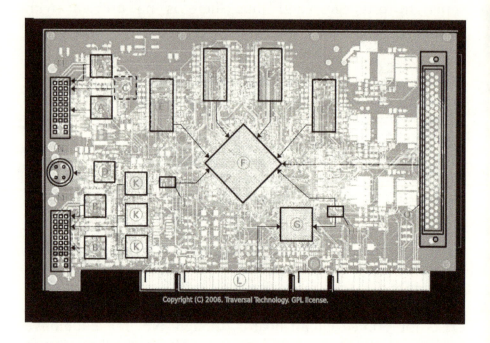

Copyright (C) 2006. Traversal Technology. GPL license.

"synthesis" tools like those used to create **FPGA** bitstreams from human-readable **Verilog** source code (the GPL requires that the Verilog source be included when the bitstream is distributed).

If we want a strong copyleft license for open hardware, we'll have to write a license which operates more along the lines of the "Production Copyleft" option above: something which invokes copyleft requirements beyond the limits of the copyrighted design. Thus far, only the TAPR Open Hardware License attempts to implement a copyleft like this, although it is a relatively untested license, and in any case, is very specific to circuit board designs.

On the other hand, we also have to be much more explicit about what should not be covered by the copyleft, in order to retain our ethical commitment to users' freedoms.

Notes:

1 See also the ReactOS website.
`http://www.reactos.org/en/index.html`

2 See also the WINE website.
`http://www.winehq.org/`

3 See the Wikipedia entry at for more information (and sources) on End User License Agreements
`http://en.wikipedia.org/wiki/EULA`

4 I asked several people working on the Open Graphics project whether manufacturing a product from an open hardware design was legally equivalent to compiling a binary from source code. There was no general consensus, showing that this is a confusing point, but some of the project participants definitely believed this either was true or should be true. Based on this, and opinions gathered through various legal and open hardware mailing lists, I believe this is a frequently misunderstood point.

5 Official online site for the TAPR Open Hardware License. The TAPR OHL does not explicitly deal with this legal formality, but it can be interpreted in terms of it. No legal precedants have been set up, however, as the TAPR OHL has never (yet) been tested in court.
`http://www.tapr.org/ohl.html`

Appendices

242

Appendix D:
Marketshare or Sharing?

In a 2008 article[1], Free Software Magazine columnist, Ryan Cartwright argued that free software isn't playing the "same game" as proprietary software is. He's right—but that begs the question: what game is GNU/Linux playing?

Thirty years of proprietary software thinking have conditioned us to think that marketshare is a critical measure of success, and so we've convinced ourselves that we have to "win" against Windows in order to "succeed." But this is simply not true. GNU/Linux can be a very great success even if it never achieves more than 1% of the installations in the world. The reason is the difference between "power" and "freedom."

The Freedom Metric

"Success" means something very different when your goal is "freedom" than it does when your goal is "power." Proprietary companies exist to make money, thus power over the marketplace—the ability to demand tribute (in the form of license fees)—is the essential definition of success. For free software, however, the goal is to provide the freedom to choose and use free software (the GNU/Linux operating system and its associated universe of applications). For those who seek to create freedom, such monetary tribute is a nice form of applause, but it is not essential to success.

Freedom cannot be forced on people. Freedom to choose GNU/Linux means also the freedom to choose Windows as well. We can argue that it's a bad deal, but we don't have the right to force people to choose one over the other. Nor should we pass value judgements on them for their choice: we don't know the basis of their decisions, nor can we claim superior knowledge of their business. In brief, we don't need power over them! Seeking it is actually counter-productive to our goal of creating a more free software ecosystem.

Hence, we have no obligation nor need to eradicate Windows in the marketplace nor to consume marketshare. That's because we aren't a massive multi-national corporation which must

Figure D.1:
The most important measure of "success" for free software is when users who want it feel free to use it
(Credit: Andy Davison / CC-By-SA 2.0)

exercise power over people in order to survive. Marketshare: defined either as sales of services or as total numbers of installations is a nice sign of success for GNU/Linux, but it is in no way essential to the end goal of achieving freedom.

Self-Reliance

Freedom is primarily achieved by providing the means for self-reliance. When individuals can provide for their own needs independently, without placing burdens on others, we are all more free.

GNU/Linux provides self-reliance in the form of software you have complete control over. Instead of having to pay a tribute in order to receive a benefit from a corporate provider, you are able to provide for your own needs using a freely-available product. In practice, of course, you really do this through voluntary sharing networks or "the community" of open source users and developers, rather than trying to operate on your own. However, you are by no means required to participate in this community, and of course, there may very well be more than one such community if one is not universally appealing (as a simple example, there are lots of Linux user groups divided by geography or language).

What Does Matter: Sharing and Standards

So what makes you free to choose free software? Essentially, what you need are quality and stability. There is also the touchier matter of interchangeable data format standards. To explain these criteria, let's consider the reasons you might be un-able to use a free software application to do a job:

• Software crashes due to bugs (quality)

• Software is too out of date (stability)

• Can't open the files (data standards)

The first two problems have nothing to do with marketshare for free software programs. They have to do with the level of development activity: How many different platforms and configurations has the software been tested in; how many people are finding bugs; and how much time is being spent on fixing them once they are found?

All of these have to do not with the percentage of people merely using the software in the marketplace, but with the absolute number of people developing and testing the program (see figure D.2). In other words, a niche program that less than 1% of the public is using, but which has a strong, highly-motivated group of developers and users may be more successful than a package which is used by 99% of the population, but has few people interested in keeping it working (of course, it's unlikely that such a popular program would not find dedicated users, but this is by no means a closely-correlated relationship).

In other words, what matters is the people who are sharing their time to work on the project. And that is enabled by the nature of the license, which allows the software itself to be shared. In other words, the strength providing the quality and stability of free software comes from the sharing of community effort and of the software itself. Marketshare, as such, has a limited impact on this for free software (the major exception is when a company makes significant money from the product and therefore decides to share developer time to work on it—but again, there is no strong correlation here: a company is free to free-ride or contribute, regardless of its income from the software).

So why do people quote marketshare as if it were the absolute most important metric? Because, for proprietary software it is: if only 1% of the public buys licenses for software A, but 99% buy licenses for software B, then B has 99 times as much money to pay developers. And that's really important for proprietary development projects, because they don't share. By not sharing the code, they not only discourage the desire to share effort, but they actually make it much more difficult (or even impossible) to do. As such, all development and testing time on proprietary software must be paid for. Thus, it is the availability of funds, driven entirely by marketshare, that determines the quality and stability of proprietary software. That's why it's sensible for proprietary software developers to quote marketshare as a selling point.

But those rules don't apply to free software—it relies on voluntary sharing to achieve the same ends. And it turns out that that is much more cost-effective.

The third item, data standards, *does* have a connection to marketshare, albeit it a tenuous one. If a single supplier wields effective monopoly control of the marketplace, it can also monopolize the formats of data that are used for communications. For example, when Microsoft had such total domination of the word processing marketplace, it created a situation in which a proprietary data format—MS Word DOC format—became a *de facto* interchange standard. Since this format was secret and only fully supported by MS Word, it created an obstacle to people wanting to use free software. A similar situation exists with respect to various DRM-encrypted file formats and video codecs used today.

Figure D.2:
This photo from the 2006 Linux Kernel Summit shows 73 people. The stability and quality of the Linux kernel depends on the factors that allow these people to share their time towards improving it. Consumer marketshare is only one of those factors, and not the most important
(Photo Credit: kernel.org / PR)

Avoiding Monopolies

Companies promoting closed data standards are openly hostile towards market freedom. They are, as the law puts it, "anti-competitive," because they put competitors at an unfair disadvantage. This creates a situation in which quality is not sufficient to allow a product to be used. It isn't just free software that suffers from this! This is a problem for all competing software.

Thus, in the interest of promoting both freedom and market efficiency, such tactics, whether intentional or not, should not be permitted. This can be achieved through legal means, primarily by not granting monopoly copyright nor trade secrecy protections for such standards. It can also be achieved by social movements to use standards which are freely available. Finally, having more than one effective competitor in the marketplace will result in natural market forces to encourage use of open formats.

However, even where marketshare matters, it matters only in the need to avoid extreme monopoly: it is not that GNU/Linux needs to have a 90% or even a 50% marketshare to be a

	Operating Systems		
Versions	Hits	Percent	
WIN	**8406**	**30.5 %**	
Windows XP	7022	25.4 %	
Windows NT	15	0 %	
Windows Me	72	0.2 %	
Windows 98	232	0.8 %	
Windows 95	1	0 %	
Windows 2003	50	0.1 %	
Windows 2000	1014	3.6 %	
MAC	**14206**	**51.5 %**	
Mac OS X	14193	51.5 %	
Mac OS	13	0 %	
Others	**4937**	**17.9 %**	
Unknown	4055	14.7 %	
Linux	870	3.1 %	
FreeBSD	12	0 %	

Figure D.3:
The one issue about marketshare that matters is that there isn't a strong enough monopoly to effectively control the marketplace
(Credit: Robert Jorgenson / CC-By-SA 2.0)

"success," it is only that allowing *one* competitor (e.g. Microsoft Windows) to have a 90% or 99% marketshare is damaging. A 10% or 15% share of the marketplace would be completely sufficient. More importantly, that 10% or 15% needn't belong to GNU/Linux—it just can't belong to Microsoft (or any other single provider). We're perfectly fine if that marketshare is controlled by Apple's OS X or Free BSD, or some other operating system, so long as it really is independent of Microsoft control.

Success for Free Software Is Having the Freedom to Use It

This is a very different situation than with proprietary software, where "success" is directly proportional to marketshare (or absolute market size). In the end, for the cause of freedom, we don't need a strong marketshare. We just need a free market and enough sharing to get the software developed.

Of course, freedom may not be everyone's goal for free software. Some people may simply want market domination, and there are companies like Canonical (maker of Ubuntu) who will benefit from increased adoption of GNU/Linux. Their financial successes—at whatever level—are beneficial to the overall success of GNU/Linux, because they mean that more money will be spent on developing GNU/Linux. However, even if such companies fail, GNU/Linux will not. Development will continue whether there is financial backing from sales of services or not, so long as there are enough people who need the software enough to share their time in keeping it working and providing new capabilities.

Notes:

1 Ryan Cartwright; "Don't compare GNU/Linux with Windows or Mac OS X, they are not in the same Game"; 2008.

    http://www.freesoftwaremagazine.com/columns/
        dont_compare_gnu_linux_windows_or_macos_they_are_not_same_game

Appendix E:
CC+ and Buying for the Commons

T his year, Creative Commons unveiled a new initiative called **CC+**. It is not a license. It's a **protocol**, although it's so simple that it almost doesn't warrant the term. Basically it specifies a standardized mechanism to sell further rights for works under Creative Commons licenses. One application of this technology could be to enable **collective patronage** models like the one that brought us the Blender free movies to be extended to a much larger pool of Creative Commons licensed material.

The CC+ Protocol

The idea behind CC+ protocol[1] is so simple it almost seems silly to formally publish it. It consists of two basic steps:

• Provide a means to mark a work as under (any) Creative Commons[2] license (you'll note that there are a number of sites that already do this).

• Provide an extra button which links to a site where further rights in the work can be purchased.

That's it. That's "CC+": a CC license plus the ability to buy more rights.

Naturally, there's a recommended RDF code, button graphics, example mock-ups and so forth, as you would expect from a Creative Commons initiative. The specifics on the CC+ protocol are available from the Creative Commons wiki site. But even so, there's not a whole lot, because it really is just that simple.

It's not a new idea, of course. Magnatune[3] and Beat Pick[4] have been doing this successfully for a few years now. What's new is that Creative Commons is now promoting this idea as a standard, to be implemented by a lot of Creative Commons friendly websites. Hopefully, we'll be seeing little CC+ boxes on a lot of content sharing websites (I'm personally hoping to see it on Jamendo[5] and Flickr[6]).

There is one extra wrinkle beyond what Magnatune and Beat Pick have been doing, and that is here by virtue of what the protocol does *not* specify: it doesn't say *anything* about how the rights-clearing site should work. In fact, the whole idea is to open up a new niche marketplace where different strategies can be tried out—strategies decoupled from the content sharing sites themselves, because the rights clearing can be done by third parties.

Rights-clearing services will compete for the attention of artists who want to use their services. Most will probably make their money by applying small surcharges to the sales, much like PayPal[7] or e-Bay.[8]

Use Case #1: Private Commercial Licenses

Now the use case that Creative Commons had in mind is the one that Magnatune and Beat Pick use: they provide download access to works licensed under one of the Creative Commons "Non-Commercial" licenses. These let you listen to the work and share it with your friends, but you can't use the work "commercially".

Figure E.1:

In the private licensing use case, CC+ permits the already-demonstrated business model of selling commercial licenses to NC-licensed material

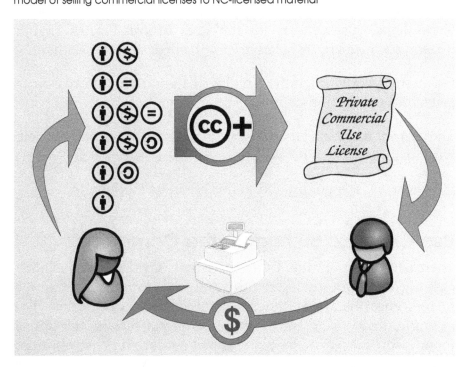

Sadly, "commercially" includes a LOT of uses you might not think of as "commercial". For example, just publishing the material on your personal webpage could be considered a violation if you use Google Adsense to offset your hosting costs!

If you are a commercial publisher, though, and you want to use the work (as an advertising jingle for example, or graphics in a proprietary software game), you can buy a private commercial license for the work. That's the normal sort of license you get when you buy a CD at the music store, for example.

This is what has already been available on a limited basis, and the CC+ initiative will simply make it more widespread. In itself it is a good thing for "free culture".

The thing that annoys me personally, though, is that if you use a non-commercially licensed work in a free software project (music or graphics in a game, for example), the result is no longer free! This may or may not be allowed at all if you used copylefted components in your software: it depends on how the content elements are integrated with the program. But even if it's legal, it's contrary to the goal of free-licensing your project, because you're held back by the license on the content.

For many people (including me) that's good enough reason to just avoid using "non-commercial" content.[9]

The *private* commercial licensing model does nothing to help with this situation.

However, CC+ is not limited to this business model!

Use Case #2: Buying for the Commons

There's nothing in the CC+ spec that says that the rights-clearing website cannot provide an option to pay a certain fee to re-license the work under a commons friendly license. For example, there could be an option to pay a certain amount of money for the work to be released under the "Attribution-ShareAlike" or "Attribution-Only" licenses,[10] or even to be released under a CC0 public domain assertion.[11]

CC+ is an opportunity to implement this, and we should seize it.

The actual fund-raising part can be a separate problem, or it could be included in the rights-clearing service. More than one possible model can be arranged here.

The Buy4Commons Protocol

The name may be a little kitschy, originating on the CC community mailing list. I'm not sure if that will stick. But let's look at what it the protocol itself would involve:

• Author (Licensor) publishes material on a content sharing site under any of By-NC-ND, By-NC-SA, By-ND, By-NC, By-SA, or By and adds a CC+ link to the rights-clearing provider

Figure E.2:

In the Buy4Commons concept, a group of individuals interested in using the material under a free license, raise money to buy rights in the work for everyone (through one of the standard free content licenses)

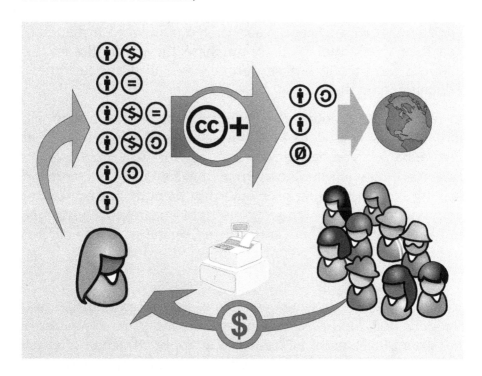

- Author chooses a price for standard private commercial licensing which effectively removes ND, NC, and SA restrictions for one licensing entity (this is use case #1 above)

- Author chooses a second price for standard public commercial licensing which offers the work under their choice of CC0, By, or By-SA license for a given "Buy4Commons" price (only one license should be selected, in order to avoid self-competition)

- Customers who follow the link, see two items for sale: an "individual private license" for x, and a "commons public license" (with the chosen specific license identified) for y.

- Customer selects one or the other. If they buy the private license for x, they license the work for their own use. If they pay y for the public license, they license it for everyone.

- Once the work is "bought for the commons," the rights-clearing site is updated to note the fact that the work is available under the public license (and the date of the purchase). Future customers visiting the CC+ link will see this and know that the license has changed (and when it changed), so they won't attempt to re-purchase the public license. Of course, the private license option may still draw customers, depending on their needs

In most cases, of course "y" will probably be more than one individual is willing to pay, but services like Fundable[12] or Pledge Bank[13] can be used to raise cash for such purchases, by projects that want to incorporate the content. I recommend leaving the fund-raising problem up to them for the present, at least (without this wrinkle, the rights-clearing site can be implemented with conventional e-Commerce "web store" technology, and no extra technical hurdles have to be overcome).

In the future, it might be desirable to go one step further and integrate the fund-raising process into the purchase process. For example, it might be desirable to apply a fraction of every "private" sale towards the "public" sale so that if a work is popular enough with private buyers, it will automatically become available for public use.

For the Common Good

I think this would be a fantastic service for the commons, and I hope someone steps up to provide it. It's obviously a viable business plan, even if only private licenses are sold, but the Buy4Commons option would make the project into more than that: a true public service.

The time to step up is now, when the CC+ initiative itself is just catching on, and before any preconceptions about the service have been formed in the minds of artists or content hosting services.

Notes:

1 CC+ protocol
  http://wiki.creativecommons.org/CCPlus

2 Creative Commons
  http://creativecommons.org

3 Magnatune (a music net label)
  http://magnatune.com

4 Beat Pick (a music net label)
  http://beatpick.com

5 Jamendo (a music sharing site)
  http://www.jamendo.com

6 Flickr (a photo sharing site)
  http://flickr.com

7 PayPal (a payment processing service)
  http://www.paypal.com

8 e-Bay (an internet auctioning service)
  http://www.ebay.com

9 "Non-free" Creative Commons licenses: Attribution-NonCommercial (CC By-NC),
  Attribution-NonCommercial-NoDerivatives (CC By-NC-ND), Attribution-NonCommercial-
  ShareAlike (CC By-NC-SA), Attribution-NoDerivatives (CC By-ND)
  http://creativecommons.org/licenses/by-nc/3.0

  http://creativecommons.org/licenses/by-nc-nd/3.0

  http://creativecommons.org/licenses/by-nc-sa/3.0

  http://creativecommons.org/licenses/by-nd/3.0

10 Free Creative Commons licenses:"Attribution-ShareAlike" (CC By-SA) or "Attribution-
   Only" (CC By) licenses.
   http://creativecommons.org/licenses/by-sa/3.0

   http://creativecommons.org/licenses/by/3.0

11 Creative Commons "CC0" public domain assertion
   http://wiki.creativecommons.org/CCZero

12 Fundable (a collective fundraising system)
   https://www.fundable.org

13 Pledge Bank (a collective fundraising system)
   http://www.pledgebank.com

Appendices

Appendix F:
Licenses

H ere are five of the most important licenses used in commons-based projects. All of them have been mentioned in the text of this book, and all of them may be considered "best practice" licenses for their particular applications:

- The GNU General Public License

- The Creative Commons Attribution-ShareAlike License

- The BSD License

- The MIT License

- The TAPR Open Hardware License

GNU General Public License (GPL)

The GNU GPL, version 2, is by far the most common license for free software (over 50% of projects use it). The Free Software Foundation released an update to this license (version 3), which is being used by a small but growing group of new projects. Furthermore, most projects use an upgrade clause in their license assertion that allows the new license to be used if desired. However, some of the terms in the new license have proved controversial, and so many projects have opted to stick with the earlier license, which it must be noted, stood for more than ten years as practically the defining document of the free software movement. I have included the version 2 license here. The version 3 license can be downloaded from the Free Software Foundation website at: http://www.fsf.org

GNU GENERAL PUBLIC LICENSE

Version 2, June 1991

Copyright (C) 1989, 1991 Free Software Foundation, Inc., 51 Franklin Street, Fifth Floor, Boston, MA 02110-1301 USA Everyone is permitted to copy and distribute verbatim copies of this license document, but changing it is not allowed.

Preamble

The licenses for most software are designed to take away your freedom to share and change it. By contrast, the GNU General Public License is intended to guarantee your freedom to share and change free software—to make sure the software is free for all its users. This General Public License applies to most of the Free Software Foundation's software and to any other program whose authors commit to using it. (Some other Free Software Foundation software is covered by the GNU Lesser General Public License instead.) You can apply it to your programs, too.

When we speak of free software, we are referring to freedom, not price. Our General Public Licenses are designed to make sure that you have the freedom to distribute copies of free software (and charge for this service if you wish), that you receive source code or can get it if you want it, that you can change the software or use pieces of it in new free programs; and that you know you can do these things.

To protect your rights, we need to make restrictions that forbid anyone to deny you these rights or to ask you to surrender the rights.

These restrictions translate to certain responsibilities for you if you distribute copies of the software, or if you modify it.

For example, if you distribute copies of such a program, whether gratis or for a fee, you must give the recipients all the rights that you have. You must make sure that they, too, receive or can get the source code. And you must show them these terms so they know their rights.

We protect your rights with two steps: (1) copyright the software, and (2) offer you this license which gives you legal permission to copy, distribute and/or modify the software.

Also, for each author's protection and ours, we want to make certain that everyone understands that there is no warranty for this free software. If the software is modified by someone else and passed on, we want its recipients to know that what they have is not the original, so that any problems introduced by others will not reflect on the original authors' reputations.

Finally, any free program is threatened constantly by software patents. We wish to avoid the danger that redistributors of a free program will individually obtain patent licenses, in effect making the program proprietary. To prevent this, we have made it clear that any patent must be licensed for everyone's free use or not licensed at all.

The precise terms and conditions for copying, distribution and modification follow.

GNU GENERAL PUBLIC LICENSE
TERMS AND CONDITIONS FOR COPYING, DISTRIBUTION AND MODIFICATION

0. This License applies to any program or other work which contains a notice placed by the copyright holder saying it may be distributed under the terms of this General Public License. The "Program", below, refers to any such program or work, and a "work based on the Program" means either the Program or any derivative work under copyright law: that is to say, a work containing the Program or a portion of it, either verbatim or with modifications and/or translated into another language. (Hereinafter, translation is included without limitation in the term "modification".) Each licensee is addressed as "you".

   Activities other than copying, distribution and modification are not covered by this License; they are outside its scope. The act of running the Program is not restricted, and the output from the Program is covered only if its contents constitute a work based on the Program (independent of having been made by running the Program). Whether that is true depends on what the Program does.

1. You may copy and distribute verbatim copies of the Program's source code as you receive it, in any medium, provided that you conspicuously and appropriately publish on each copy an appropriate copyright notice and disclaimer of warranty; keep intact all the notices that refer to this License and to the absence of any warranty; and give any other recipients of the Program a copy of this License along with the Program.

   You may charge a fee for the physical act of transferring a copy, and you may at your option offer warranty protection in exchange for a fee.

2. You may modify your copy or copies of the Program or any portion of it, thus forming a work based on the Program, and copy and distribute such modifications or work under the terms of Section 1 above, provided that you also meet all of these conditions:

   a) You must cause the modified files to carry prominent notices stating that you changed the files and the date of any change.

   b) You must cause any work that you distribute or publish, that in whole or in part contains or is derived from the Program or any part thereof, to be licensed as a whole at no charge to all third parties under the terms of this License.

   c) If the modified program normally reads commands interactively when run, you must cause it, when started running for such interactive use in the most ordinary way, to print or display an announcement including an appropriate copyright notice and a notice that there is no warranty (or else, saying that you provide a warranty) and that users may redistribute the program under these conditions, and telling the user how to view a copy of this License. (Exception: if the Program itself is interactive but does not normally print such an announcement, your work based on the Program is not required to print an announcement.)

These requirements apply to the modified work as a whole. If identifiable sections of that work are not derived from the Program, and can be reasonably considered independent and separate works in themselves, then this License, and its terms, do not apply to those sections when you distribute them as separate works. But when you distribute the same sections as part of a whole which is a work based on the Program, the distribution of the whole must be on the terms of this License, whose permissions for other licensees extend to the entire whole, and thus to each and every part regardless of who wrote it.

Thus, it is not the intent of this section to claim rights or contest your rights to work written entirely by you; rather, the intent is to exercise the right to control the distribution of derivative or collective works based on the Program.

In addition, mere aggregation of another work not based on the Program with the Program (or with a work based on the Program) on a volume of a storage or distribution medium does not bring the other work under the scope of this License.

3. You may copy and distribute the Program (or a work based on it, under Section 2) in object code or executable form under the terms of Sections 1 and 2 above provided that you also do one of the following:

a) Accompany it with the complete corresponding machine-readable source code, which must be distributed under the terms of Sections 1 and 2 above on a medium customarily used for software interchange; or,

b) Accompany it with a written offer, valid for at least three years, to give any third party, for a charge no more than your cost of physically performing source distribution, a complete machine-readable copy of the corresponding source code, to be distributed under the terms of Sections 1 and 2 above on a medium customarily used for software interchange; or,

c) Accompany it with the information you received as to the offer to distribute corresponding source code. (This alternative is allowed only for noncommercial distribution and only if you received the program in object code or executable form with such an offer, in accord with Subsection b above.)

The source code for a work means the preferred form of the work for making modifications to it. For an executable work, complete source code means all the source code for all modules it contains, plus any associated interface definition files, plus the scripts used to control compilation and installation of the

executable. However, as a special exception, the source code distributed need not include anything that is normally distributed (in either source or binary form) with the major components (compiler, kernel, and so on) of the operating system on which the executable runs, unless that component itself accompanies the executable.

If distribution of executable or object code is made by offering access to copy from a designated place, then offering equivalent access to copy the source code from the same place counts as distribution of the source code, even though third parties are not compelled to copy the source along with the object code.

4. You may not copy, modify, sublicense, or distribute the Program except as expressly provided under this License. Any attempt otherwise to copy, modify, sublicense or distribute the Program is void, and will automatically terminate your rights under this License. However, parties who have received copies, or rights, from you under this License will not have their licenses terminated so long as such parties remain in full compliance.

5. You are not required to accept this License, since you have not signed it. However, nothing else grants you permission to modify or distribute the Program or its derivative works. These actions are prohibited by law if you do not accept this License. Therefore, by modifying or distributing the Program (or any work based on the Program), you indicate your acceptance of this License to do so, and all its terms and conditions for copying, distributing or modifying the Program or works based on it.

6. Each time you redistribute the Program (or any work based on the Program), the recipient automatically receives a license from the original licensor to copy, distribute or modify the Program subject to these terms and conditions. You may not impose any further restrictions on the recipients' exercise of the rights granted herein. You are not responsible for enforcing compliance by third parties to this License.

7. If, as a consequence of a court judgment or allegation of patent infringement or for any other reason (not limited to patent issues), conditions are imposed on you (whether by court order, agreement or otherwise) that contradict the conditions of this License, they do not excuse you from the conditions of this License. If you cannot distribute so as to satisfy simultaneously your obligations under this License and any other pertinent obligations, then as a consequence you may not distribute the Program at all. For example, if a patent license would not permit royalty-free redistribution of the Program by all those who receive copies directly or indirectly through you, then the only way you could satisfy both it and this License would be to refrain entirely from distribution of the Program.

If any portion of this section is held invalid or

unenforceable under any particular circumstance, the balance of the section is intended to apply and the section as a whole is intended to apply in other circumstances.

It is not the purpose of this section to induce you to infringe any patents or other property right claims or to contest validity of any such claims; this section has the sole purpose of protecting the integrity of the free software distribution system, which is implemented by public license practices. Many people have made generous contributions to the wide range of software distributed through that system in reliance on consistent application of that system; it is up to the author/donor to decide if he or she is willing to distribute software through any other system and a licensee cannot impose that choice.

This section is intended to make thoroughly clear what is believed to be a consequence of the rest of this License.

8. If the distribution and/or use of the Program is restricted in certain countries either by patents or by copyrighted interfaces, the original copyright holder who places the Program under this License may add an explicit geographical distribution limitation excluding those countries, so that distribution is permitted only in or among countries not thus excluded. In such case, this License incorporates the limitation as if written in the body of this License.

9. The Free Software Foundation may publish revised and/or new versions of the General Public License from time to time. Such new versions will be similar in spirit to the present version, but may differ in detail to address new problems or concerns.

Each version is given a distinguishing version number. If the Program specifies a version number of this License which applies to it and "any later version", you have the option of following the terms and conditions either of that version or of any later version published by the Free Software Foundation. If the Program does not specify a version number of this License, you may choose any version ever published by the Free Software Foundation.

10. If you wish to incorporate parts of the Program into other free programs whose distribution

conditions are different, write to the author to ask for permission. For software which is copyrighted by the Free Software Foundation, write to the Free Software Foundation; we sometimes make exceptions for this. Our decision will be guided by the two goals of preserving the free status of all derivatives of our free software and of promoting the sharing and reuse of software generally.

NO WARRANTY

11. BECAUSE THE PROGRAM IS LICENSED FREE OF CHARGE, THERE IS NO WARRANTY FOR THE PROGRAM, TO THE EXTENT PERMITTED BY APPLICABLE LAW. EXCEPT WHEN OTHERWISE STATED IN WRITING THE COPYRIGHT HOLDERS AND/OR OTHER PARTIES PROVIDE THE PROGRAM "AS IS" WITHOUT WARRANTY OF ANY KIND, EITHER EXPRESSED OR IMPLIED, INCLUDING, BUT NOT LIMITED TO, THE IMPLIED WARRANTIES OF MERCHANTABILITY AND FITNESS FOR A PARTICULAR PURPOSE. THE ENTIRE RISK AS TO THE QUALITY AND PERFORMANCE OF THE PROGRAM IS WITH YOU. SHOULD THE PROGRAM PROVE DEFECTIVE, YOU ASSUME THE COST OF ALL NECESSARY SERVICING, REPAIR OR CORRECTION.

12. IN NO EVENT UNLESS REQUIRED BY APPLICABLE LAW OR AGREED TO IN WRITING WILL ANY COPYRIGHT HOLDER, OR ANY OTHER PARTY WHO MAY MODIFY AND/OR REDISTRIBUTE THE PROGRAM AS PERMITTED ABOVE, BE LIABLE TO YOU FOR DAMAGES, INCLUDING ANY GENERAL, SPECIAL, INCIDENTAL OR CONSEQUENTIAL DAMAGES ARISING OUT OF THE USE OR INABILITY TO USE THE PROGRAM (INCLUDING BUT NOT LIMITED TO LOSS OF DATA OR DATA BEING RENDERED INACCURATE OR LOSSES SUSTAINED BY YOU OR THIRD PARTIES OR A FAILURE OF THE PROGRAM TO OPERATE WITH ANY OTHER PROGRAMS), EVEN IF SUCH HOLDER OR OTHER PARTY HAS BEEN ADVISED OF THE POSSIBILITY OF SUCH DAMAGES.

END OF TERMS AND CONDITIONS

How to Apply These Terms to Your New Programs

If you develop a new program, and you want it to be of the greatest possible use to the public, the best way to achieve this is to make it free software which everyone can redistribute and change under these terms.

To do so, attach the following notices to the program. It is safest to attach them to the start of each source file to most effectively convey the exclusion of warranty; and each file should have at least the "copyright" line and a pointer to where the full notice is found.

```
<one line to give the program's name
and a brief idea of what it does.>
Copyright (C) <year>  <name of author>
```

This program is free software; you can redistribute it and/or modify it under the terms of the GNU General Public License as published by the Free Software Foundation; either version 2 of the License, or (at your option) any later version.

This program is distributed in the hope that it will

be useful, but WITHOUT ANY WARRANTY; without even the implied warranty of MERCHANTABILITY or FITNESS FOR A PARTICULAR PURPOSE. See the GNU General Public License for more details.

You should have received a copy of the GNU General Public License along with this program; if not, write to the Free Software Foundation, Inc., 51 Franklin Street, Fifth Floor, Boston, MA 02110-1301 USA.

Also add information on how to contact you by electronic and paper mail.

If the program is interactive, make it output a short notice like this when it starts in an interactive mode:

```
Gnomovision version 69, Copyright (C)
year name of author
Gnomovision comes with ABSOLUTELY NO
WARRANTY; for details type `show w'.
This is free software, and you are
welcome to redistribute it
under certain conditions; type `show
c' for details.
```

The hypothetical commands `show w' and `show c' should show the appropriate parts of the General Public License. Of course, the commands you use may be called something other than `show w' and `show c'; they could even be mouse-clicks or menu items--whatever suits your program.

You should also get your employer (if you work as a programmer) or your school, if any, to sign a "copyright disclaimer" for the program, if necessary. Here is a sample; alter the names:

```
Yoyodyne, Inc., hereby disclaims all
copyright interest in the program
`Gnomovision' (which makes passes at
compilers) written by James Hacker.
<signature of Ty Coon>, 1 April 1989
Ty Coon, President of Vice
```

This General Public License does not permit incorporating your program into proprietary programs. If your program is a subroutine library, you may consider it more useful to permit linking proprietary applications with the library. If this is what you want to do, use the GNU Lesser General Public License instead of this License.

Creative Commons Attribution-ShareAlike License

The Creative Commons licenses are intended primarily for aesthetic works: art, music, literature, or other creative content. For such works, there is often no good definition of what "source code" might mean, and at other times it is simply impractical to include it. For example, at one extreme, a motion picture's source code might be considered to include not only all of the footage used in making it, but also all of the special effects fixtures, software, props, sets, and even actors—since without them, you can't really make fundamental changes to the film. At the other extreme, a digital video of the film is a directly-editable work, so the film itself can serve as source code for many purposes. Many positions in between are equally sensible.

These ambiguities are common with digital content, so the Creative Commons ShareAlike license module simply sidesteps the issue by not requiring any particular form of source code. Instead, it simply requires that the distribution medium not actively impede copying and modification, by insisting that the file be distributed without DRM encryption that prevents such use (in principle, a DRM format would be okay, so long as the key is provided).

The Creative Commons licenses all include an Attribution module, which insists on proper credit being given to the author, but also allows the author to disclaim derivatives that they do not want to be associated with. This makes more sense for content, since it is more likely to contain material which may be politically or socially objectionable to some parties (indeed, this sort of corruption is often one of the first fears artists new to free content express about releasing their work).

Creative Commons Legal Code

Attribution-ShareAlike 3.0 Unported

CREATIVE COMMONS CORPORATION IS NOT A LAW FIRM AND DOES NOT PROVIDE LEGAL SERVICES. DISTRIBUTION OF THIS LICENSE DOES NOT CREATE AN ATTORNEY-CLIENT RELATIONSHIP. CREATIVE COMMONS PROVIDES THIS INFORMATION ON AN "AS-IS" BASIS. CREATIVE COMMONS MAKES NO WARRANTIES REGARDING THE INFORMATION PROVIDED, AND DISCLAIMS LIABILITY FOR DAMAGES RESULTING FROM ITS USE.

License

THE WORK (AS DEFINED BELOW) IS PROVIDED UNDER THE TERMS OF THIS CREATIVE COMMONS PUBLIC LICENSE ("CCPL" OR "LICENSE"). THE WORK IS PROTECTED BY COPYRIGHT AND/OR OTHER APPLICABLE LAW. ANY USE OF THE WORK OTHER THAN AS AUTHORIZED UNDER THIS LICENSE OR COPYRIGHT LAW IS PROHIBITED.

BY EXERCISING ANY RIGHTS TO THE WORK PROVIDED HERE, YOU ACCEPT AND AGREE TO BE BOUND BY THE TERMS OF THIS LICENSE. TO THE EXTENT THIS LICENSE MAY BE CONSIDERED TO BE A CONTRACT, THE LICENSOR GRANTS YOU THE RIGHTS CONTAINED HERE IN CONSIDERATION OF YOUR ACCEPTANCE OF SUCH TERMS AND CONDITIONS.

1. Definitions

1. **"Adaptation"** means a work based upon the Work, or upon the Work and other pre-existing works, such as a translation, adaptation, derivative work, arrangement of music or other alterations of a literary or artistic work, or phonogram or performance and includes cinematographic adaptations or any other form in which the Work may be recast, transformed, or adapted including in any form recognizably derived from the original, except that a work that constitutes a Collection will not be considered an Adaptation for the purpose of this License. For the avoidance of doubt, where the Work is a musical work, performance or phonogram, the synchronization of the Work in timed-relation with a moving image ("synching") will be considered an Adaptation for the purpose of this License.

2. **"Collection"** means a collection of literary or artistic works, such as encyclopedias and anthologies, or performances, phonograms or broadcasts, or other works or subject matter other than works listed in Section 1(f) below, which, by reason of the selection and arrangement of their contents, constitute intellectual creations, in which the Work is included in its entirety in unmodified form along with one or more other contributions, each constituting separate and independent works in themselves, which together are assembled into a collective whole. A work that constitutes a Collection will not be considered an Adaptation

(as defined below) for the purposes of this License.

3. **"Creative Commons Compatible License"** means a license that is listed at http://creativecommons.org/ compatiblelicenses that has been approved by Creative Commons as being essentially equivalent to this License, including, at a minimum, because that license: (i) contains terms that have the same purpose, meaning and effect as the License Elements of this License; and, (ii) explicitly permits the relicensing of adaptations of works made available under that license under this License or a Creative Commons jurisdiction license with the same License Elements as this License.

4. **"Distribute"** means to make available to the public the original and copies of the Work or Adaptation, as appropriate, through sale or other transfer of ownership.

5. **"License Elements"** means the following high-level license attributes as selected by Licensor and indicated in the title of this License: Attribution, ShareAlike.

6. **"Licensor"** means the individual, individuals, entity or entities that offer(s) the Work under the terms of this License.

7. **"Original Author"** means, in the case of a literary or artistic work, the individual, individuals, entity or entities who created the Work or if no individual or entity can be identified, the publisher; and in addition

   (i) in the case of a performance the actors, singers, musicians, dancers, and other persons who act, sing, deliver, declaim, play in, interpret or otherwise perform literary or artistic works or expressions of folklore;

   (ii) in the case of a phonogram the producer being the person or legal entity who first fixes the sounds of a performance or other sounds; and,

   (iii) in the case of broadcasts, the organization that transmits the broadcast.

8. **"Work"** means the literary and/or artistic work offered under the terms of this License including without limitation any production in the literary, scientific and artistic domain, whatever may be the mode or form of its expression including digital form, such as a book, pamphlet and other writing; a lecture, address, sermon or other work of the same nature; a dramatic or dramatico-musical work; a choreographic work or entertainment in dumb show; a musical composition with or without words; a cinematographic work to which are assimilated works expressed by a process analogous to cinematography; a work of drawing, painting, architecture, sculpture, engraving or lithography; a photographic work to which are assimilated works expressed by a process analogous to photography; a work of applied art; an illustration, map, plan, sketch or three-dimensional work relative to geography,

topography, architecture or science; a performance; a broadcast; a phonogram; a compilation of data to the extent it is protected as a copyrightable work; or a work performed by a variety or circus performer to the extent it is not otherwise considered a literary or artistic work.

9. "**You**" means an individual or entity exercising rights under this License who has not previously violated the terms of this License with respect to the Work, or who has received express permission from the Licensor to exercise rights under this License despite a previous violation.

10. "**Publicly Perform**" means to perform public recitations of the Work and to communicate to the public those public recitations, by any means or process, including by wire or wireless means or public digital performances; to make available to the public Works in such a way that members of the public may access these Works from a place and at a place individually chosen by them; to perform the Work to the public by any means or process and the communication to the public of the performances of the Work, including by public digital performance; to broadcast and rebroadcast the Work by any means including signs, sounds or images.

11. "**Reproduce**" means to make copies of the Work by any means including without limitation by sound or visual recordings and the right of fixation and reproducing fixations of the Work, including storage of a protected performance or phonogram in digital form or other electronic medium.

2. Fair Dealing Rights

Nothing in this License is intended to reduce, limit, or restrict any uses free from copyright or rights arising from limitations or exceptions that are provided for in connection with the copyright protection under copyright law or other applicable laws.

3. License Grant

Subject to the terms and conditions of this License, Licensor hereby grants You a worldwide, royalty-free, non-exclusive, perpetual (for the duration of the applicable copyright) license to exercise the rights in the Work as stated below:

1. to Reproduce the Work, to incorporate the Work into one or more Collections, and to Reproduce the Work as incorporated in the Collections;

2. to create and Reproduce Adaptations provided that any such Adaptation, including any translation in any medium, takes reasonable steps to clearly label, demarcate or otherwise identify that changes were made to the original Work. For example, a translation could be marked "The original work was translated from English to Spanish," or a modification could indicate "The original work has been modified.";

3. to Distribute and Publicly Perform the Work including as incorporated in Collections; and,

4. to Distribute and Publicly Perform Adaptations.

5. For the avoidance of doubt:

1. **Non-waivable Compulsory License Schemes**. In those jurisdictions in which the right to collect royalties through any statutory or compulsory licensing scheme cannot be waived, the Licensor reserves the exclusive right to collect such royalties for any exercise by You of the rights granted under this License;

2. **Waivable Compulsory License Schemes**. In those jurisdictions in which the right to collect royalties through any statutory or compulsory licensing scheme can be waived, the Licensor waives the exclusive right to collect such royalties for any exercise by You of the rights granted under this License; and,

3. **Voluntary License Schemes**. The Licensor waives the right to collect royalties, whether individually or, in the event that the Licensor is a member of a collecting society that administers voluntary licensing schemes, via that society, from any exercise by You of the rights granted under this License.

The above rights may be exercised in all media and formats whether now known or hereafter devised. The above rights include the right to make such modifications as are technically necessary to exercise the rights in other media and formats. Subject to Section 8(f), all rights not expressly granted by Licensor are hereby reserved.

4. Restrictions

The license granted in Section 3 above is expressly made subject to and limited by the following restrictions:

1. You may Distribute or Publicly Perform the Work only under the terms of this License. You must include a copy of, or the Uniform Resource Identifier (URI) for, this License with every copy of the Work You Distribute or Publicly Perform. You may not offer or impose any terms on the Work that restrict the terms of this License or the ability of the recipient of the Work to exercise the rights granted to that recipient under the terms of the License. You may not sublicense the Work. You must keep intact all notices that refer to this License and to the disclaimer of warranties with every copy of the Work You Distribute or Publicly Perform. When You Distribute or Publicly Perform the Work, You may not impose any effective technological measures on the Work that restrict the ability of a recipient of the Work from You to exercise the rights granted to that recipient under the terms of the License. This Section 4(a) applies to the Work as incorporated in a Collection, but this does not require the Collection apart from the Work itself to be made subject to the terms of this License. If You create a Collection, upon notice from any Licensor You must, to the extent practicable, remove from the Collection any credit as required by Section 4(c), as requested. If You create an Adaptation, upon notice from any Licensor You must, to the extent practicable,

remove from the Adaptation any credit as required by Section 4(c), as requested.

2. You may Distribute or Publicly Perform an Adaptation only under the terms of:

(i) this License;

(ii) a later version of this License with the same License Elements as this License;

(iii) a Creative Commons jurisdiction license (either this or a later license version) that contains the same License Elements as this License (e.g., Attribution-ShareAlike 3.0 US));

(iv) a Creative Commons Compatible License.

If you license the Adaptation under one of the licenses mentioned in (iv), you must comply with the terms of that license. If you license the Adaptation under the terms of any of the licenses mentioned in (i), (ii) or (iii) (the "Applicable License"), you must comply with the terms of the Applicable License generally and the following provisions:

(I) You must include a copy of, or the URI for, the Applicable License with every copy of each Adaptation You Distribute or Publicly Perform;

(II) You may not offer or impose any terms on the Adaptation that restrict the terms of the Applicable License or the ability of the recipient of the Adaptation to exercise the rights granted to that recipient under the terms of the Applicable License;

(III) You must keep intact all notices that refer to the Applicable License and to the disclaimer of warranties with every copy of the Work as included in the Adaptation You Distribute or Publicly Perform;

(IV) when You Distribute or Publicly Perform the Adaptation, You may not impose any effective technological measures on the Adaptation that restrict the ability of a recipient of the Adaptation from You to exercise the rights granted to that recipient under the terms of the Applicable License. This Section 4(b) applies to the Adaptation as incorporated in a Collection, but this does not require the Collection apart from the Adaptation itself to be made subject to the terms of the Applicable License.

3. If You Distribute, or Publicly Perform the Work or any Adaptations or Collections, You must, unless a request has been made pursuant to Section 4(a), keep intact all copyright notices for the Work and provide, reasonable to the medium or means You are utilizing:

(i) the name of the Original Author (or pseudonym, if applicable) if supplied, and/or if the Original Author and/or Licensor designate another party or parties (e.g., a sponsor institute, publishing entity, journal) for attribution ("Attribution Parties") in Licensor's copyright notice, terms of service or by other reasonable means, the name of such party or parties;

(ii) the title of the Work if supplied;

(iii) to the extent reasonably practicable, the URI, if any, that Licensor specifies to be associated with the Work, unless such URI does not refer to the copyright notice or licensing information for the Work; and

(iv) consistent with Section 3(b), in the case of an Adaptation, a credit identifying the use of the Work in the Adaptation (e.g., "French translation of the Work by Original Author," or "Screenplay based on original Work by Original Author"). The credit required by this Section 4(c) may be implemented in any reasonable manner; provided, however, that in the case of an Adaptation or Collection, at a minimum such credit will appear, if a credit for all contributing authors of the Adaptation or Collection appears, then as part of these credits and in a manner at least as prominent as the credits for the other contributing authors. For the avoidance of doubt, You may only use the credit required by this Section for the purpose of attribution in the manner set out above and, by exercising Your rights under this License, You may not implicitly or explicitly assert or imply any connection with, sponsorship or endorsement by the Original Author, Licensor and/or Attribution Parties, as appropriate, of You or Your use of the Work, without the separate, express prior written permission of the Original Author, Licensor and/or Attribution Parties.

4. Except as otherwise agreed in writing by the Licensor or as may be otherwise permitted by applicable law, if You Reproduce, Distribute or Publicly Perform the Work either by itself or as part of any Adaptations or Collections, You must not distort, mutilate, modify or take other derogatory action in relation to the Work which would be prejudicial to the Original Author's honor or reputation. Licensor agrees that in those jurisdictions (e.g. Japan), in which any exercise of the right granted in Section 3(b) of this License (the right to make Adaptations) would be deemed to be a distortion, mutilation, modification or other derogatory action prejudicial to the Original Author's honor and reputation, the Licensor will waive or not assert, as appropriate, this section, to the fullest extent permitted by the applicable national law, to enable You to reasonably exercise Your right under Section 3(b) of this License (right to make Adaptations) but not otherwise.

5. Representations, Warranties and Disclaimer

UNLESS OTHERWISE MUTUALLY AGREED TO BY THE PARTIES IN WRITING, LICENSOR OFFERS THE WORK AS-IS AND MAKES NO REPRESENTATIONS OR WARRANTIES OF ANY KIND CONCERNING THE WORK, EXPRESS, IMPLIED, STATUTORY OR OTHERWISE,

INCLUDING, WITHOUT LIMITATION, WARRANTIES OF TITLE, MERCHANTIBILITY, FITNESS FOR A PARTICULAR PURPOSE, NONINFRINGEMENT, OR THE ABSENCE OF LATENT OR OTHER DEFECTS, ACCURACY, OR THE PRESENCE OF ABSENCE OF ERRORS, WHETHER OR NOT DISCOVERABLE. SOME JURISDICTIONS DO NOT ALLOW THE EXCLUSION OF IMPLIED WARRANTIES, SO SUCH EXCLUSION MAY NOT APPLY TO YOU.

6. Limitation on Liability

EXCEPT TO THE EXTENT REQUIRED BY APPLICABLE LAW, IN NO EVENT WILL LICENSOR BE LIABLE TO YOU ON ANY LEGAL THEORY FOR ANY SPECIAL, INCIDENTAL, CONSEQUENTIAL, PUNITIVE OR EXEMPLARY DAMAGES ARISING OUT OF THIS LICENSE OR THE USE OF THE WORK, EVEN IF LICENSOR HAS BEEN ADVISED OF THE POSSIBILITY OF SUCH DAMAGES.

7. Termination

1. This License and the rights granted hereunder will terminate automatically upon any breach by You of the terms of this License. Individuals or entities who have received Adaptations or Collections from You under this License, however, will not have their licenses terminated provided such individuals or entities remain in full compliance with those licenses. Sections 1, 2, 5, 6, 7, and 8 will survive any termination of this License.

2. Subject to the above terms and conditions, the license granted here is perpetual (for the duration of the applicable copyright in the Work). Notwithstanding the above, Licensor reserves the right to release the Work under different license terms or to stop distributing the Work at any time; provided, however that any such election will not serve to withdraw this License (or any other license that has been, or is required to be, granted under the terms of this License), and this License will continue in full force and effect unless terminated as stated above.

8. Miscellaneous

1. Each time You Distribute or Publicly Perform the Work or a Collection, the Licensor offers to the recipient a license to the Work on the same terms and conditions as the license granted to You under this License.

2. Each time You Distribute or Publicly Perform an Adaptation, Licensor offers to the recipient a license to the original Work on the same terms and conditions as the license granted to You under this License.

3. If any provision of this License is invalid or unenforceable under applicable law, it shall not affect the validity or enforceability of the remainder of the terms of this License, and without further action by the parties to this agreement, such provision shall be reformed to the minimum extent necessary to make such provision valid and enforceable.

4. No term or provision of this License shall be deemed waived and no breach consented to unless such waiver or consent shall be in writing and signed by the party to be charged with such waiver or consent.

5. This License constitutes the entire agreement between the parties with respect to the Work licensed here. There are no understandings, agreements or representations with respect to the Work not specified here. Licensor shall not be bound by any additional provisions that may appear in any communication from You. This License may not be modified without the mutual written agreement of the Licensor and You.

6. The rights granted under, and the subject matter referenced, in this License were drafted utilizing the terminology of the Berne Convention for the Protection of Literary and Artistic Works (as amended on September 28, 1979), the Rome Convention of 1961, the WIPO Copyright Treaty of 1996, the WIPO Performances and Phonograms Treaty of 1996 and the Universal Copyright Convention (as revised on July 24, 1971). These rights and subject matter take effect in the relevant jurisdiction in which the License terms are sought to be enforced according to the corresponding provisions of the implementation of those treaty provisions in the applicable national law. If the standard suite of rights granted under applicable copyright law includes additional rights not granted under this License, such additional rights are deemed to be included in the License; this License is not intended to restrict the license of any rights under applicable law.

Creative Commons Notice

Creative Commons is not a party to this License, and makes no warranty whatsoever in connection with the Work. Creative Commons will not be liable to You or any party on any legal theory for any damages whatsoever, including without limitation any general,special, incidental or consequential damages arising in connection to this license. Notwithstanding the foregoing two (2) sentences, if Creative Commons has expressly identified itself as the Licensor hereunder, it shall have all rights and obligations of Licensor.

Except for the limited purpose of indicating to the public that the Work is licensed under the CCPL, Creative Commons does not authorize the use by either party of the trademark "Creative Commons" or any related trademark or logo of Creative Commons without the prior written consent of Creative Commons. Any permitted use will be in compliance with Creative Commons' then-current trademark usage guidelines, as may be published on its website or otherwise made available upon request from time to time. For the avoidance of doubt, this trademark restriction does not form part of the License.

Creative Commons may be contacted at http://creativecommons.org

Free, Non-Copyleft Licenses:
BSD, MIT, and Apache

One of the oldest free licenses is the license that was used for BSD Unix, which has come to be known as the "BSD License". An earlier form of this license which contained a clause insisting on certain kinds of advertising was considered too burdensome, and was subsequently dropped, resulting in the "3 clause" BSD that appears below.

The license used by MIT for its contributions to the X Windows software is generally called the MIT License, though it is sometimes referred to as the "MIT/X11" or "X11" license. It has essentially the same effect as the BSD and is more compact (some people feel it is better worded).

The Apache license was used for the webserver of the same name. It is a much longer license, and is not included here, but it often used for add-ons to Apache. All three licenses are compatible with each other and with the GPL, since they do not include copyleft terms.

The BSD License

Copyright (c) <YEAR> <COPYRIGHT HOLDER>

All rights reserved.

Redistribution and use in source and binary forms, with or without modification, are permitted provided that the following conditions are met:

* Redistributions of source code must retain the above copyright notice, this list of conditions and the following disclaimer.

* Redistributions in binary form must reproduce the above copyright notice, this list of conditions and the following disclaimer in the documentation and/or other materials provided with the distribution.

* Neither the name of the <ORGANIZATION> nor the names of its contributors may be used to endorse or promote products derived from this software without specific prior written permission.

THIS SOFTWARE IS PROVIDED BY THE COPYRIGHT HOLDERS AND CONTRIBUTORS "AS IS" AND ANY EXPRESS OR IMPLIED WARRANTIES, INCLUDING, BUT NOT LIMITED TO, THE IMPLIED WARRANTIES OF MERCHANTABILITY AND FITNESS FOR A PARTICULAR PURPOSE ARE DISCLAIMED. IN NO EVENT SHALL THE COPYRIGHT HOLDER OR CONTRIBUTORS BE LIABLE FOR ANY DIRECT, INDIRECT, INCIDENTAL, SPECIAL, EXEMPLARY, OR CONSEQUENTIAL DAMAGES (INCLUDING, BUT NOT LIMITED TO, PROCUREMENT OF SUBSTITUTE GOODS OR SERVICES; LOSS OF USE, DATA, OR PROFITS; OR BUSINESS INTERRUPTION) HOWEVER CAUSED AND ON ANY THEORY OF LIABILITY, WHETHER IN CONTRACT, STRICT LIABILITY, OR TORT (INCLUDING NEGLIGENCE OR OTHERWISE) ARISING IN ANY WAY OUT OF THE USE OF THIS SOFTWARE, EVEN IF ADVISED OF THE POSSIBILITY OF SUCH DAMAGE.

The MIT License

Copyright (c) <YEAR> <COPYRIGHT HOLDER>

Permission is hereby granted, free of charge, to any person obtaining a copy of this software and associated documentation files (the "Software"), to deal in the Software without restriction, including without limitation the rights to use, copy, modify, merge, publish, distribute, sublicense, and/or sell copies of the Software, and to permit persons to whom the Software is furnished to do so, subject to the following conditions:

The above copyright notice and this permission notice shall be included in all copies or substantial portions of the Software.

THE SOFTWARE IS PROVIDED "AS IS", WITHOUT WARRANTY OF ANY KIND, EXPRESS OR IMPLIED, INCLUDING BUT NOT LIMITED TO THE WARRANTIES OF MERCHANTABILITY, FITNESS FOR A PARTICULAR PURPOSE AND NONINFRINGEMENT. IN NO EVENT SHALL THE AUTHORS OR COPYRIGHT HOLDERS BE LIABLE FOR ANY CLAIM, DAMAGES OR OTHER LIABILITY, WHETHER IN AN ACTION OF CONTRACT, TORT OR OTHERWISE, ARISING FROM, OUT OF OR IN CONNECTION WITH THE SOFTWARE OR THE USE OR OTHER DEALINGS IN THE SOFTWARE.

TAPR Open Hardware License

The TAPR OHL is a very new license, and has not yet seen widespread use. It is not necessarily the hardware license that will succeed in the end, but it is unique in that it attempts to impose a production copyleft as described in Appendix C: that is to say, a copyleft clause which requires the recipient of the design to release design data with products manufactured from the design (or from derivatives of the design).

Certain terms of this license may not be legally enforceable through copyright, although the license also involves patent law.

Unfortunately, the TAPR OHL is very specific to printed circuit board designs. On the one hand, this is convenient in that it permits the copyright terms to be spelled out very concretely, increasing the likelihood that they will be upheld if challenged in court. On the other hand, they would need to be rewritten if they were to be applied to other sorts of hardware designs.

The TAPR Open Hardware License

Version 1.0 (May 25, 2007)

Copyright 2007 TAPR - http://www.tapr.org/OHL

PREAMBLE

Open Hardware is a thing—a physical artifact, either electrical or mechanical—whose design information is available to, and usable by, the public in a way that allows anyone to make, modify, distribute, and use that thing. In this preface, design information is called "documentation" and things created from it are called "products."

The TAPR Open Hardware License ("OHL") agreement provides a legal framework for Open Hardware projects. It may be used for any kind of product, be it a hammer or a computer motherboard, and is TAPR's contribution to the community; anyone may use the OHL for their Open Hardware project.

Like the GNU General Public License, the OHL is designed to guarantee your freedom to share and to create. It forbids anyone who receives rights under the OHL to deny any other licensee those same rights to copy, modify, and distribute documentation, and to make, use and distribute products based on that documentation.

Unlike the GPL, the OHL is not primarily a copyright license. While copyright protects documentation from unauthorized copying, modification, and distribution, it has little to do with your right to make, distribute, or use a product based on that documentation. For better or worse, patents play a significant role in those activities. Although it does not prohibit anyone from patenting inventions embodied in an Open Hardware design, and of course cannot prevent a third party from enforcing their patent rights, those who benefit from an OHL design may not bring lawsuits claiming that design infringes their patents or other intellectual property.

The OHL addresses unique issues involved in the creation of tangible, physical things, but does not cover software, firmware, or code loaded into programmable devices. A copyright-oriented license such as the GPL better suits these creations.

How can you use the OHL, or a design based upon it? While the terms and conditions below take precedence over this preamble, here is a summary:

- You may modify the documentation and make products based upon it.
- You may use products for any legal purpose without limitation.
- You may distribute unmodified documentation, but you must include the complete package as you received it.
- You may distribute products you make to third parties, if you either include the documentation on which the product is based, or make it available without charge for at least three years to anyone who requests it.
- You may distribute modified documentation or products based on it, if you:
  - License your modifications under the OHL.
  - Include those modifications, following the requirements stated below.
  - Attempt to send the modified documentation by email to any of the developers who have provided their email address. This is a good faith obligation—if the email fails, you need do nothing more and may go on with your distribution.
- If you create a design that you want to license under the OHL, you should:
  - Include this document in a file named LICENSE (with the appropriate extension) that is included in the documentation package.
  - If the file format allows, include a notice like "Licensed under the TAPR Open Hardware License (www.tapr.org/OHL)" in each documentation file. While not required, you should also include this notice on printed circuit board artwork and the product itself; if space is limited the notice can be shortened or abbreviated.

Appendices

- Include a copyright notice in each file and on printed circuit board artwork.
- If you wish to be notified of modifications that others may make, include your email address in a file named "CONTRIB.TXT" or something similar.

- Any time the OHL requires you to make documentation available to others, you must include all the materials you received from the upstream licensors. In addition, if you have modified the documentation:

  - You must identify the modifications in a text file (preferably named "CHANGES.TXT") that you include with the documentation. That file must also include a statement like "These modifications are licensed under the TAPR Open Hardware License."
  - You must include any new files you created, including any manufacturing files (such as Gerber files) you create in the course of making products.
  - You must include both "before" and "after" versions of all files you modified.
  - You may include files in proprietary formats, but you must also include open format versions (such as Gerber, ASCII, Postscript, or PDF) if your tools can create them.

TERMS AND CONDITIONS

1. Introduction

1.1 This Agreement governs how you may use, copy, modify, and distribute Documentation, and how you may make, have made, and distribute Products based on that Documentation. As used in this Agreement, to "distribute" Documentation means to directly or indirectly make copies available to a third party, and to "distribute" Products means to directly or indirectly give, loan, sell or otherwise transfer them to a third party.

1.2 "Documentation" includes:

(a) schematic diagrams;

(b) circuit or circuit board layouts, including Gerber and other data files used for manufacture;

(c) mechanical drawings, including CAD, CAM, and other data files used for manufacture;

(d) flow charts and descriptive text; and

(e) other explanatory material.

Documentation may be in any tangible or intangible form of expression, including but not limited to computer files in open or proprietary formats and representations on paper, film, or other media.

1.3 "Products" include:

(a) circuit boards, mechanical assemblies, and other physical parts and components;

(b) assembled or partially assembled units (including components and subassemblies); and

(c) parts and components combined into kits intended for assembly by others;

which are based in whole or in part on the Documentation.

1.4 This Agreement applies to any Documentation which contains a notice stating it is subject to the TAPR Open Hardware License, and to all Products based in whole or in part on that Documentation. If Documentation is distributed in an archive (such as a "zip" file) which includes this document, all files in that archive are subject to this Agreement unless they are specifically excluded. Each person who contributes content to the Documentation is referred to in this Agreement as a "Licensor."

1.5 By (a) using, copying, modifying, or distributing the Documentation, or (b) making or having Products made or distributing them, you accept this Agreement, agree to comply with its terms, and become a "Licensee." Any activity inconsistent with this Agreement will automatically terminate your rights under it (including the immunities from suit granted in Section 2), but the rights of others who have received Documentation, or have obtained Products, directly or indirectly from you will not be affected so long as they fully comply with it themselves.

1.6 This Agreement does not apply to software, firmware, or code loaded into programmable devices which may be used in conjunction with Documentation or Products. Such software is subject to the license terms established by its copyright holder(s).

2. Patents

2.1 Each Licensor grants you, every other Licensee, and every possessor or user of Products a perpetual, worldwide, and royalty-free immunity from suit under any patent, patent application, or other intellectual property right which he or she controls, to the extent necessary to make, have made, possess, use, and distribute Products. This immunity does not extend to infringement arising from modifications subsequently made by others.

2.2 If you make or have Products made, or distribute Documentation that you have modified, you grant every Licensor, every other Licensee, and every possessor or user of Products a perpetual, worldwide, and royalty-free immunity from suit under any patent, patent application, or other intellectual property right which you control, to the extent necessary to make, have made, possess, use, and distribute Products. This immunity does not extend to infringement arising from modifications subsequently made by others.

2.3 To avoid doubt, providing Documentation to a third party for the sole purpose of having that party make Products on your behalf is not considered "distribution," and a third party's act of making Products solely on your behalf does not cause that party to grant the immunity described in the preceding paragraph.

2.4 These grants of immunity are a material part of this Agreement, and form a portion of the consideration given by each party to the other. If any court judgment or legal agreement prevents you from granting the immunity required by this Section, your rights under this Agreement will terminate and you may no longer use, copy, modify or distribute the Documentation, or make, have made, or distribute Products.

3. Modifications

You may modify the Documentation, and those modifications will become part of the Documentation. They are subject to this Agreement, as are Products based in whole or in part on them. If you distribute the modified Documentation, or Products based in whole or in part upon it, you must email the modified Documentation in a form compliant with Section 4 to each Licensor who has provided an email address with the Documentation. Attempting to send the email completes your obligations under this Section and you need take no further action if any address fails.

4. Distributing Documentation

4.1 You may distribute unmodified copies of the Documentation in its entirety in any medium, provided that you retain all copyright and other notices (including references to this Agreement) included by each Licensor, and include an unaltered copy of this Agreement.

4.2 You may distribute modified copies of the Documentation if you comply with all the requirements of the preceding paragraph and:

(a) include a prominent notice in an ASCII or other open format file identifying those elements of the Documentation that you changed, and stating that the modifications are licensed under the terms of this Agreement;

(b) include all new documentation files that you create, as well as both the original and modified versions of each file you change (files may be in your development tool's native file format, but if reasonably possible, you must also include open format,such as Gerber, ASCII, Postscript, or PDF, versions);

(c) do not change the terms of this Agreement with respect to subsequent licensees; and

(d) if you make or have Products made, include in the Documentation all elements reasonably required to permit others to make Products, including Gerber, CAD/CAM and other files used for manufacture.

5. Making Products

5.1 You may use the Documentation to make or have Products made, provided that each Product retains any notices included by the Licensor (including, but not limited to, copyright notices on circuit boards).

5.2 You may distribute Products you make or have made, provided that you include with each unit a copy of the Documentation in a form consistent with Section 4. Alternatively, you may include either

(i) an offer valid for at least three years to provide that Documentation, at no charge other than the reasonable cost of media and postage, to any person who requests it; or

(ii) a URL where that Documentation may be downloaded, available for at least three years after you last distribute the Product.

6. NEW LICENSE VERSIONS

TAPR may publish updated versions of the OHL which retain the same general provisions as the present version, but differ in detail to address new problems or concerns, and carry a distinguishing version number. If the Documentation specifies a version number which applies to it and "any later version," you may choose either that version or any later version published by TAPR. If the Documentation does not specify a version number, you may choose any version ever published by TAPR. TAPR owns the copyright to the OHL, but grants permission to any person to copy, distribute, and use it in unmodified form.

7. WARRANTY AND LIABILITY LIMITATIONS

7.1 THE DOCUMENTATION IS PROVIDED ON AN "AS-IS" BASIS WITHOUT WARRANTY OF ANY KIND, TO THE EXTENT PERMITTED BY APPLICABLE LAW. ALL WARRANTIES, EXPRESS OR IMPLIED, INCLUDING BUT NOT LIMITED TO ANY WARRANTIES OF MERCHANTABILITY, FITNESS FOR A PARTICULAR PURPOSE, AND TITLE, ARE HEREBY EXPRESSLY DISCLAIMED.

7.2 IN NO EVENT UNLESS REQUIRED BY APPLICABLE LAW WILL ANY LICENSOR BE LIABLE TO YOU OR ANY THIRD PARTY FOR ANY DIRECT, INDIRECT, INCIDENTAL, CONSEQUENTIAL, PUNITIVE, OR EXEMPLARY DAMAGES ARISING OUT OF THE USE OF, OR INABILITY TO USE, THE DOCUMENTATION OR PRODUCTS, INCLUDING BUT NOT LIMITED TO CLAIMS OF INTELLECTUAL PROPERTY INFRINGEMENT OR LOSS OF DATA, EVEN IF THAT PARTY HAS BEEN ADVISED OF THE POSSIBILITY OF SUCH DAMAGES.

7.3 You agree that the foregoing limitations are reasonable due to the non-financial nature of the transaction represented by this Agreement, and acknowledge that were it not for these limitations, the Licensor(s) would not be willing to make the Documentation available to you.

7.4 You agree to defend, indemnify, and hold each Licensor harmless from any claim brought by a third party alleging any defect in the design, manufacture, or operation of any Product which you make, have made, or distribute pursuant to this Agreement.

License Comparison

The quick reference chart below compares the most popular licenses you will see in free culture and commons-based projects. A few important non-free licenses are also included. You should probably think very hard before using any licenses that are not listed here for the reasons discussed in "Rule #1." Reference URLs are provided for each license, which you should see for the full text and more information about each license.

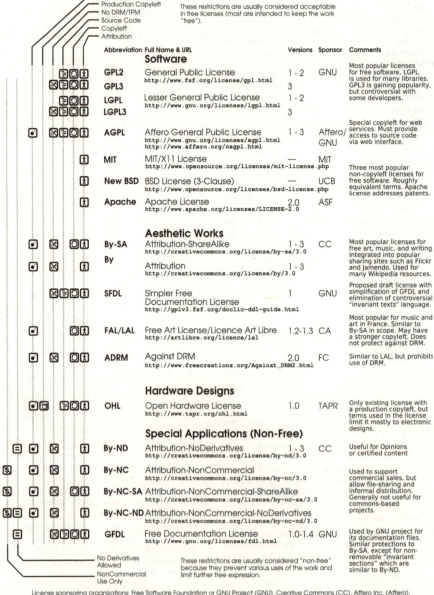

Addresses Related Rights (e.g. Performance)
Production Copyleft
No DRM/TPM
Source Code
Copyleft
Attribution

These restrictions are usually considered acceptable in free licenses (most are intended to keep the work "free").

Abbreviation	Full Name & URL	Versions	Sponsor	Comments
Software				
GPL2	General Public License http://www.fsf.org/license/gpl.html	1 - 2	GNU	Most popular licenses for free software. LGPL is used for many libraries. GPL3 is gaining popularity, but controversial with some developers.
GPL3		3		
LGPL	Lesser General Public License http://www.gnu.org/licenses/lgpl.html	1 - 2		
LGPL3		3		
AGPL	Affero General Public License http://www.gnu.org/licenses/agpl.html http://www.affero.org/oagpl.html	1 - 3	Affero/ GNU	Special copyleft for web services. Must provide access to source code via web interface.
MIT	MIT/X11 License http://www.opensource.org/licenses/mit-license.php	—	MIT	Three most popular non-copyleft licenses for free software. Roughly equivalent terms. Apache license addresses patents.
New BSD	BSD License (3-Clause) http://www.opensource.org/licenses/bsd-license.php	—	UCB	
Apache	Apache License http://www.apache.org/licenses/LICENSE-2.0	2.0	ASF	
Aesthetic Works				
By-SA	Attribution-ShareAlike http://creativecommons.org/license/by-sa/3.0	1 - 3	CC	Most popular licenses for free art, music, and writing. Integrated into popular sharing sites such as Flickr and Jamendo. Used for many Wikipedia resources.
By	Attribution http://creativecommons.org/license/by/3.0	1 - 3		
SFDL	Simpler Free Documentation License http://gplv3.fsf.org/doclic-ddl-guide.html	1	GNU	Proposed draft license with simplification of GFDL and elimination of controversial "invariant texts" language.
FAL/LAL	Free Art License/Licence Art Libre http://artlibre.org/licence/lal	1.2-1.3	CA	Most popular for music and art in France. Similar to By-SA in scope. May have a stronger copyleft. Does not protect against DRM.
ADRM	Against DRM http://www.freecreations.org/Against_DRM2.html	2.0	FC	Similar to LAL, but prohibits use of DRM.
Hardware Designs				
OHL	Open Hardware License http://www.tapr.org/ohl.html	1.0	TAPR	Only existing license with a production copyleft, but terms used in the license limit it mostly to electronic designs.
Special Applications (Non-Free)				
By-ND	Attribution-NoDerivatives http://creativecommons.org/license/by-nd/3.0	1 - 3	CC	Useful for Opinions or certified content
By-NC	Attribution-NonCommercial http://creativecommons.org/license/by-nc/3.0			Used to support commercial sales, but allow file-sharing and informal distribution. Generally not useful for commons-based projects.
By-NC-SA	Attribution-NonCommercial-ShareAlike http://creativecommons.org/license/by-nc-sa/3.0			
By-NC-ND	Attribution-NonCommercial-NoDerivatives http://creativecommons.org/license/by-nc-nd/3.0			
GFDL	Free Documentation License http://www.gnu.org/licenses/fdl.html	1.0-1.4	GNU	Used by GNU project for its documentation files. Similar protections to By-SA, except for non-removable "invariant sections" which are similar to By-ND.

No Derivatives Allowed
NonCommercial Use Only

These restrictions are usually considered "non-free" because they prevent various uses of the work and limit further free expression.

License sponsoring organizations: Free Software Foundation or GNU Project (GNU), Creative Commons (CC), Affero Inc. (Affero), Massachussetts Institute of Technology (MIT), University of California at Berkeley (UCB), Apache Software Foundation (ASF), Copyleft Attitude (CA), Free Creations (FC), Tucson Area Personal Radio (TAPR). TAPR is usually known by the acronym since it is now an international ham radio organization.

Glossary

aesthetic works
Aesthetic works are those which are valued for their intrinsic beauty, such as a novel or a painting.

application
A software application is an interactive program that is used purposely in order to accomplish a task. Common applications include web browsers (e.g. Firefox), word processors (e.g. OpenOffice.org Writer), and graphics programs (e.g. Inkscape or GIMP).

Application Specific Integrated Circuit (ASIC)
An ASIC is a chip which has an orderly array of logic devices on it, which can be "programmed" at the factory, using a hardware description language, similar to the ones used for FPGAs

architecture
Generally, architecture refers to a particular hardware design for a central processing unit or CPU. Software must be compiled to a separate binary format for each architecture.

attribution
Attribution is the practice of identifying the author or copyright holder for a work.

Attribution License
The Creative Commons Attribution license requires only that the author be identified when the work is used.

Attribution-ShareAlike License
The Creative Commons Attribution-ShareAlike license requires not only that the author be identified, but also that all derivatives of the work be released under the same terms.

backlink
A link back to an original source. The method Creative Commons has used to count how many CC licensed works there are on the world wide web has been to search for pages with backlinks to their license "deed" pages.

Basic Input/Output System (BIOS)
Firmware common to most personal computers which provides the startup software during the boot sequence and which provides low-level control of the computer, especially those aspects that depend on the particular hardware used.

bazaar
A mode of development in which changes are released as often as possible to minimize the feedback cycle between users and developers, and in which many people have the ability to contribute. Also, a community of developers so organized.

Berkeley Software Distribution (BSD)
A free-licensed distribution of the Unix operating system. BSD descends directly from the source code used for proprietary Unix operating systems used in the 1970s through 1990s. It is maintained under a non-copyleft license. As with Linux, there are multiple distributions, the largest being FreeBSD and NetBSD.

binary executable

A binary is a program in a ready form to be executed by the computer, typically the result of compiling and linking source code. It is usually not the prefered form for making changes to the program (compare source code).

Blender Foundation

Organization formed to support development of the Blender 3D modelling program after it was released under a free license.

bottom-up design

An engineering approach in which smaller components are developed first (with little or no overall understanding of how they might interact), and then successively more complex designs are developed using what has already been created. Contrasts with top-down design.

bug-tracking system

Any system used to keep track of faults (or bugs) in software, but especially one which uses a numbered "ticket" system, in which each bug receives a ticket number to which comments, tests, and fixes can be attached. Typically allows for searching, prioritizing, and assigning the bugs to different developers based on what part of the software is expected to be involved.

cathedral

A mode of development in which there is a fairly rigid planning, development, and release cycle, or any project which is managed in this way.

central processing unit (CPU)

The main computing element in a computer, usually a microchip (see also microprocessor).

chilling effect

A term used in legal discussions of the freedom of speech. A chilling effect is any effect that prevents (or chills) individuals from expressing themselves freely. Fear of copyright or patent prosecution is one such effect.

collective patronage

Centuries ago, the arts were largely dependent on "patronage," that is to say, financing by individual wealthy sponsors. One advantage of this system is that it did not rely on intellectual property ideas, since artists were commissioned in advance. *Collective* patronage systems are modern systems which allow a group of people to sponsor a project. There are many possible methods, including the various street performer protocols and even the original form of limited-term copyright monopolies in the USA (when copyright terms were only a few years).

commercial

Applications or software which are primarily created in order to make money. Not all commercial software is proprietary, however, there is also commercial free software (Such as Red Hat Linux, Moodle, or Zope).

commons-based enterprise

Large scale commons-based peer production efforts may be regarded as a new kind of enterprise-scale institution, alongside corporate and government enterprises.

commons-based peer production

A method of collaboratively creating information products, based on the use of a free license and the resulting parity between the people who work on the project (peers).

computer-aided design (CAD)

Programs that help with the creation of engineering design drawings (especially for mechanical design).

computer-aided manufacturing (CAM)

Programs that directly control manufacturing machines such as robotic drills, pick-and-place machines, mills, or lathes in order to manufacture parts automatically.

copyleft

A "copyleft" is a licensing provision which exists to ensure that the original license terms are applied to derivatives of the work.

copyright-like protection

There are a few cases where a legal regime similar to copyright has been extended to products that do not qualify for traditional copyright privileges. Examples include integrated circuit masks (used to photographically etch chips). Sound recordings and photographs may also be covered by copyright-like legislation in jurisdictions where ordinary copyright does not include them.

core

In hardware design, a "core" (or "IP core") is a logic gate design that may be incorporated into a larger design and implemented in an FPGA, an ASIC, or any other logic gate technology.

Creative Commons

Organization started by lawyer Lawrence Lessig in 2002 to promote and maintain licenses for aesthetic content.

Debian Free Software Guidelines (DFSG)

A set of guidelines established by the Debian Project for determining whether the license of any given piece of software is "free enough" to be included in the Debian GNU/Linux distribution.

Debian GNU/Linux

A distribution of GNU/Linux produced as a community project by the Debian Project.

Debian Project

A volunteer organization which packages and maintains the world's largest distribution of

GNU/Linux. It is also a parent distribution for many more specialized GNU/Linux distributions.

Definition of Free Cultural Works

A standard for free-licensed works of an aesthetic or creative nature, meant to include and extend the standards established for free software, prepared as the principle *raison d'etre* of the Freedom Defined project.

developer

Anyone who works on creating or improving a design.

developer documentation

Documentation which is primarily intended to help people to work on improving or making changes to a design, as opposed to merely using it for its intended purpose. Free culture projects depend heavily on developer documentation because without it, contributing to the project is often too hard. The condition of developer documentation is often a critical indicator to which projects will succeed and which will fail.

digital divide

The notion that there is some minimal level of disposable income above which people can afford the investment in technology to be able to use it and learn more. Below it, people are simply too poor to afford the technology and so do not benefit from electronic improvements to education and society.

digital rights management (DRM)

Any of several encryption technologies designed to interfere with the ability to copy or analyze software or content data. Although it is ostensibly promoted to protect copyright privileges, it often interferes with legal uses of the material, thus effectively promoting a more restrictive copyright system. Opponents have suggested that the acronym should really stand for "digital restrictions management."

distribution

A collection of software or other data, such as an operating system that is released as one packaged entity. Usually, there is an implication that the included packages have been tested for consistent interaction and quality.

dual-boot

A computer which can be started up with two different operating systems. There are also multi-boot systems.

facilitators

Some people are unable or unwilling to contribute directly to a project, but are still interested in talking about it. Such people can contribute significantly to the visibility, memory, and enthusiasm of the community, regardless of whether they are materially contributing code.

factoring

See re-factoring.

Field Programmable Gate Arrays (FPGA)

A chip which contains an array of gates which can be written to, in a way analogous to writing data into a memory chip, but for which each cell represents a logic gate and its connections to the gates around it. By writing a prepared set of data to the chip, a hardware logic circuit can be programmed into it.

firmware

Software stored in permanent memory (which doesn't get erased when the power is removed) is called firmware (the idea being that it is midway between software and hardware, although today things are more complicated, since both firmware and hardware can sometimes be reprogrammable. The term firmware is reserved for procedural code, rather than circuitry).

flagship applications

Some applications, especially in the proprietary/ commercial development world show a tendency to grow larger and larger, with lots of extra features added on to them. This is encouraged by the way in which the software is sold as a unit, but it often interferes with modularity and interoperability with other programs, because the one application is trying to "do it all."

flow activity

A psychological term describing a state of contentment and fascination that occurs when an activity has just the right amount of challenge for a person: not hard enough to create frustration yet not so easy as to create boredom. People generally seek "flow" in their leisure activities, and many games are designed to produce this feeling.

Forth

A programming language, noted for its extremely terse syntax and close relationship to how computers actually process data.

founder

The person who started a project originally.

four freedoms

According to Richard Stallman's Free Software Definition, there are four essential freedoms that users need to have with software to make it free. They are the freedom to use the work for any purpose, the freedom to study the source code (or design) of the work, the freedom to make and share copies of the work, and the freedom to improve the work and share those improvements.

free license

A license which grants free use for distribution and modification of works, as described by the Free Software Definition, the Debian Free Software Guidelines, the Freedom Definition, or the Open Source Definition. Usually if license doesn't satisfy all of them (as opposed to most of the important free licenses, which do), it's necessary to specify which you meant, as in the expression "DFSG Free", which is frequently seen in Debian discussions.

free software

In this book, the expression "free software" is always used in the jargon sense of "software offered under a free license" as described in the Free Software Foundation's "Free Software Definition." This is a somewhat unfortunate choice of jargon, as it is frequently misunderstood, but it is generally the preferred term used within the free software development community. For most practical purposes, the term is synonymous with "open source software".

Free Software Definition

The original standard for the meaning of free software, in terms of licensing requirements, provided by the Free Software Foundation

Free Software Foundation

The formal organization created by Richard Stallman to support the GNU Project and promote free software in general.

Freedom Defined

The Freedom Defined wiki was created as a community response to the perceived lack of leadership by the Creative Commons in creating normative standards for freedom of cultural, creative, and aesthetic works. Its principle function is to maintain a definition of what "freedom" should mean in reference to cultural works, and to list licenses which are believed to satisfy that standard. It is roughly analogous to the Open Source Initiative for software.

freeware

Any software which is available at no licensing cost, *not* necessarily free or open source software.

GNU Project

A project to create a complete Unix-like operating system from scratch, using all free software, started by Richard Stallman in the 1980s.

GNU General Public License (GPL)

The most popular free software license, created by Richard Stallman for the GNU project, and later revised with the help of lawyer Eben Moglen.

GNU Lesser General Public License (LGPL)

A popular license for libraries which allows them to be used with proprietary software so long as the library itself is unaltered. Used to be called the Library General Public License.

GNU/Linux

The operating system formed by combining the Linux kernel with the GNU utilities and libraries. Also called **Linux**.

hacker

Hacker has acquired more than one meaning, but in this book it means a programmer with little formal software engineering training who works on free software.

hardware description languages (HDL)

Formal languages for specifying the requirements for a logic circuit. Specialized programs can "synthesize" a circuit which meets the specification, following formal design rules, in much the same way that a compiler can create binary code from source code. Thus, HDLs can be thought of as "source code" for digital integrated circuits

homebrew

A generic term for any small scale design or production, by analogy with the original meaning of beer brewed at home.

intellectual freedom

The freedom to exchange information is one of the most fundamental tenants of our society and is necessary for scientific, technical, and social progress. It is usually enshrined in the concept of "freedom of speech."

intellectual property

Intellectual property is a legal fiction created to allow people to charge money for the intellectual efforts that they make. It treats certain kinds of information products as if they were tangible objects to be bought and sold.

kernel

The minimal core part of an operating system that manages time-sharing between programs, hardware devices, and file systems.

LGPL

See **GNU Lesser General Public License**.

library

A software library is a collection of reusable programs and subroutines which other programs depend on for basic functionality. In the GNU/Linux environment, many libraries are dynamically-linked "shared objects" which can be installed once and used by many programs. There are also "static libraries" that are combined with programs (or "linked") during the compilation process.

license

The terms under which a program, design, or other copyrightable content may be used.

license assertion

A statement by the copyright holder which asserts that a certain license applies to a certain work. Clear license assertions are very important to free culture, because the whole point of a free license is to avoid having to ask for permission when using a work.

license proliferation

In the commons environment, too many licenses can be a serious problem, as conflicts may arise, particularly with copyleft clauses. This is less of a problem with proprietary licenses, because it is always assumed that you will have to contact the licensor in order to use the work. For free licensed works, however, such problems negate the advantage of the free license.

Linux

Linux is an operating system "kernel" written by Linus Torvalds (the name is derived from "Linus" plus "UX," which is a common abbreviation for Unix). In popular use it also represents the entire operating system and often the applications that are used with it, although some purists prefer the term GNU/Linux.

mailing list

A popular way to organize discussion groups online, mailing lists are much older than the world wide web (they date back at least to the early 1980s), and are essentially just automated servers which send emails they receive to all the members of a group.

maintainer

The person primarily responsible for keeping a program or design up-to-date. The first maintainer of a project is usually its founder, but many projects move on to new maintainers when the founder loses interest in the project for some reason.

microcontroller (MCU, µC, or uC)

A microcontroller is a **microprocessor** which includes specialized input/output hardware so that it can be used as a complete or nearly complete computer. Microcontrollers are typically used in embedded devices (devices which you don't normally think of as a computer, such as a television or car, but which have digital computing devices in them).

microprocessor (MPU)

A microprocessor is a **central processing unit** implemented on a single integrated circuit.

netbook

A very small laptop computer, larger than a personal data assistant (PDA). Generally uses flash memory instead of a harddrive and rarely has any optical (CD or DVD) drives. The first netbook was the One Laptop Per Child XO, though the term was coined for later competitors.

Open Cores

A design sharing site for open hardware chip designs (or **cores**).

open hardware

Hardware whose design documentation is available under a free license, an analog to free software.

open source

Whereas the term "free software" focuses on the license terms, "open source" focuses on the fact of having the source code. Both the Open Source Definition and the Free Software Definition require both source code availability and a free license, however, so they are equivalent except for minor differences in what is considered an acceptable license (the few obscure licenses which fall into the gap are rarely used and should be avoided).

Open Source Definition (OSD)

A definition of software licenses which are worthy of the label "Open Source" according to the Open Source Initiative.

Open Source Initiative (OSI)

An organization, started by Bruce Perens and Eric Raymond, to promote free software to businesses in a less "confrontational" way than had been pursued by the Free Software Foundation.

operating system

A basic collection of software that defines a platform, such as Microsoft Windows or GNU/Linux, on which application software depends for basic services such as accessing files, running programs, or controlling input/output hardware. What is considered to be included in an operating system varies from a minimal definition preferred by computer scientists up to an environment complete with graphical user interface and web browser (as with Windows).

package

A software package is a convenient bundle of software for one task, often consisting of the binary executable and various configuration files, typically stored in an archive format, sometimes with installation tools or templates included. Software distributions usually consist of lots of packages for each of the programs they include.

packager

A developer who doesn't really contribute to program itself, but rather prepares it for use with other programs by adding meta-data, compressing it, automating the build process, checking dependencies, and so on. GNU/Linux distributions are primarily the creation of packagers.

permissions culture

A culture in which virtually every action requires permission to be requested before doing it. Opponents of restrictive copyright regimes claim that copyright interferes with personal freedoms by requiring this kind of constant permission seeking.

productive leisure

A state in which a person is essentially having fun, but is involved in some kind of productive activity.

proprietary

Although not strictly accurate, "proprietary" is used to distinguish from "free" when describing license terms. It means that the license terms are sold on a per-user basis by the copyright holder. Often joined with commercial.

protocol

A defined set of steps to be followed, as in an electronic communication.

Python

A programming language which is known primarily for clear, consistent, and explicit syntax.

re-factoring

Reorganizing a design or a program to improve re-usability without really changing its function. Generally the goal is to reduce dependencies between different parts of the design, though sometimes it is possible to eliminate redundant elements. Common examples are moving functionality into plugins; creating a modular or open bus system; or converting two nearly identical modules into one.

resource description framework (RDF)

RDF is a formal language which represents a serie of semantic statements following a sentence-like noun-verb-noun format (or object-relationship-object). Each noun and verb is represented by a unique identifier which often resembles a web address. In this way, a very large number of concepts and relationships can be described in a way which can be interpreted by software.

sale value

The value of a thing as a product to sell (i.e. what you can charge for it).

separation of concerns

A design principle, in which the design is constructed so that tasks (or concerns) of the design are concentrated in separate areas. The idea is to reduce the number of things you have to work on when tracking down a problem or adding functionality.

set-top box

A specialized computer for multimedia processing. So-named because it is typically sold as a box that will be put on top of your television set.

small sharp tools

An expression which comes from the Unix programmer culture, suggesting that programs should be small and focused on one single purpose (like most Unix command line utility programs).

source code

The prefered form of representation of a program for the purpose of making changes. Typically this code must be either compiled into a binary exectuable or run by an interpreter.

Source Lines Of Code (SLOC)

SLOC are used as a metric of the size and complexity of a software package, and can, in bulk, be used to estimate the effort required to create it. It obviously can be inaccurate in specific cases, but is a good objective metric which is easy to measure.

stack

A collection of software in which each piece is meant to run "on top of" (i.e. depends upon) the others. The idea is that the separate elements are included with the specific goal of running one or a few top-level functions.

street performer protocol (SPP)

Any of several methods for electronically mimicking the behavior of a street performer putting out a hat to collect donations. More sophisticated examples (such as Rational Street Performer Protocol or RSPP), implement details such as matching funds and minimum and maximum donations.

synthesis

In logic chip design, synthesis is the step when a logical description of a circuit's function (described using a hardware description language) is converted into an actual network of logic gates which will achieve the desired behavior. It is analogous to compiling source code into binary code for software.

TAPR Open Hardware License (TAPR OHL)

A new, relatively untried, copyleft license for hardware circuitboard designs. Its most interesting feature is that it attempts to apply copyleft to the products created using the design, which would not normally be affected by copyright terms.

technological protection measures (TPM)

See digital rights management.

top-down design

An engineering approach in which you start with a plan for the large scale project you want to achieve, then successively break the problem down into smaller and smaller elements to be implemented. Contrasted with bottom-up design.

use value

The value of a thing as a tool to use (i.e. what value you can generate with it).

user documentation

Documentation intended simply to help you use a program (or product) to do what it is intended to do (as opposed to altering the design). See also developer documentation.

user interface (UI)

The way in which a program works with or is controlled by the human user.

utilitarian works

A utilitarian work is one whose value consists mostly of use value: in other words, what you can do with it.

utility

A software utility is a simple program which does one task, often with a simple command-line interface. Common Unix/Linux utilities include the `less` program which shows the contents of files, the `tar` utility which creates archives, and so on.

Verilog

A particular **hardware description language**.

version control system

A software system for tracking changes made to any body of data, but especially program source code. Popular version control systems used with free software include CVS and Subversion (both of which use a centralized client-server design) and GIT and Bazaar (which use a distributed peer-to-peer design).

website

A collection of web pages made available by a web server to users of the world wide web via internet browsers. Almost any collaborative project will need one of these.

Glossary

Index

utilitarian projects 8
utilitarian works **29**, 30

V

Val Henson 201
vandalism 23
Verilog 240
version control 115, 120, 209
version control system 191
very high level languages 211
VHDL 62
view source key 73
Viking Landers 14f
virtual reality 195
volunteers 111, 113
Voyager 14f, 15
VRML 195

W

web 2.0 181
web browser 17
web store 199, 256
weblogs 189
website 115, 122
wiki 191
Wikipedia **19**, 25, 27, 161, 163f, 166, 169, 171, 173
    English 19, 20f, 26f
    growth 20f, 21
    log engine 19

quality 22
size 20f, 21
Wikipedians 22
wikis 209
window tabs 139
Wine 230
women **201**, 203
    in computer science 223, 222f
    in free software 222f, 224
    visibility 223
word counts 24, 26f, 26
work 171
workflow 191
works
    expressive 227
    functional 227
workshop (as analog to project) 122, 123f
writing 91f

X-Z

X 16f, 133, 133f
X Server 16
X3D 195
XML 141
XO **71**, **72**, 74f, 75f, 78, 79f, 81
Yahoo Groups 182
Yong-Le Encyclopedia 20, 26f, 27
zero sum game 139
Zope 44, 147
Zope.org 118

Boldface entries indicate more extensive discussion. Figure references are indicated by an "f" after the page number.

www.ingramcontent.com/pod-product-compliance
Lightning Source LLC
Chambersburg PA
CBHW051225050326
40689CB00007B/801

* 9 780578 032726 *